HENRY BRADSHAW SOCIETY

Founded in the Year of Our Lord 1890

for the editing of Rare Liturgical Texts.

AF717598

VOL. XXV.

ISSUED TO MEMBERS FOR THE YEAR 1903,

AND

PRINTED FOR THE SOCIETY

BY

HARRISON AND SONS, ST. MARTIN'S LANE

PRINTERS IN ORDINARY TO HIS MAJESTY.

All that appertein to the clerkes to say or syng at the ministracion of the Communion, and when there is no Communion. At Confirmacion. At Matrimonie. The visitacion of the sicke. At buriall of the dedde. At the purificacion of womē. And the first daie of Lent.

At the Communion

Clerke.

First the Psalme appoyncted for the Introite.

Priest.

Almightie God. &c.

Answere.

iii. Lorde haue mercie vpon vs.
iii. Christ haue mercie vpon vs.
iii. Lorde haue mercie vpon vs.

Priest.

Glory to God on high.

Answere.

And in yearth peace, good will towardes menne.

Wee praise thee, wee blesse thee, wee worship thee, wee glorifie thee, we geue thankes to thee, for thy greate glory, O

British Museum, C. 36. d. 1.

© Henry Bradshaw Society 1903

All Rights Reserved. Except as permitted under current legislation no part of this work may be photocopied, stored in a retrieval system, published, performed in public, adapted, broadcast, transmitted, recorded or reproduced in any form or by any means, without the prior permission of the copyright owner

First Published for the Henry Bradshaw Society 1903
by The Boydell Press
an imprint of Boydell & Brewer Ltd
PO Box 9, Woodbridge, Suffolk IP12 3DF, UK
and of Boydell & Brewer Inc.
668 Mt Hope Avenue, Rochester, NY 14620, USA
website: www.boydellandbrewer.com

Transferred to digital printing

ISBN 978-1-870252-60-7

ISSN 0144-0241

This publication is printed on acid-free paper

THE CLERK'S BOOK OF 1549.

EDITED BY

J. WICKHAM LEGG,

Fellow of the Royal College of Physicians and of the Society of Antiquaries of London.

London.

1903.

TABLE OF CONTENTS.

PREFACE.

It would hardly be honest of me to present the following pages to the Society with my name prefixed as Editor, unless I made it clear that in them I have done little but play the part of the rhapsodist, one who stitches and strings together the information brought to him by others. Mr. Cuthbert Atchley is chief amongst those who have so kindly furnished me with material; in fact, the book ought really to be called his, and I do not know of any reason why he should not have edited the work in his own name, except that he does not live in London, and thus could not have daily access to the only copy of the Clerk's Book that is at present known to exist. In arranging the materials for the introduction so freely offered to me, and in choosing them, I have not in all cases followed Mr. Atchley's recommendations, and he is free from all responsibility for defects thus ensuing; but I must express my very sincere thanks and heart-felt gratitude for the generosity with which he has placed the results of his prolonged researches so completely at my disposal.

In investigations which I have made on my own behalf I have been much helped by the lists of *Parish and other accounts*, which have been published by Mr. B. L. Hutchins in *Notes and Queries*, 1899 and 1900, Ninth Series, Vol. IV. and Vol. V. I have found the references to the churchwardens' accounts very valuable.

I am also much indebted to Mr. James Christie's work, which has for its title, *Some Account of Parish Clerks*, printed at the expense of the Company of Parish Clerks in 1893, but not published.

Illustrations of the duties of clerks taken from foreign sources have been hardly, if at all, admitted to this work. It was felt that such could be very much better dealt with by continental writers, who would have command of the manuscript and printed sources of such illustrations; a lesser reason is, also, that the introduction and notes would be enlarged beyond what was desirable as an accompaniment to so small a work as the Clerk's Book, which, again, is also itself merely English.

In printing the records of the fifteenth and sixteenth centuries that appear as appendices, I have followed a plan which I cannot flatter myself will meet with general approval. I have given no indication of the contractions that I have expanded. I have done this not without a good deal of consideration and some misgivings. My aim has been, not thereby to give a better look to the page, but rather to avoid a promise of accuracy which, it may be feared, would not be invariably borne out in the performance.

Finally, I would acknowledge with much gratitude the help so kindly given me by many friends and correspondents. To the Rev. Christopher Wordsworth I am indebted for much information, especially about the clerk's duties at Barrow on the Humber and the holy loaf at Stanford in the Vale; to the Rev. F. M. Beaumont, for allowing the constitutions of the clerks at Coventry to be deposited in the British Museum, which enabled me to transcribe these documents afresh from the originals; to the Rev. Dr. Macray for transcripts of documents in the Bodleian Library; to the Rev. J. R. Hughes for transcripts of documents from the parish records at Rempstone; to Mr. J. A. Herbert for transcripts from manuscripts in the British Museum; to Mr. Robert Brown, Junior, F.S.A., for a fresh transcript of the clerk's duties at Barrow on the Humber; to the Rev. Dr. J. T. Fowler for access to a printed book in the Library of the University of Durham; to the Rev. J. Erskine Binney for access to the documents containing the dispute at Morebath. For information and encouragement I am also indebted to the

Rev. Arthur Brinckman, Mr. Alfred W. Pollard, Mr. Francis B. Bickley, Mr. Falconer Madan, the Rev. Sidney E. Dodderidge, Mr. Francis F. Giraud, Mr. J. Brooking Rowe, the Rev. H. Aldrich Cotton, and the Rev. A. L. Palmes.

Dr. Edwin Freshfield must be specially mentioned for the abundant information that he has given me, as well as for the great kindness that I have always received at his hands.

To our Treasurer, Mr. Dewick, and our Secretary, Mr. Wilson, I am again, as so often before, under very deep obligations. Their advice and time have been most ungrudgingly bestowed upon me; and only those who have received similar favours at their hands can measure my indebtedness to their goodness and generosity.

J. WICKHAM LEGG.

INTRODUCTION.

The book of which a part is now reprinted was purchased for the British Museum in the autumn of 1876. Beyond this I am able to say little of the history of the copy. It was, indeed, in actual use in Cheshire early in the seventeenth century; but besides this, nothing else seems to be at present known.

Six years after the purchase of this volume, attention was called to it by Mr. Maskell in the second edition of *Monumenta Ritualia*. In a note to the *Ordo ad faciendum Sponsalia* he gave a short account of the contents of the book; but he does not make it quite plain how it is more "a connecting link between the old rituals and the reformed Prayer book," than the first prayer book of Edward VI. itself.[1]

I do not know that anyone else has described it in print.

The book is in 4°, the leaves now measuring 189 by 140 millimeters, but they have been cut down by the binder. The size of a page of 25 lines including headline and catchword is 159 by 93 millimeters. It is printed wholly in black, with the exception of the title page, and the first quire, parts of which are in red, as the holy days in the calendar. The type is black letter; but when a capital W has to be used, it is in nearly all cases Roman. There is only one column. The number of lines in a full page varies from 25 to 26, 25 being more usual.

The book is composed of two parts; each has a separate title page and signatures. The first part is that containing the book for the clerk, now edited; the second, the psalter. Both parts have eight leaves to the quire, except the last quire of the psalter, which has only six. To the last quire (*d*) of the handbook the last leaf is wanting; its place is now taken by a blank leaf of modern paper, but the last leaf was probably also blank. The signatures of the clerk's book are in small black letter, with the exception of the first which is a cross; the signatures of the psalter are in capital black letter, from A to T.

There is no pagination. There are forty leaves in the clerk's book, counting the blank leaf at its end. There are 150 in the psalter.

The structure of the book may be thus expressed:

$$✠\ a\text{—}d^{8}=40 \text{ ff.}$$
$$\text{A—S}^{8}\ \text{T}^{6}=150 \text{ ff.}$$

The lines of the title are printed alternately in red and black, excepting the two lowest, and the title is surrounded by a border of

[1] William Maskell, *Monumenta Ritualia Ecclesiae Anglicanae*, Oxford, 1882, vol. i. p. 60, note 20.

architectural design; a lintel supported by two columns which rest upon an ornamental base. Parts of this border are in red; (i.) a figure on the left side of the upper border; (ii.) two roundels, one in the extreme left of the lower border, another in the middle right hand portion of the side border; (iii.) the printer's device within a wreath in the middle of the lower border.

The title page of the whole book has been reprinted below.[1] The title page of the psalter is as follows:

The Psal- || ter or Psalmes of Da- || uid, after the transla- || cion of the greate || Bible, poyn- || ted as it shal- || be song in || Churches || [an ornamental leaf] M.D. xlix.

The colophon which occupies the verso of the last leaf is:

Imprinted by || Richard || Grafton, prin- || ter to the || Kinges || Maies- || tie || Mense Augustij || 1549 || Cum priuilegio ad imprimendum solum ||

The binding is in purple morocco, and modern; lettered on the back: *Psalter. Ordre for Mattyns, &c.* Lower down is *R. Grafton, August.* 1549. From the crown impressed on the inside of the cover, it may be inferred that the book was bound in this way after its entrance into the British Museum. Its press mark is: C. 36 d. 1.

This book seems to be of very considerable rarity. As yet, no other copy has been found. The bulk of the work is made up of a psalter, distributed for Mattins and Evensong, as in the first Prayer Book of King Edward VI. Prefixed to the psalter are "diverse things" which are set out below,[2] under six headings: the first five of which are verbal reproductions of the orders with the same name in Edward VI.'s first book; but the sixth sets forth "all that shall appertain to the clerks to say or sing" at the Communion, Matrimony, the Visitation of the Sick, the Burial of the Dead, the Purification of Women, and the first day of Lent. All under the sixth heading show considerable difference from the like offices in Edward VI.'s first prayer book, the greater part of that which is to be said by the priest being left out, while that said by the clerks only is printed in full. The orders under this last heading are thus emphatically for the use of the clerk, not of the priest, nor of the people, and thus to the collection may very well be given the name of *The Clerk's Book.*

It should be noticed that the psalter has not been reprinted in the following edition.

The order how the psalter is appointed to be read, is necessary for the clerk's instruction in accompanying the priest in the recitation of the psalter. The Kalendar, which contains the lessons for every day in the year, would tell the clerk the lesson or lessons which he was to read in the church. Mattins, Evensong, *Quicunque vult*, the Litany and Suffrages, would need the answer of the clerk at almost every line. These are all printed at length. But the offices which follow, "All that appertain to the clerks to say or sing" only give at length the clerk's portion.

It may, perhaps, be noticed that there is no reference given in the

[1] See below, p. 1.

[2] See below, p. 2.

part that has come down to us to the variable parts of the communion service, which fell to the lot of the clerk in the different seasons of the Christian year. For example, it was his business to sing the introit, and a leaf or so would have sufficed to set forth the psalms assigned to this. Then he was also to read the Epistle,[1] and yet none of those for the Christian seasons is set forth. It does not seem likely that the book ever contained either introits or epistles, for such are not in the table of contents, even considering that the last leaf before the psalter is wanting.

The earlier editions of Edward VI.'s first book did not contain psalters, and thus it became advisable to provide psalters for use with the book, such as the latter part of the work before us. In the churchwardens' accounts about 1549, we find purchases of psalters together with the new service book. For example, at North Elmham in 1549, they paid sixteen shillings and fourpence "for ij books and ij Sawlters for the order of the new sett forthe by the Kyngs Maiesties Coñ."[2]

At Ludlow in 1549, they "payde for the parishe bookes, viz. iiij Mase bookes, one Paraffraces, and viij Salters xxxvj *s*."[3] And at Hawkhurst in Kent, about the same time they "payde to Sir Petur for ij books of Salmes and a boke of prayer for peace vij *d*."[4] and again in 1550–51, they bought two psalter books, but these were three shillings and tenpence.[5] Also at St. Dunstan's, Canterbury, in 1549–50, it seems likely that the same books were bought, as they "paid for ij Salters iij *s*. viij *d*."[6] much the same price. Also in 1548–49 at St. Matthew's, Friday Street, they "payd for iij newe sawters bokes ij *s*. vj *d*." and in 1549–50 "for iij sawter Boockes at ij *s*. vj *d*. the pece." In 1547–48, they bought a book of the common prayer and "two sawter bokes for the churche" for which they paid four shillings.[7]

At Wing, Buckinghamshire, in 1549, they "payd for two sawter bokes iij *s*. iiij *d*."[8]

At Bridlington in Yorkshire, amongst other goods they had in 1552, a Bible, a Paraphrase, a Communion book, and "two Englesse Satters" or Psalters.[9] In the same collection, other psalters are mentioned[10]; though not precisely said to be English, yet their enumeration with English books makes it likely that they were in the vernacular.

Mr. H. A. Wilson, our Secretary, has pointed out to me that a book akin to the Clerk's Book is in the Library of the University of Durham.

[1] See below, p. 35.

[2] A. G. Legge, *Ancient Churchwardens' accounts in the parish of North Elmham*, Norwich, 1891, p. 51.

[3] *Churchwardens' Accounts of the Town oj Ludlow*, Ed. Thos. Wright, Camden Society, 1869, p. 38.

[4] *Archaeologia Cantiana*, 1863, vol. v. p. 61.

[5] p. 66.

[6] *Archaeologia Cantiana*, 1887, vol. xvii. p. 112.

[7] *Journal of the British Archaeological Association*, 1869, vol. xxv. p. 373.

[8] *Archaeologia*, 1855, vol. xxxvi. p. 230.

[9] *The Inventories of Church Goods. . . . York*, etc. Surtees Society, 1897, p. 31.

[10] p. 169.

By the courtesy of the Rev. Dr. Fowler, I have been enabled to examine the book, the press mark of which is: Routh Collection, xvii. E. 28. (2.)

The title page is almost identical with that of the Clerk's Book. It is thus:

The Psal- || ter, or Psalmes of Dauid, cor- || *rected, and poincted, as they shal-* || be song in Churches, aftre the || *Translation of the greate* || Byble.

Hereunto is added, diuers || *thinges as maie apeare on the* || nexte side, wheare is expressed || *the contentes of thys* || Booke.

Anno Do. MDLII. || Mense Martij. || Cum priuilegio ad imprimen- || dum solum. ||

The title is surrounded by an architectural design the same as that which surrounds the title of the Clerk's Book, only the pieces are reversed; the upper border is here the lower, and the right border the left, and *vice versâ.*

Of the psalter, A i. which was probably the title page, is missing. After the one hundred and fiftieth psalm at the bottom of the verso of R. viii. is: The ende of this Booke. || Imprinted by Richard Grafton, Printer to the || Kynges Maiestie. ||

There is no pagination. The signatures of the earlier portion are red a, black a, b, c, d, e, in black letter. Of these the first four quires are in eights, d is in four and e is in two.

The psalter is in eights from A to R. but A i. and A vii. are now wanting.

The type is black letter, and is printed in black ink throughout with the exception of the title page and certain initial letters in the table for the order of the psalter and parts of the kalendar including the festivals. It is in single columns. The first part of the book is in smaller type than the psalter.

There are 32 lines in a full page of the first part, the size of which, including catchwords and headlines, is 163 by 94 millimeters.

At the end of the first part, the verso of the last leaf (e. ii.) is blank.

The margins have been cut down by the binder. The binding is of brown calf, probably of the first half of the eighteenth century. A label on the back is lettered: *Common Prayer, K. Edward VI.*

It is bound up with an imperfect primer of 1551, quarto, Richard Grafton. This is described by Mr. Hoskins.[1] After the psalter come *Certain Sermones or Homelies,* Richard Grafton, 1551, which are followed by the *Pystles and Gospels, of euery Sonday and holydaye in the yere,* apparently of Sarum use, but with no title or colophon remaining.

In spite of the identity of the titles of the two books the contents are not the same. The contents given on the verso of the title of the Clerk's Book agree verbally with those of the psalter from Durham as far as Cap. V. the Litany and suffrages. Then instead of Cap. VI. *All that shall appertain, &c.,* there is in the Durham book: vi. *All the collectes vsed throughoute the yeare at the Communion, and when*

[1] Edgar Hoskins, *Horae,* London, 1901, p. 68.

there is no Communion. Thus the part which marks off the Clerk's Book[1] from other known books disappears, and is replaced by the introits and collects of the first prayer book of Edward VI. from the first Sunday in Advent to All Saints with proper psalms and lessons on certain festivals. These are followed by the two collects for the King and the general confession and prayer of humble access in the communion service, with the thanksgiving after communion *Almighty and euerlastyng God, wee moste hartily thanke the*, and the blessing. After this are collects to be said after the offertory, the prayers for rain and fair weather, with which the first part ends.

I have not discovered any noteworthy variations from the Clerk's Book in the early part, such as the kalendar; or in Mattins, Evensong, and the Litany.

An English psalter printed in the year before the Clerk's Book, that is, in 1548, follows the lines of the Latin books, and has little in common with those just described. Its title page is:

The Psal || ter or Boke || of the psalmes, || where vnto is added the || Letany and cer- || tayne other de- || uout pra- || yers.

Set forth wyth the || Kynges moste || gracious ly- || cence [an ornamental leaf].

Anno Do. M.D. . XLVIII. || Mensis Iulij. ||

The colophon is:

Imprinted at London || by me Roger Car, for An- || thoni Smyth dwellyng || in Pauls church || yarde. ||

The book is in 8° and consists of 187 pages numbered, to which are added 18 unnumbered, and these contain the litany. The press mark of the only copy known to me is: C. 25, b. 2, in the British Museum. The binding, apparently contemporary with the printing, is preserved.

The contents of this book are the psalter, the canticles at lauds, also *Benedicite*, *Benedictus*, *Magnificat*, *Nunc Dimittis*, *Te Deum*, and *Quicunque vult*, all in a translation different from that in Edward VI.'s first prayer book. After these comes the Litany, which retains the invocations of the Blessed Virgin, angels, patriarchs, apostles, and other orders of saints. The psalter follows the numbering of the Vulgate.

At St. Margaret's, Westminster, they bought about August 10th, 1548, eight psalters in English for which they paid 13*s.* 4*d.*[2] It seems quite possible that these may have been copies of the psalter now described, which was published in July. Leave had been given on April 22nd, 1547, to Grafton and Whitchurch to print books concerning the divine service in English or Latin.[3] These eight psalters may have been copies of such books, they were not merely copies of the old Latin psalter. The first book of Edward VI. did not come into use

[1] See below, p. 2.

[2] J. Nichols, *Illustrations*, London, 1797, p. 13.

[3] Rot. Pat. 1 Ed. VI. Pars. 4 m. 7. Quoted by Gasquet and Bishop, *Edward VI.* etc. 1890, chap. iv. p. 58.

until Whitsunday, 1549, nearly a year after these psalters were bought, and compline had been sung in English in the King's chapel as early as Easter, 1547, and there were English mattins and evensong at St. Paul's and elsewhere in 1548.[1] It seems just possible that English services in which these psalters were used might have been sung after August, 1548, at St. Margaret's, Westminster.

There is a rhyming translation of the psalter by Robert Crowley, which was published on September 20, 1549, a copy of which Mr. Madan has shown me in Brasenose College Library. Its title page is:

The Psalter of || *Dauid newely translated into Englysh* || metre in such sort that it maye the more || decently, and wyth more delyte of the || mynde, be reade and songe of al men. || *Whereunto is added a note* of four || *partes, wyth other thynges,* || as shall appeare in the || Epistle to the || Readar. || ✠

Translated and Imprinted by || Robert Crowley in the yere of || our Lorde. *M.D. xlix. the* || *xx. daye of September.* || And are to be solde || in Eley rentes in || Holburne. || ✠

Cum Priuilegio ad Imprimendum solum.

There is no colophon: the greater part of the book is in black letter. It is in 4°. The pages are unnumbered. The structure may be thus expressed:

$$+, ++, \text{A—Z, Aa—Uu}^4.$$

The leaves measure 190 × 131 millimeters. The size of the page including headline and catchword is 156 × 84 mm.

The book has been rebacked in modern times, but the sides are apparently contemporary with the printing. The clasps have disappeared.

The contents of the book are a calendar: the address to the christian reader in which the author tells us he has added to the end of the book all the canticles that are usually sung in the church, and that in translating he has followed the version of Leo Judas[2]: the four parts, Countertenor, Tenor, Plainsong, and Bass: a dedication to Owen Oglethorpe, then President of Magdalen College, Oxford: the psalter, following the numbering of the Hebrews: and after the 150th psalm a rhyming version of *Magnificat*, *Nunc dimittis*, *Benedictus*, *Benedicite*, *Te Deum*, which is called *the songe of Nicetus the bishope*, and *Quicunque vult*. With this the book ends.

It does not seem that the psalms or canticles were to be sung as we now sing a modern metrical hymn; but in a cadence just as the prayer book psalms are sung either to Anglican or Gregorian chants. But it would be an assumption if, without further evidence, it were stated that

[1] F. A. Gasquet and Edm. Bishop, *Edward VI. and the Book of Common Prayer*, London, 1890, Ch. xi. p. 181.

[2] According to Hoefer (*Nouvelle Biographie générale*, Paris, 1858. t. xxvii. p. 134) Leo Judas was born in 1482 and died in 1542. He was the natural son of a priest, not of Jewish parentage. I have seen his *Biblia*, in the editions of Froschover and Etienne, in the Bodleian Library.

these rhyming psalms and canticles were intended to be sung in the place of the psalms and canticles of the Edwardian prayer book. It is true that the early editions of Edward's First Prayer book did not contain the psalter. But under a Tudor it would have been dangerous to use a book of private adventure which possessed not even the authority conveyed by the licence to Grafton and Whitchurch spoken of above.[1]

The clerk, a church minister inferior to the deacon and priest, has been known in England since the days of St. Augustine and King Ethelbert. Rules as to his marriage and manner of living are given by St. Gregory the Great to St. Augustine of Canterbury[2]; and he is spoken of in the laws of King Ethelbert, which probably determine that his property shall be returned threefold when wrongfully taken from him.[3]

These officers existed also at the same time in other parts of Western Christendom. They are spoken of by St. Isidore of Sevile, and they were part of the clerical body clearly marked off from the lay folk.[4] In 655 the third canon of the ninth council of Toledo speaks of the *minister* together with the priest; and in 666 the eighteenth canon of the council of Merida enjoins the parish priest to have about him clerks, with whom he could discharge his duty of praising God.[5] The office of the clerk was thus to praise God by singing psalms and canticles, and he was described by St. Isidore under the name of *psalmista*, and men were ordained to this office without the intervention of the bishop, solely by the command of the priest.[6] The *psalmista* in St. Isidore's enumeration of the clerical degrees is the fourth from the lowest, the *ostiarius*.[7]

[1] See above, p. xv.

[2] St. Gregory the Great, *Epistolae*, lib. xi. 64. (studio et labore Monachorum O.S.B. Venetiis, 1771, t. viii. p. 297.)

[3] B. Thorp, *Ancient Laws . . . England*, London, 1840, p. 1. This seems to be the interpretation of Bede. (*Hist. Eccles.* lib. ii. cap. v. Oxon. 1896, Ed. C. Plummer, vol. i. p. 90.) In the laws of King Edgar (Thorp, p. 395) it is ordered that every priest at the synod have his clerk.

[4] Isidorus, *de Eccles. offic.* lib. ii. capp. 1 and 12. Venetiis, 1558.

[5] Mansi, *Sacrorum Conciliorum* etc. Florentiae, 1765, t. xi. coll. 27 and 86.

[6] Solent autem ad hoc officium etiam absque conscientia Episcopi sola iussione presbyteri eligi quique, quos probabile, in cantandi arte esse constiterit. (*op. cit.* cap. 12.) Here is an echo of the tenth canon of the fourth council of Carthage: Psalmista id est cantor potest absque scientia episcopi sola iussione presbyteri officium suscipere cantandi, dicente sibi presbytero: Vide, ut quod ore cantas, corde credas, et quod corde credis, operibus comprobes. (H. T. Bruns, *Canones Apostolorum*, etc. Berolini, 1839, pars I. p. 142.) Gallican canons which are now often quoted as *Statuta ecclesiae antiqua*, or *statuta antiqua ecclesiae Arelatensis*. This form appears in the English pontificals of Egbert (Surtees Society, 1853, p. 10.) and St. Dunstan, (National Library, Paris, MS. Latin 943, fo. 45.) and Archbishop Robert. (Henry Bradshaw Society, 1903, p. 115.)

[7] Letter of St. Isidore *de gradibus* in J. Saenz de Aguirre, *Collectio maxima conciliorum omnium Hispaniae*, ed. J. Catalani, Romae, 1753, t. iii. p. 455.

The clerk being one of the clergy, the lay folk were forbidden by the penitential of Theodore to take the clerk's duties. The layman was not to read the mass lesson at the altar, nor to sing *alleluia* at the rood screen; but he was only to recite psalms and responds, without *alleluia*.[1] From this we may gather something of the duties of the clerk in the time of Theodore. He could read the mass lesson or epistle, and sing the *alleluia* or chant between the epistle and gospel, and this we find distinctly expressed in the ninth century by Pope Leo IV. Every priest was to have a clerk who should be a scholar and able to read the epistle or lesson, and to answer at mass, and who should also be sufficient to sing the psalms, that is, to take his part in the divine service, what we now call the breviary, or choir offices.

> Omnis presbyter clericum habeat scholarem, qui epistolam, vel lectionem legat, et ad missam respondeat, cum quo et psalmos cantet.[2]

Hincmar, archbishop of Rhemes, a contemporary of Leo IV. in a series of questions which remind us of modern Visitation articles, asks if each church have a clerk who can keep a school, read the epistle, and sing.

> xi. Si habeat clericum qui possit tenere scholam, aut legere epistolam, aut canere valeat, prout necessarium sibi videtur.[3]

Four centuries later these requirements from the clerk pass into the general body of the canon law, in the decretals of Gregory IX. Every rector is to have a clerk to sing the divine service with him, and to read the epistle or lesson, one who is sufficient to teach in the school, and who is to warn the parishioners to send their children to the church to be instructed in the Christian faith.

> Ut quisque presbyter, qui plebem regit, clericum habeat, qui secum cantet, et epistolam et lectionem legat, et qui possit scholas tenere, et admonere suos parochianos, ut filios suos ad fidem discendam mittant ad ecclesiam, quos ipse cum omni castitate erudiat.[4]

Thus the three main duties of the clerk are to be able to sing; to read the epistle; and to teach.

The ability to sing appears amongst the earliest of the clerk's qualifications.[5] Leo IV. distinctly states that it is the psalms which he has to sing; and the psalms being the main portion of the divine service, it will

[1] § 14. Laicus in aecclesia iuxta altare non debet lectionem recitare ad missam, nec in pulpito alleluia cantare, sed psalmos tantum aut responsoria, sine Alleluia. (B. Thorpe, *Ancient Laws . . . England*, London, 1840, p. 304.)

[2] Leonis IV. papae *homilia*; Migne, *Patrologia*, 1852. t. 115. col. 677. The variants of Martène and Labbe are given in this edition, but they are of no great importance. See also *Commonitorium cuiusque episcopi ad sacerdotes* xiii. in Martène and Durand, *Veterum Scriptorum* etc. Parisiis, 1733. t. vii. col. 2.

[3] Hincmari Rhemensis archiepiscopi *Capitula quibus de rebus magistri et decani per singulas ecclesias inquirere episcopo renuntiare debeant*. Migne, *Patrologia*, 1852. t. 125. col. 779. Cf. Regino, *de ecclesiasticis disciplinis*, ed. S. Baluse, Paris, 1671. p. 24. No. 26.

[4] *Decret. Gregorii IX.* lib. iii. tit. i. cap. iii. in Æ. L. Richter, *Corpus Iuris Canonici*, Lipsiae, 1839, pars ii. col. 433.

[5] Isidore, *de eccles. off.* lib. ii. cap. 12.

be the divine service which the clerk is to sing with the priest and to recite with him.

Then he is to read the epistle or the prophetical lesson, or one of the lessons at Mattins.

Lastly, he is to be of sufficient education to keep the parish school.

Ability to Sing.—St. Gregory in his answer to St. Augustine of Canterbury, says that clerks are not only to be of good life and conversation but to be diligent in singing the psalms. The same accomplishment is noted throughout: in Leo IV. Hincmar, and the canon law.[1] Lyndwood twice notes that one of the parish clerk's duties is to sing; and to sing the responds and Grails,[2] that is, parts of Mass and of the divine service.

According to the rules, at Coventry in 1462 the clerks were to sing at high mass and evensong.[3] So at Faversham in 1506 they were to be diligent to sing and do their duty at all services to be sung by note.[4] Also at St. Michael's, Cornhill, some time before 1538, it was ordained that the priests and clerks should be in the quire singing there from the beginning of Mattins, Mass, and Evensong.[5] A priest was made Ruler or Dean of the Quire, who appointed two Rectors for every high or solemn feast, apparently out of the clerks. But nothing much is said about singing in the rules of St. Stephen's, Coleman Street, written in 1542, where it is counted among such small things that can hardly be set down on paper.[6]

At Coventry the first clerk was to be *rector chori* on the south side, the second on the north, on feast days.[7] This was an office that was not despised even by royal persons. We read that our King Richard I. delighted in the divine service at the great festivals; and that he went up and down the quire, stirring them up by hand and voice to sing the louder.[8] And we all of us remember an incident in the life of Sir Thomas More when Lord Chancellor, his acting as parish clerk, and wearing a surplice.[9]

[1] See above, p. xviii.
[2] W. Lyndwood, *Provinciale*, lib. iii. tit. *de concessione praebendae* cap. *a nostris maioribus*, verba *clericis* and *sciant*.
[3] See below, Appendix I. §§ 4 and 6, pp. 57 and 58.
[4] See below, Appendix V. § 4, p. 76.
[5] See below, Appendix VI. § 6, p. 83.
[6] See below, Appendix VIII. § 17, p. 91.
[7] See below, Appendix I. §§ 6 and 50, pp. 58 and 61.
[8] Ralph of Coggeshall, *Chronicon Anglicanum*, Rolls Series, 1875, p. 97. Circa divinum officium in praecipuis solemnitatibus plurimum delectabatur . . . atque per chorum huc illucque deambulando, voce ac manu, ut altius concreparent, excitabat.
[9] "This good Duke of *Norfolke* comming on a tyme to *Chelsey* to dyne with *Syr Thomas More*, found him in the Church, singing in the Quier, with a Surplisse on his backe: to whome (after Masse was done) as they went towardes his house, together arme in arme, the Duke said: Gods body, Gods body, my Lord Chancellour, what turned Parish Clarke? You dishonor the King and his Office very much. Nay (quoth *Syr Thomas More* smyling vpon the Duke) your Grace may not thinke that the King your Maister and myne, wilbe offended with me for seruing God his Maister, or therby accompt his Seruice any way dishonoured." (William Roper, *The Mirrour of Vertue . . . the life of Syr Thomas More*, Paris, 1626. p. 83. It is to the same effect though not verbatim in § xvii. p. 64 of the London edition of 1729.)

Immediately after the accession of Elizabeth, the clerks seem to be held responsible by Parkhurst for the character of the music, that it be modest and distinct. Grindal speaks only of ability to read. The Canons of 1603 speak of the clerk's "competent skill in singing (if it may be.)"[1] And thence the demand upon this point becomes very usual in the visitation articles until the eighteenth century.

An instance of the misbehaviour of a parish clerk not only in doing servile work on a Sunday and in refusing to kneel at proper times, but also in making a jest of the music in church, is found in James I.'s reign.

> *Eastham. Contra Thomam Milborne.* Presentatur, for spreadinge mowle hills with a shovell in the churchyard upon the Sundaye next Septuagesima last being the xiiith daye of Februarie 1613 and that betweene morninge and eveninge prayer; and was then taken at worke by the minister and other of the parishioners, and for that he doth not kneele on his knees in tyme of devine service when as it is fittinge he should and the rather in that he is the parishe clerke who ought to give good example therby unto others that are negligent therin, and he hath often tymes bene admonished for to kneele by the minister but he doth altogether refuse it. And for that he singeth the psalmes in the church with such a jesticulus tone and altisonant voyce, viz. squeakinge like a gelded pigg which doth not onlie interrupt the other voyces, but is altogether dissonant and disagreeing unto any musicall harmonie and he hath been requested by the minister to leave it, but he doth obstinatlie persist and contynue therein.[2]

But the great rebellion, among other evils, seems to have caused a decrease in the qualifications and education, especially the musical education, of the parish clerk. So, at least, John Playford complains:

> But at this day the *Best*, and almost all the *Choice Tunes* are lost, and out of use in our *Churches*: nor must we expect it otherwayes, when in and about this great City, in above One hundred Parishes, there is but few *Parish Clerks* to be found that have either Ear or Understanding to Set one of these *Tunes* Musically as it ought to be: It having been a Custom during the late Wars, and since, to Chuse men into such places, more for their *Poverty* than *Skill* and *Ability*; Whereby this part of God's Service hath been so ridiculously performed in most places, that it is now brought into Scorn and Derision by many people.[3]

And apparently the scandal went on in the following century; for a parish clerk, in a work published by the company, in 1731, says:

> My Meaning is this: The *Parish-Clerk* is oftentimes chosen rather for his *Poverty*, to prevent a Charge to the *Parish*, than either for his *Virtue* or *Skill*; or else for some other By-end or Purpose, more than for the immediate Honour and Service of *Almighty God* and his *Church*.[4]

Playford adds that it was in his time the custom for the clerk to read out every line of the hymn before it was sung, a practice which some of us no doubt can remember in our youth, though it has now almost entirely disappeared. The parish clerk just quoted tells us of the

[1] See below, Appendix XI. pp. 98 and 99.

[2] W. H. Hale, *A Series of precedents . . . extracted from Act books of Ecclesiastical Courts in the Diocese of London*, London, 1847, p. 238.

[3] John Playford. *Psalms and Hymns in solemn musick* London, Godbid, 1671. fo. Preface a 2. [B.M. Music G. 80.]

[4] *The Parish Clerks Guide . . .* by B. P. Parish Clerk, London, reprinted by John March for the Company of Parish-Clerks, 1731, p. 19.

custom of "bespeaking" the psalm with these words, *Let us Sing to the Praise and Glory of God*, which has likewise gone out of use. He justifies it with this analogy: "As the *Priest* has his *Oremus*, *Let us pray*, so the Clerk has his *Cantemus*."[1] It seems clear that down to this date one of the chief duties of the parish clerk was to sing.

Ability to Read the Epistle and Lesson.—This portion of the clerk's duties is one of the best pieces of evidence that we have of the good education required of those who undertook the clerk's office. For he who could read the Latin epistle or a lesson at Mattins must have possessed an education not far short of the parson himself.

Leo IV. and the Decretals of Gregory IX. mention the reading of the epistle or lesson amongst the duties of the clerk; Hincmar the epistle only, but doubtless under the name of epistle is included the prophetical lesson. For in the life of St. Godric, there is a story which may well represent the practice of the twelfth century; a young clerk who wished to become a soldier and abandon his clerical profession, was made to read *Misit rex Herodes*, the epistle, as it is called, at the mass on Lammas day, and thus, to his shame, discover his clerkly abilities.[2] *Misit rex Herodes* is a portion of scripture taken from the Acts of the Apostles, and read in many uses on Lammas day as the lesson in place of the epistle.

John of Athon incidentally mentions this duty of the clerk when speaking of a disputed election, for when the clerk appointed by the parson began to read the epistle the clerk named by the parishioners snatched the book from the other's hand, and smote him to the earth with effusion of blood.[3]

In 1411 Clifford Bishop of London sanctioned an arrangement by which the Vicar of Elmstead was to find one clerk to help him to celebrate private masses on week days, and on holy days to read the epistle.[4]

Lyndwood, who wrote later than John of Athon, affirms more than once that it is the business of the clerk to read the epistle.[5] He had also to sing the grail and the responds.

In practice we find the parish clerk reading the epistle at Coventry,[6]

[1] B. P. *op. cit.* p. 32.

[2] *Libellus de vita et miraculis S. Godrici*, Surtees Society, 1847, cap. cix. p. 226.

[3] John of Athon, *Constitutiones Othoboni*, *de residentia Archiepiscoporum*, cap. *Pastor bonus*, verb. *sanctae obedientiae*, Appendix to Lyndwood, *Provinciale*, Oxon. 1679. p. 119.

[4] Ric. Newcourt, *Repertorium*, Lond. 1710, vol. ii. p. 243.

[5] Lyndwood, *Provinciale* Lib. iii. tit. *de concessione praebendae*, cap. *a nostris maioribus*, ad verba *Clericis* and *sciant*, Oxon. 1679. pp. 142, 143. By the Customary of St. Augustine's Canterbury, written in the first half of the fourteenth century, the novices soon after their profession were to read the lessons and epistles, sing the grails and responds, and to serve in other matters of less importance. (*Customary of the Benedictine Monasteries of St. Augustine, Canterbury, and St. Peter, Westminster*, Ed. by Sir Edward Maunde Thompson, H.B.S. 1902, vol. i. p. 273.)

[6] See below, Appendix I. p. 61. § 54.

St. Nicholas, Bristol,[1] and Faversham.[2] At St. Nicholas, Bristol, he had to pay a fine of twopence, apparently every day that he failed to sing.

John de Burgo notes that it is lawful for a clerk only in minor orders to read the epistle in the mass, if a subdeacon be not at hand. But at the same time he is not to read solemnly with the ornaments of a subdeacon.[3]

So the right of the clerk to read the epistle was not to be exercised without restriction. In 1229 the eleventh constitution of W. de Bloys orders that no one shall read the epistle who is not a subdeacon except in case of necessity.[4] Necessity in the hands of a canonist has a very elastic meaning, and most likely the constitution only means that the clerk may not read the epistle if a subdeacon be present, as John de Burgo holds.

At the introduction of the first book of Edward VI. there seems to have been no break with this custom of the past. The clerk's book now edited certainly contemplates in more places than one, the reading of the epistle and of the lesson by the clerk. In the communion service itself, the epistle is directed to be read either by the priest or clerk.[5] Accordingly at the communion of the sick, the epistle is given in full, plainly that the clerk may have it ready before him to read, while merely the first words of the rest of the service are given.[6]

So too at the communion when there is a burial the epistle is given in full for the same reason.[7] At the burial service, the priest or clerk is to read the lesson.[8] Thus it can hardly be doubted that the clerk continued under Edward VI.'s first book the old office of reading the epistle at mass and one or more of the lessons at mattins. Of this latter there is evidence from the accounts of St. Margaret's, Westminster, where in 1553 they paid thirteen shillings and fourpence "for the pulpit, where the Curate and the Clark did read the chapters at service time."[9] And at Ludlow in 1551 they paid three shillings and fourpence to the deacons, under which name the parish clerks appear, "for readynge the first chapter."[10]

The practice also prevailed under Elizabeth. In the metropolitical visitations of Grindal, whether as Archbishop of York or of Canterbury, he inquires whether the parish clerk is able to read the first lesson and the

[1] See below, Appendix III. p. 68, § 23.
[2] See below, Appendix V. p. 76, § 4.
[3] John de Burgo, *Pupilla oculi*, pars vii. *de sacramento ordinis*, cap. v. *sub fine*, Argentini, Knoblouch, 1514, fo. cii.
[4] Ut nullus epistolam legat in ecclesia nisi fuerit subdiaconus nisi causa necessitatis. (D. Wilkins, *Concilia*, London, 1737. t. i. p. 624.) He was bishop of Worcester.
[5] See below, p. 35.
[6] See below, p. 46.
[7] See below, p. 52.
[8] See below, p. 49.
[9] J. Nichols, *Illustrations of the Manners*, etc. London, 1797. p. 14.
[10] *Churchwardens' Accounts of the Town of Ludlow*, ed. Thomas Wright, Camden Society, 1869. p. 47.

epistle.[1] Aylmer, Bishop of London, makes this same inquiry in 1577,[2] and William Wickham, Bishop of Lincoln, asks the same question in 1585[3] and 1588,[4] and another bishop of the same see, William Chaderton, also puts the same in 1598.[5]

After 1603, the inquiry whether the parish clerk be able to read the first lesson and epistle does not seem to be continued. Yet clerks not in holy orders continued in certain cathedral churches to read both epistle and gospel, for it is forbidden by Laud at Winchester in his metropolitical visitation of that church. It is quite reasonable that this should be forbidden in a church with a large staff. It has been seen that John de Burgo only allowed the clerk in minor orders to read the epistle in the absence of the subdeacon, and in a church like Winchester a clerk in holy orders ought never to be wanting to assist the celebrant.[6]

But clerks in minor orders to whom the duty of reading the gospel and epistle was assigned continued after the Restoration of Church and State in 1660. There has been printed a list of the chapter at Worcester in October, 1661 : after the clerks in holy orders come the lower clerks :

School-master	John Toy.
Usher	Stephen Richardson.
Deacon or gospeller	Humphrey Withie.
Subdeacon or epistler	John Laight.
Precentor	Philip Tinker.
Sacrist	John Sayre.[7]

That the custom of allowing clerks not in holy orders to read the epistle had not died out in the middle of the nineteenth century is shown by the following passage from one who claims to have been a scholar of Merton College, Oxford.

> When I was an undergraduate at Merton College nearly fifty years ago, it was the custom, if there were but one priest at the altar, for one of the scholars to read the Epistle from the lowest chancel step on the Epistle side. . . . That the custom existed at that time I am certain, for I was the unfortunate scholar who read it.[8]

Mr. F. C. Eeles has given me the following statement :

> At Keighley in the West Riding of Yorkshire it was the custom some thirty or forty years ago for the parish clerk to wear a black gown and bands. He

[1] *The remains of Edmund Grindal*, Parker Society, 1843, p. 142, § 21. and p. 168, § 39.

[2] *Appendix E to second report of the Royal Commission on Ritual*, 1868. p. 420. § 31. The epistle does not appear in 1586. (p. 430.)

[3] *Articles . . . Dieocss† of Lincoln*, London, 1585, § 24.

[4] *Idem*, London 1588. § 41.

[5] *Idem*, Cambridge, John Legat, 1598, § 33.

[6] Item Dominus iniunxit, quod nullus dicti chori praesumat legere epistolas sive evangelium, nisi prius sit in sacris ordinibus constitutus. (*Works of . . . William Laud*, Anglo-Catholic library, 1853. vol. v. p. 478.)

[7] John Noake, *The Monastery and Cathedral of Worcester*, London and Worcester, 1866. p. 569.

[8] *Church Times*, March 30. 1899. p. 377 col. ii. A letter to the editor, signed *Mertonensis*.

read the first lesson and the epistle. To read the latter he left his seat below the pulpit and went up to the altar and took down the book from behind; after reading the epistle within the altar rails he replaced the book and returned to his place. Keighley parish church retained a number of old customs at that time; *e.g.* the people who sat facing across the church turned to the east at the *Gloria's*, the older people used to bow towards the altar on entering the church, and the altar was decorated with a large display of plate. This was told me by a man who was born and brought up there, and who remembers fasting communion being practised in his own family.

The reading of the lesson also continued into our own time. Ambrose Fisher replying to those who complained that their forces were exhausted in reading the service before they got to the really important part of divine worship, the sermon, says that "one of the Chapters is in many churches read by the Clark."[1] John Johnson says: "those Singing-Men, who read the first Lesson, are called *Lay-Clerks* (a contradictory name.)"[2]

Giles Jacob says of parish clerks: "Their business consists chiefly in responses to the minister, reading lessons, singing psalms."[3] In Cornwall, in the first half of the nineteenth century, it was said: "A very short time since, parish clerks used to read the first lesson."[4] The reading of the epistle and of the first lesson by the clerk must have been given up on account of an increasing want of education in these church officers. But this ability to read is an essential part of their duty, and no parish clerk ought to be appointed hereafter who is unable satisfactorily to perform it.

ABILITY TO TEACH.—It has been seen that together with ability to sing the psalms and read the epistle the clerk was also to be of sufficient capacity to teach the children of the parishioners.[5] Perhaps this is the least prominent of the clerk's duties in the middle ages. It is sometimes said that in 1237 the Constitutions of Alexander, Bishop of Coventry, require the clerk to be a teacher; but it looks uncertain. It is true that scholars are named who take about the holy water in country places, but there is no exact indication that these scholars are to teach.[6] An ordination of John Peckham touching the church of Bakewell is hardly more to the point. He requires that two clerks (*clerici scholastici*) shall take round the holy water on Sundays and other festivals; but on week days they are to engage in *disciplinis scholasticis*,[7] but whether this means that they are to teach or be taught is not at all clear. It may mean that the two clerks kept the school.

1 Ambrose Fisher, *A defence of the Liturgie*, London, 1630. p. 7.
2 John Johnson, *Clergy-man's Vade-mecum*, London, 1709. Ch. xxiii. vol. i. p. 203.
3 Giles Jacob, *New Law Dictionary*, ninth edition, London, 1772. *s.v.* parish clerk.
4 R. Polwhele, *Traditions and Recollections*, 1826, vol. i. p. 606. note. So also T. D. Fosbroke, *Encyclopaedia of Antiquities*, London, 1825, vol. ii. p. 680.
5 See above, p. xviii.
6 Constitutiones Alexandri Covent. episcopi, in D. Wilkins, *Concilia*, London, 1737. t. i. p. 641. The passage is given at length below, p. li.
7 W. Dugdale, *Monasticon*, ed. Caley, Ellis, and Bandinel, Lond. 1830. vol. vi. part iii. p. 1246. See the passage quoted below, p. lii.

There is an allusion in Matthew Paris to the keeping of school by the parish clerk *multis diebus scolas exercens* in the woeful story of the exaction of the officer of the Roman court.[1]

This instance comes from the thirteenth century. But during the fourteenth and fifteenth centuries I have been able to gather no evidence of teaching by the clerk. In the sixteenth there are these few. In 1506, at Faversham, the clerks or one of them had to teach the children to read and sing in the quire and to do service.[2] Also at St. Giles', Reading, in 1544–45, they "payd to Whitborne the clerk towardes his wages and he to be bound to teche ij children for the quere xij*s*."[3]

There may be an allusion to the clerk's teaching of children at St. Nicholas, Bristol, when he is told to take no book out of the quire for children to learn.[4]

In Elizabethan times Dr. Raine notes that the parish clerk of Woodhorne, Amor Oxley, was an eminent schoolmaster[5]; but it is probably a mere coincidence.

In the succeeding centuries there is still less material.

White Kennett tells us that the parish clerk ought to instruct the children in reading and writing and rehearsing the church catechism.[6]

A writer in the *Gentleman's Magazine*[7] at the beginning of the nineteenth century complains of the ignorance of the parish clerk of his time, and suggests as a remedy that they should be taken hereafter from a better class, such as would make good parish schoolmasters.[7]

To these three chief duties were added, in the later middle ages, a multitude of others, many of them servile, until in our days, instead of the parish clerk being the man of the best education in the parish next to the parson, he has sunk to a lower level than that of a domestic servant.

As the clerk was bound to attend the priest in the divine service, it was considered that it was also his duty to be with the priest in all clerical functions, to assist him in the ministration of sacraments and sacramentals; in short, wherever the priest went on duty within or without the church the clerk also went.

Some of these lesser duties of the parish clerk may now be spoken of, first considering that which is given him by Lyndwood, as the most important.

TO ASSIST IN MINISTERING SACRAMENTS AND SACRAMENTALS.—This duty is spoken of by Lyndwood, who says that no one can have a doubt

[1] Matthew Paris, *Chronica Maiora*, Rolls Series, 1880. ed. H. R. Luard, vol. v. p. 172. See below, p. lii. for the whole story.

[2] See below, Appendix V. p. 77, § 10.

[3] W. L. Nash, *Churchwardens' Account book for the parish of St. Giles' Reading*, 1881. p. 74.

[4] See below, Appendix III. p. 69, § 33.

[5] *The Injunctions . . . of Richard Barnes*, Surtees Society, 1850. p. 45.

[6] White Kennett, *Parochial Antiquities*, Oxford, 1695. Glossary *sub voce* Clericus Sacerdotis.

[7] *Gentleman's Magazine*, 1801. vol. 71. p. 1090.

that this ministration belongs to the divine service.[1] Thus if the clerk be bound to help the priest in the divine service he must be bound also to help him in ministering sacraments and sacramentals.

At Faversham the first of the clerks' duties is that one of them shall diligently attend the Vicar or his deputy in the ministration of sacraments and sacramentals at all times both by day and night.[2] Also at St. Stephen's, Coleman Street, the clerks were at no time to be out of the way, but one was to be always ready to minister sacraments and sacramentals to anyone that should need them, to wait upon the curate, and to give him warning: and that none of the clerks should go or ride out of town without special licence of the Vicar and churchwardens.[3]

Included in this greater duty is the lesser duty:

To attend on the parson visiting the sick.—Lyndwood speaks of this, recommending that the clerk be clad in a surplice and carry the light.[4] At Coventry the clerk is to go with the priest when he visits the sick in his ward.[5] So also at All Saints, Bristol.[6] At St. Nicholas, Bristol, the Suffragan went, bearing the surplice, book, oil fat, and stole.[7] At St. Michael's, Cornhill, the clerks were to be "redye at all visitacions accustomed."[8]

At Wighton, a church belonging to York minster, the parishioners present, about the year 1470, that the parish clerk absents himself when the Vicar visits the sick, and sends only a boy with the Vicar.[9]

Bale, in the following century, profanely describes the visitation of the sick.

> Than came he, ful lyke a religious confessour, wyth hys cake God in a boxe, and the parish clarke or sexten wyth a bell and a lanterne.[10]

The parish clerk was accustomed to go with the priest to visit the sick in the eighteenth century; for we find it incidentally mentioned in a tract published by the company of parish clerks. We, that is the parish clerks, are

> always conversant in Holy Places, in Holy Things; such as are the Holy Sacraments of *Baptism* and the *Lord's Supper*; yea, and in the most serious Things too, such as the *Visitation of the Sick*, where we do often attend, and at the *Burial of the Dead*.[11]

[1] *Provinciale*, lib. iii. tit. *de concessione praebendae*, cap. *a nostris maioribus*, ad verb. *deservire*, Oxon. 1679, p. 142.
[2] See below, Appendix V. p. 75, § 1.
[3] See below, Appendix VIII. p. 91, §§ 12, 13.
[4] *Provinciale*, lib. iii. tit. *de reliquiis*, cap. *Dignissimum*, ad verba *saltem* and *lumine praevio*, Oxon. 1679, p. 249.
[5] See below, Appendix I. p. 59, § 36, p. 62, § 61.
[6] See below, Appendix II. p. 65, § 2.
[7] See below, Appendix III. p. 68, § 21.
[8] See below, Appendix VI. p. 82, § 5.
[9] *Fabric-Rolls of York Minster*, Surtees Society, 1859, p. 257.
[10] John Bale, *A declaration of Edmonde Bonners articles*, London, Frauncys Coldocke, 1561, fo. 80.
[11] *The Parish-Clerk's Guide*, by B. P. Parish-Clerk, London, Company of Parish Clerks, 1731. p. 16.

MINOR DUTIES.—It has been said just above that the minor duties of the clerk became multitudinous. The greater part of these are named in the following extract from the Statutes of the collegiate church of St. Mary Ottery, where the duties are arranged under eight heads, as follows:

> Item eciam sacrista idem in periculo anime sue et in virtute sacramenti prestiti sepius moneat et inducat aquebaiulos et alios duos clericos ecclesie nuncupatos quod diligentes sint, solliciti, et devoti circa
> campanas pulsandas,
> luminaria accendenda,
> vestimenta plicanda,
> altaria ornanda,
> ignem et carbones preparandos et querendos,
> ecclesiam mundandam,
> sconsas et boettas illuminandas,
> et in privatis missis sacerdotibus ministrandum.[1]

The duties of the clerks, then, would be these: i. to ring the bells; ii. to light the ritual lamps and candles; iii. to fold up the vestments; iv. to array the altars; v. to fetch and make ready fire and coal; vi. to keep the church clean; vii. to light the lanterns and sconses; and viii. to serve the priest at low mass.

1. *To ring the bells.*—In Germany this was considered so important a part of the clerk's duty that it seems to have given him his name of *Campanarius.*[2] Even to this day it is part of the duty of the *ostiarius*, the lowest of the minor orders as the modern Roman pontifical still testifies, and the Latin edition of the Canons of 1603 gives the name of *ostiarius* to the parish clerk.[3]

At St. Stephen's Bristol in 1393, the clerk was paid for tolling the bell.[4] The duty is prominent amongst the constitutions of clerks from that of Coventry in 1462, to that of Barrow on Humber in 1713, and in the visitation articles of the seventeenth and early eighteenth centuries. At Coventry besides ringing the day bell, and for mattins, high mass, and evensong, they had to ring for the sacring of the high mass, and at procession, for compline in Lent, and for none on Saturdays and holy day eves.[5]

There was, besides, the ringing at funerals and obits, and upon All Souls' eve. Also the bells were to be rung when the bishop, the king,

[1] George Oliver, *Monasticon Dioecesis Exoniensis*, Exeter, 1846, p. 271. § 46.

[2] Labbe and Cossart, *Sacrosancta Concilia*, Venetiis, 1731. t. xiv. col. 1286. Council of Cologne, 1300. canon xvii. *Ne campanarii sint illiterati.* Prohibemus item ne deinceps campanarii in villis et ecclesiis parochialibus ibidem assumantur, nisi literati, qui in defectu respondentis ad altare, cum camisiis lineis assistant, in missis deservientes presbytero, ne ministrator carent socio sibi respondente. Also for the same word see the Council of Triers in 1238, in Martène and Durand, *Veterum Scriptorum* etc., Parisiis, 1733, t. vii. col. 128. Canon xvi. Campanarii sine camisia in superiori non serviant in ecclesia vel alias in divinis.

[3] *Constitutiones sive Canones ecclesiastici*, London, John Norton, 1604. Canon 91.

[4] T. P. Wadley, *Notes or abstracts of the wills . . . at Bristol*, Bristol and Gloucestershire Society, 1886, p. 42.

[5] See below, Appendix I. Coventry, p. 57, §§ 2, 4, p. 58, §§ 5, 9, p. 60, §§ 39, 41, 42. Also p. 61, § 49, 52, p. 62, § 66, p. 63, §§ 74, 75, 77, 79.

the queen, and the prince, came[1]; this reminds us that it was ordered at St. Margaret's, Lothbury, in 1571, that the clerk should ring a peal at the passing by of the queen's majesty, by water or land.[2]

With the exception of these lesser details, the rules were very much the same at St. Nicholas, Bristol, but they had also to ring the bells to keep off thunder and to the lady mass in Lent.[3]

At Faversham, the duty of ringing the bells seems to fall more into the hands of the sexton than of the clerk[4]; but the clerks were to help the sexton when he had need.[5] At St. Stephen's, Coleman Street, the sexton rang curfew,[6] and also for mattins, as the clerks were to give him help if he wanted it, and they also rang the bells for mass, evensong, the Lent compline, and curfew when the sexton was away, and to all manner of divine service after the use and custom of the city of London.[7]

In 1510, the parishioners of Wighton complain of

> a faut that our parish clerk that he hath not done his dewtie to the kirk, that is to say, ryngyng of the morne bell and the evyn bell.

There is added immediately, surely by the clerk himself,

> and also a nother fawt, he fyndes that powr mene pays hym not his wages.[8]

In 1548, they paid at Ludlow twelve pence to the deacons "for ryngynge day belle after Easter at Mr. baylifes commaundyment."[9]

In 1571, at St. Margaret's Lothbury, the duty of ringing the bells is divided between the clerk and the sexton, the sexton ringing the morning and evening bell, while the clerk rings for burials, apparently as being the more profitable, and also the passing bell.[10]

At Barrow on Humber, the clerk had to attend at churchings and burials and to toll a bell and ring a little, according to the accustomed manner.[11]

Dr. W. D. Macray has given me an abstract of a document in the Bodleian Library which is the official record, dated December 12th, 1471, of the foundation by Thomas Peyton in the church of Iselham, Cambridgeshire, of the ringing by the parish clerk of the smallest of four bells, the one called Gabriel, immediately after the death of any parishioner. But it was not to be rung unseasonably, in the silence of the night.[12]

[1] p. 59, § 31, p. 63, § 75.
[2] See below, Appendix IV. p. 74.
[3] See below, Appendix III. p. 68, § 20.
[4] See below, Appendix V. p. 78, § 19 and p. 79, §§ 20, 21.
[5] p. 77, § 11.
[6] See below, Appendix VIII. p. 90, § 3.
[7] p. 91, § 14, and p. 92, §§ 23, 26.
[8] *Fabric Rolls of York Minster*, Surtees Society, 1859, p. 265.
[9] *Churchwardens' Accounts of the Town of Ludlow*, Ed. Thos. Wright, Camden Society, 1869, p. 35
[10] See below, Appendix IV. pp. 72 and 73.
[11] See below, Appendix XIV. p. 109, § 2.
[12] Bodleian Library, Cambridgeshire charter 60.

In the visitation articles of the seventeenth century, it is often enquired if the clerk ring the passing bell, as well as the bell before divine service.[1] The tolling of the bell before prayers appears in the visitation articles of Fleetwood, Bishop of St. Asaph, in 1710.[2] The duty of ringing morning and afternoon bells and curfew is expressly mentioned at Barrow on Humber in 1713.[3]

It must have been the custom for the clerk to carry about a little bell before a funeral; for we find it forbidden in 1583, by the Injunctions of Middleton, Bishop of St. David's, a convinced puritan :

> 2. Item, that the Clark nor his deputie, do carie about the Towne, a little bell called the Sainctes bell before the Buriall, after the vse of Popishe superstition.[4]

Besides ringing the bells, the clerk had also to take care of them, and see that all things connected with them, such as the ropes, baldricks, and clappers were in good order.[5] They were also to grease them.[6] At Ludlow in 1564 they paid the deacon for mending the bellropes.[7]

Attention to the church clock was also part of the clerk's duties, as the proverb testifies: The clock goes as it pleases the clerk. At Cawood in 1510, we find him keeping the clock, ringing curfew at due times appointed by the parish, and also ringing the day bell.[8] At Pilton also he kept the clock.[9] At St. Giles', Reading, in 1534, they paid Stevyn Bisbrige 2*s.* 6*d.* "for kepying of the clock ed chyme for a yere" and to the same man 6*s.* 8*d.*, "for his service in the quere for a yere." Thus he was a clerk, but it is not likely that he was the parish clerk.[10]

2. *To light the lamps.*—These must be the ritual lamps and candles. At St. Nicholas, Bristol, the suffragan was to have a torch ready for the masses, daily; and he put out all the lights in the quire and on the altars. Further, he was charged with all other lights and the quire light; also he kept two lamps burning, and saw that they had oil. The undersuffragan provided two torches at the high mass sacring on Sundays.[11] At St. Stephen's, Coleman Street, the sexton was to light

1 See below, Appendix XI. pp. 100 and 101.
2 Appendix XI. p. 102.
3 See below, Appendix XIV. p. 109, § 2, p. 110, §§ 3, 4, 7, 9, 10. Cf. also p. 102, § 7.
4 *Appendix E. to Second Report of the Royal Commission on Ritual*, 1868, p. 427.
5 Coventry, Appendix I. §§ 22, 57, 58, St. Nicholas Bristol, Appendix III. § 36, St. Margaret, Lothbury, Appendix IV. p. 74. St. Michael's, Cornhill, Appendix VI. p. 83. Barrow on Humber, Appendix XIV. § 2.
6 Coventry, Appendix I. §§ 29, 57. Barrow on Humber, Appendix XIV. § 2.
7 *Churchwardens' Accounts of the Town of Ludlow*, Ed. Thos. Wright, Camden Society, 1869, p. 119.
8 *Fabric Rolls of York Minster*, Surtees Society, 1859, p. 266.
9 *Churchwardens' Accounts*, Somerset Record Society, 1890, p. 70.
10 W. L. Nash, *The Churchwardens' Account Book . . . of St. Giles, Reading*, 1881, Part i. p. 49.
11 See below, Appendix III. p. 66, § 3, p. 69, § 35, p. 68, 30. The text of § 30 seems somewhat obscure.

the candles every Sunday and holiday in the year and put them out again.[1]

At Coventry the senior clerk had to tend the lamp and to fetch oil for it.[2]

At Faversham the clerk had to see that a light was in the quire while any mass was being sung, and the sexton had to see that it was kept up day and night, and that oil was supplied. The sexton also had to light the tapers and beams (the lights on the beams) according to the solemnity of the feast, at first evensong, mattins, mass, and last evensong.[3]

At Coventry the under clerk had to deliver to the woman about to be churched a taper, and bread for holy bread.[4]

At St. Nicholas, Bristol, clerk and suffragan had to tend the light before the sepulchre until Easter Even.[5]

Early in the sixteenth century, the Founders' Company in the city of London paid twelvepence a year to the Sexton for attending to their light and for ringing.[6] About the same time they paid fourpence to the Clerk and Sexton at St. Michael's, Bishops Stortford, for keeping the lamps at Easter.[7]

3. *To fold up the vestments.*—In the latter half of the fifteenth century, at Yatton, there is a reward of fourpence "paide to T. Clerke for foldyng of the vestments," every year.[8] At Coventry the clerks had to see the book, chalice, and vestment laid up in the vestry after mass, and to fold up the albes and vestments every Sunday and holiday.[9]

At St. Nicholas, Bristol, this duty had to be done on week days as well as on principal feasts.[10] At Faversham the ornaments for the principal feast which were kept in the treasury had to be taken thence and brought back again by the clerks.[11] At All Saints, Bristol, the clerk was to be true and profitable unto the church in keeping and guiding (guarding ?) the vestments, books, jewels and all other ornaments.[12]

In the late seventeenth century a parish clerk, writing about his duties, tells us that "the clerk is to take care . . . of the Holy Vestments, that they be decently kept."[13] And at Barrow on Humber it was part of the

1 See below, Appendix VIII. p. 90, § 2.

2 See below, Appendix I. p. 59, § 32.

3 See below, Appendix V. p. 76, § 2 and p. 79, §§ 22, 23.

4 See below, Appendix I. p. 63, § 73.

5 See below, Appendix III. p. 67, § 16.

6 *Archaeological Journal*, 1886, vol. xliii, p. 170.

7 J. L. Glasscock, *Records of St. Michael's Parish Church, Bishop's Stortford*, London, 1882, p. 11.

8 *Churchwardens' Accounts*, Somerset Record Society, edited by Bishop Hobhouse, 1890, p. 113.

9 See below, Appendix I. p. 57, §§ 1, 37, p. 61, § 55.

10 See below, Appendix III. p. 67, §§ 9, 18.

11 See below, Appendix V. p. 76, § 4.

12 See below, Appendix II. p. 64, § 1.

13 *The Parish Clerk's Vade Mecum*, by B. P. Parish Clerk, London, Benj. Motte, 1694, Preface to the Reader.

clerk's business to lay up carefully the communion cloth, carpet, and surplice.[1]

Allied to this is the duty of mending and washing the vestments. At St. Nicholas, Bristol, the suffragan had to see that the albes, amices, towels and altar cloths were washed, at the expense of the churchwardens.[2] In the tract issued by the Ecclesiological Society, instructing parish clerks in their duties, they are told that it is their business to see that "the surplices are clean and in good repair."[3]

4. *To array the altars.*—At Coventry the clerks had to wait upon the churchwardens at the first evensong of every principal feast to array the high altar with the cloths necessary for it; and the second clerk made ready the high altar every day for the priest to sing high mass.[4] At St. Nicholas, Bristol, both clerk and suffragan saw the altars dressed on principal feasts.[5] At St. Stephen's, Coleman Street, the clerks had to bring forth the copes, vestments, and apparels for the altars, on festival days, with the jewels for the altars, and disarray them again as the season required.[6] At Faversham the clerks had to apparel the altars daily where any priest was to sing mass, high mass, or morrow mass, or after. Also to apparel the altars against every principal feast with such apparel as belongeth to them.[7]

At Morebath one of the points agreed on in 1536 was that the clerk should help the churchwarden to make up the vestments and to dress the altars.[8]

At Coventry the clerks had to help the churchwardens at the beginning of Lent to cover the altar, and rood, with Lent cloths and to hang up the Lenten veil between the choir and the presbytery and to take them down again when the Easter had come.[9] The Lenten cloths, Mr. W. H. St. John Hope has shown with great fulness, were white in colour.[10]

5. *To fetch and make ready fire and coal.*—Not a hundred years ago fire had to be struck with flint and steel, a troublesome affair. Thus in the early ages it had to be provided for as the duty of a special officer. The fetching of fire occurs in many of the clerks' constitutions.

At St. Nicholas, Bristol, he is to fetch fire for the censers in a fire-plate, and not in the censer.[11] At Faversham they had to see that light or fire was in the chancel, the clerk during the time of mass, the sexton

[1] See below, Appendix XIV. p. 109, § 1.
[2] See below, Appendix III. p. 58, § 26.
[3] *A few words to the Parish Clerks and Sextons of Country Parishes*, Third Ed. London, 1846, p. 7, § 11.
[4] See below, Appendix I. p. 58, § 19, p. 63, § 80.
[5] See below, Appendix III. p. 67, § 10.
[6] See below, Appendix VIII. p. 91, § 15.
[7] See below, Appendix V. p. 76, §§ 2, 3, p. 77, § 9.
[8] See below, Appendix VII. p. 88, § 13.
[9] See below, Appendix I. p. 59, §§ 38, 25.
[10] *Transactions of St. Paul's Ecclesiological Society*, 1886–1890, vol. ii. p. 233.
[11] See below, Appendix III. p. 68, § 24.

by day and night.[1] At St. Michael's, Cornhill, they had to provide for fire on all such feasts as incense was offered.[2] At St. Stephen's, Coleman Street, the sexton fetched fire in time of need, and the clerks had to see it ready in the censers before it was needed.[3]

At Coventry the second deacon had to see that the churchwardens provided the coals and fire on Easter Even.[4]

6. *To keep the church clean.*—This is of all time. At Coventry the first deacon had to sweep the floor of the quire and nave and the second clerk the floor of the south aisle, and to clean the corresponding leads, and to clear away the snow from the gutters lest the pipes be stopped.[5] Both had to attend to the snow on the steeple.[6] At All Saints, Bristol, the church roofs, windows, pillars, walls and floor, stalls and seats, and specially the altar, were to be kept clean by the clerk.[7]

At St. Nicholas, Bristol, the under clerk had to sprinkle the church with water every Saturday to keep it from dust, to make tidy the crypt, the stair, and the church doors, to clear away cobwebs and dust from the altars and imagery. Both clerk and suffragan had to sweep the glass windows, church walls, and pillars, once a quarter, and the seats in the church when they were called upon.[8]

At Faversham every week the clerks had to make clean the quire, the Trinity chapel, and specially over the altars, and to brush away the cobwebs. The sexton had to make clean the body of the church and the aisles every week, and every day to see the church made clean "for skomeryng of doggs."[9]

At St. Stephen's, Coleman Street, the sexton had to sweep the church once a week at the least, and cast water on the ground "for Rasynge of dust, and to sweep the church roof four times in the year."[10] The clerks had to sweep all the images and glass windows twice a year, at Easter and the translation of St. Stephen, and to keep tidy the alleys of the church yard.[11]

In the Visitation articles we find enquiries made if the clerk keep the church clean. Grindal askes if the parish clerk keep the books and ornaments of the church fair and clean, and if he cause the church and quire, the communion table, pulpit, and font, to be made decent and clean.[12] Much the same enquiries go on in the seventeenth century. Cosin asks if the clerk keep the church or chapel clean from noisome dust, cobwebs, litter, straw or any other annoyance[13]: and in 1710

[1] See below, Appendix V. p. 76, § 3 and p. 79, § 22.
[2] See below, Appendix VI. p. 82, § 4.
[3] See below, Appendix VIII. p. 90, §§ 5, 16.
[4] See below, Appendix I. p. 62, § 63.
[5] See below, Appendix I. p. 58, §§ 11, 12, and p. 61, § 53.
[6] p. 59, § 21.
[7] See below, Appendix II. p. 65, § 4.
[8] See below, Appendix III. p. 67, §§ 6, 7, 10, 12, p. 69, § 39.
[9] See below, Appendix V. p. 76, § 7, and p. 79, §§ 24, 25.
[10] See below, Appendix VIII. p. 90, §§ 1, 7.
[11] p. 92, § 27.
[12] See below, Appendix XI. p. 98.
[13] Appendix XI. p. 100.

Fleetwood asks if the clerk keep the church clean, and mentions the good keeping of this part of their duty as a reason for due payment of their salary and perquisites, as if it had become the chief, if not the only, duty they had.[1]

At Barrow on Humber the clerk had to see that the church, chancel, and seats, were swept, and kept handsome and decent.[2]

Mr. Beresford Hope gives as evidence of the apathy with which elementary propriety in church matters was regarded in the reign of King George IV. the fact that the parish clerk used to sweep the church out during service time.[3]

In the little tract published by the Ecclesiological Society and addressed to parish clerks they are told that "the first thing which it is your business to do, or to see done, is the keeping the church clean."[4]

7. *To light the lanterns and sconses*, that is, the means of lighting up the church when it was dark. Of this duty we find but little mention in the clerk's constitutions. At Coventry the second clerk was to bring out sconses for the winter time to light the quire, but nothing is said of his duty in lighting the candles set in the sconses.[5] At St. Stephen's, Coleman Street, it is said that the sexton, every Sunday and holiday, is to light the candles and put them out again; but the rule makes no distinction between ordinary and ceremonial lights.[6]

8. *To serve the priest at low mass.*—This might almost be considered one of the essential parts of a clerk's duty; for he was to read the epistle at mass, and thus of necessity he must serve the priest. The evidence for this has been given above. In England, the reading of the epistle by the clerk, and of his serving at the altar, had fallen into very great disuse in the early nineteenth century. Yet not wholly: for besides the instances given above of the clerk reading the epistle in recent times, certain correspondents of the newspapers tell us also of his waiting at the altar, as the following extracts set forth.

> It was, I remember, at this date, [thirty-five years before 1876] customary for the parish clerk (not in orders) to take his place within the communion rails as assistant, or acolyte, if that word would have been understood in those days.
>
> I well remember the importation of what would be called an "Evangelical curate," who strongly objected to this, and the clerk was forthwith ejected from his post at the "altar table," as we Northerns called it, greatly to his indignation.[7]

Mr. J. B. Wilson writes in 1880:

> Up to a few years ago at Lower Sapey Church in Worcestershire, when the parson left the reading-desk at the end of Morning Prayer, and took up

[1] Appendix XI. p. 102.
[2] See below, Appendix XIV. p. 108, § 2.
[3] A. J. B. Beresford Hope, *Worship in the Church of England*, London, 1875, sec. ed. p. 8.
[4] *A few words to the parish clerks and sextons of country parishes*, London, 1846. Third Ed. p. 4, § 5.
[5] See below, Appendix I. p. 63, § 72.
[6] See below, Appendix VIII. p. 90, § 2.
[7] A letter signed F. B. G. in the *Guardian*, May 31, 1876, p. 711, under "Reservation for the sick."

his position at the north side of the altar, it was the custom for the clerk also to go within the rails and kneel down at the south side of the altar.[1]

Dr. F. G. Lee asserts that it was customary for the parish clerk in many Oxfordshire and Buckinghamshire churches to attend upon the parson at the communion table, and to kneel either at or within the rails, and that in some cases he wore a surplice.[2]

There has been a recent revival of the practice in several English parishes. In the early days of the ecclesiological revival it was, however, thought very improper that the clerk should go inside the altar rails. He is told in a tract published by the Ecclesiological Society that

> If old customs were kept up as they ought to be, you would never be allowed to go within the altar-rails; and this I hope may some day be the case again. In the meantime, I would not go there needlessly: and when there, would behave so as to show that I knew myself to be on very holy ground.[3]

At this point we leave the duties named in the Statutes of St. Mary Ottery. But there are still some few to be spoken of.

Opening and shutting church.—At Coventry the senior clerk had to open the church doors every day at six o'clock,[4] while the junior needed only to be in the church half-an-hour before seven. At All Saints, Bristol, the clerk had to open and shut the church at due times, and also to search the church.[5] So at St. Nicholas, Bristol, with a search for fear of sleepers.[6] At Morebath it was agreed that when service was done, the clerk should knock at the church door half-an-hour after; then if any would abide in the church so that the door stood open all night, the hurt to the church should fall upon them and not on the clerk.[7]

At St. Michael's, Cornhill, it was ordered in 1596 that the church door should be kept shut in the weekdays after service, whereby boys and others may be kept forth from doing damage.

The Latin edition of the canons of 1603 gives the title *De Ostiariis sive Clericis Parochialibus* to Canon 91, which deals with the office of parish clerk.[9] The *ostiarius* in prae-Reformation times was held to be the lowest or first conferred of the minor orders, and according to St. Isidore he held the keys of the church, which he opened and shut.[10]

In the same century as these canons were passed Christopher Hervey calls the sexton by the name of the "Churches key-keeper."[11]

[1] *Notes and Queries*, May, 1880, 6th Series, vol. i. p. 356.

[2] *Notes and Queries*, *ibid.*, p. 522.

[3] *A few words to the parish clerks and sextons of country parishes*, third edition, London, 1846, p. 6, § 11.

[4] See below, Appendix I. p. 57, § 1.

[5] See below, Appendix II. p. 64, § 1.

[6] See below, Appendix III. p. 66, §§ 1, 2.

[7] See below, Appendix VII. p. 84, § 1.

[8] *The Accounts of the Churchwardens . . . St. Michael, Cornhill*, 1872, p. 253.

[9] *Constitutiones sive Canones Ecclesiastici*, London, John Norton, 1604.

[10] *Epistola B. Isidori*, in J. Saenz de Aguirre, *Collectio maxima conciliorum*, ed. J. Catalani, Romae, 1753, t. iii. p. 455.

[11] See below, p. xlvii.

To carry the pax round the church.—This is one of the duties of the clerk which we find all over England. It is spoken of incidentally in the marriage service of the rites of Sarum,[1] York,[2] and Hereford,[3] almost in the same words in all: "clericus statim a presbytero pacem accipiens, proferat aliis sicut solitum est." He carries the pax to the others as it has been accustomed.

Thomas Becon says that "the boye or parrish clark carrieth the *Pax* aboute," for the people to kiss.[4] Also in the injunctions for the Deanery of Doncaster[5] we are told that "the Clarke in the like manner shall bring down the *Paxe*."

To keep the registers.—Thomas Cromwell in 1536 ordered registers to be kept of the weddings, christenings, and burials;[6] and there is evidence that this duty was performed by the parish clerk. For example, at St. Stephen's, Coleman Street, in 1542, the clerks were every week to certify to the curate the names of those married, baptized, and buried, under pain of a penny fine.[7] At St. Margaret's, Lothbury, it was ordered in 1571,[8] the clerk should keep the register of christenings, weddings, and buryings, perfectly, and should present the same every Sunday to the churchwardens to be perused by them, and to have for his pains 3*s.* 4*d.* yearly.

In 1563 at St. Margaret's, Westminster, they bought

> a quier of paper, for the clerks to make weekly certificates unto the court of all buryals and christenings.[9]

A duty of the parish clerk in the city of London, beginning before the injunctions of Thomas Cromwell and lasting into the middle of the nineteenth century, was the drawing up of the bills of mortality. This was a weekly return of the number of deaths in each parish, sent to the Lord Mayor of London and to the King's Council. Probably it was some such return that is spoken of in the entry of St. Margaret's, Westminster, just named.

The history of the bills of mortality has been dealt with at length by Mr. James Christie,[10] and it does not seem necessary to go further into this matter in the present edition.

SOCIAL AND ECCLESIASTICAL POSITION.—It has been seen that King Richard I. delighted to take the place of *rector chori*,[11] and John of Athon

[1] *Missale . . . Sarum*, ed. F. H. Dickinson, Burntisland, 1861–83, col. 844*.
[2] *Missale . . . Ebor.* Surtees Society, 1874. Vol. ii. p. 192.
[3] *Missale . . . Herford.* ed. Henderson, Leeds, 1874, p. 443.
[4] Thomas Becon, *The displayeng of the Popysh Masse*, in *Workes*, London, 1563, vol. iii. fo. xlix. *b*.
[5] See below, Appendix IX. p. 94.
[6] D. Wilkins, *Concilia*, Lond. 1737, t. iii. p. 816.
[7] See below, Appendix VIII. § 10, p. 91.
[8] See below, Appendix IV. p. 72.
[9] J. Nichols, *Illustrations of the Manners*, etc. London, 1797, p. 17.
[10] James Christie, *Some account of Parish Clerks*, 1893, privately printed by James Vincent, pp. 132–147.
[11] See above, p. xix.

lays down the rule that any clerk, even if he be the son of a king, must not be ashamed to go up to the book and read and sing in the church.[1]

It may be noticed also that in the time of Henry VII. a canon of Newburgh did not think it beneath his dignity to ask for the place of parish clerk for his brother.[2] And it does not seem to be universally true that the office of parish clerk was considered vile and mean in the unreformed church as Ayliffe would suggest.[3] We have seen the instances to the contrary given above. And later on, in the seventeenth century, there is an instance, for the knowledge of which I am indebted to Mr. J. Brooking Rowe, of the parish clerk being in the holy order of a deacon: one Hobbes, parish clerk of Plymouth at the beginning of the troubles in King Charles the First's reign.

> Hobbes,—: He was in Deacon's *Orders*, and so must have a Place in this List; Although he was no other than *Parish-Clerk* of *Plymouth*: And having one Day *Buried* a *Corpse* by the *Common-Prayer*, he was Threatned, that if he came again with his *Mass-Book*, to *Bury* any body, he should be thrown into the same *Grave*: Which worked so much upon his Spirits, that partly with Fear, and partly with Grief, he Died soon after.[4]

Upon this Mr. J. Brooking Rowe has the following note:

> It is interesting to find Walker's story of William Hobbs, the clerk of St. Andrew's, confirmed. He was frightened to death while burying a corpse in the yard, the Puritans threatening to throw him into the grave if he came there again with his mass-book, that is, the book of common prayer. In the earliest book we find him clerk, receiving £7 per annum, in addition to burial and other fees, and £2 10*s*. for keeping the burial account, and 10*s*. for keeping the register. He died in 1643; and the balance of his salary was paid to his widow. His successor, Henry Champlyn, who was appointed to keep the register by the mayor in 1653, appears to have been the clerk until 1683, and was, I believe, succeeded by his son, who was clerk until 1716, the two thus holding office for about 73 years.[5]

Later on in the same century, in the reign of James II. the Act of Parliament which erects the new parish of St. James, Piccadilly, directs that the clerk of the new church shall be in priest's orders, and shall receive thirty pounds a year from the pew rents.[6] Mr. James Christie, examining the records of the Company of Parish Clerks in the city of London, is able to tell us that the parish clerks in orders, by which it may be inferred was meant holy orders, were recognised specially in a minute of 1689. Many such in the following century, he adds, joined the Company, and up to 1823 their membership is recognised.[7]

[1] Unde quicunque sis, etiamsi filius Regis, ex quo Clericali Militiae es ascriptus, non erubescas in Ecclesia ad librum accedere, legere, et cantare; quod si per te nescias, sequere scientes. (Constitutio Othonis, tit. *de Institutione Vicariorum* § *de iam vero*, verb. *ecclesiis*. Appendix to Lyndwood, *Provinciale*, 1679, p. 28.)

[2] *Plumpton Correspondence*, edited by Thomas Stapleton, Camden Society, 1839, p. 66.

[3] John Ayliffe, *Parergon Iuris Canonici Anglicani*, London, 1726, p. 409.

[4] John Walker, *An attempt towards recovering an account of the numbers and sufferings of the Clergy*, London, 1714. Appendix, p. 418.

[5] J. Brooking Rowe, *The Church of St. Andrew, Plymouth*, Plymouth, 1875, p. 45.

[6] See below, Appendix XI. p. 101.

[7] James Christie, *Some account of parish Clerks*, 1893, privately printed by James Vincent, p. 212.

In 1844 an Act was passed by which it was definitely made lawful for a person in the holy orders of Deacon or Priest to be elected parish clerk; but to such person it gave no freehold, but only the same rights as a stipendiary curate.[1] At All Hallows Barking, a priest has served the office of parish clerk since 1884.

The courts do not seem to agree in opinion whether the parish clerk be a spiritual person or not. In the case recorded by Godolphin it was held, apparently by the Court of King's Bench, that the parish clerk is a mere layman.[2] But afterwards there was another case, in the third year of Queen Anne, where one Judge seems to have held that the clerk was not a spiritual person, while other Judges held that he was an ecclesiastical person and in inferior orders.

> In the Case of *Parker* and *Clerk*, 3 *Annae*, where Prohibition was pray'd to stay Proceedings in the Spiritual Court, of a Parish Clerk against the Church-wardens, for soe much money due to him yearly, and by them leviable upon the Parishioners; it was said by *Holt*, Without doubt, the Spiritual Court has noe original Jurisdiction here, if they doe not make the Clerk a Spiritual person, which will be hard to doe; but others said, they look'd upon the Clerk to be an Ecclesiastical person, and in inferior Orders, and that as such, he might sue in the Spiritual Court for a stipend or pension.[3]

It must be owned that it seems more reasonable to agree with the second thoughts of the Court of Queen's Bench in the time of Queen Anne rather than to assert a contradiction in terms, as John Johnson calls it, by speaking of a lay clerk.[4] In 1710 Fleetwood, Bishop of St. Asaph, points out that the parish clerk was heretofore in some low sort of Orders and that they still kept the name of *Clerici*.[5]

The following remarks, made by Dr. Raine, the editor of Dr. Barnes' *Injunctions*, may help us to understand in some degree the position of parish clerks in the north of England towards the end of the sixteenth century.

> At the end of this Visitation of Northumberland, it is worthy of remark, that in many parishes or chapelries, in which was settled a house of old descent and note and coat armour, we have one of the same family name acting as parish clerk, a fact which is not to be observed in the Visitation of the county of Durham, to which we proceed. The following list, derived from the preceding pages, leads to the conclusion that either the persons here specified were in such circumstances as to make even a parish-clerkship acceptable, or that they thus officiated because no parishioner of the humbler class was able to read.

Here follow the names of some sixteen parish clerks. Dr. Raine then adds:

> We have, moreover, as parish clerk of Woodhorne, Amor Oxley, who was an eminent schoolmaster. Edward Stanley, parish clerk of Chillingham, was a young gentleman in the household of Sir Thomas Grey.[6]

[1] See below, Appendix XI. p. 102.
[2] See below, Appendix XIII. p. 107.
[3] Edm. Gibson, *Codex Iuris Ecclesiastici Anglicani*, tit. ix. cap. xiv. Oxford, 1761. t. i. p. 214. note d.
[4] John Johnson, *Clergy-mans' Vade-mecum*, London, 1709. Ch. xxiii. p. 203.
[5] See below, Appendix XI. p. 102.
[6] *The Injunctions and other Ecclesiastical proceedings of Richard Barnes, Bishop of Durham*, Surtees Society, 1850, p. 45. Chancellor's Visitation 1577–8.

It may be that these varying statements may be explained by supposing that the parish-clerkship was an office sometimes filled by men of education and position, sometimes taken by men who had scarcely the qualifications to enable them barely to exercise their duties. This may be seen in many professions and callings; and the parish clerk does not seem an exception.

Exemption from Juries.—By the 6th George IV. cap. 50, § 2, made in the year of our Lord 1825, a number of persons are exempt from serving on juries: "all officers of Customs and Excise; all Sheriffs, Officers, High Constables and Parish Clerks shall be and are hereby absolutely freed and exempted from being returned and from serving on any Juries." It is believed that this Act is still in force. A gentleman of large property in Wales was summoned upon the Grand Jury oftener than he liked. He procured himself to be appointed parish clerk; he claimed exemption on this ground and the claim was allowed by Mr. Justice Blackburn. And in 1888 a man resident in West Kensington received a jury notice; at the foot was a statement of various grounds of exemption; one of these was the holding of the office of parish clerk. Having been appointed to this office in his father's parish, he claimed exemption, and obtained it.

VESTURE.—The clerks who accompany Maximianus in the well-known mosaics at St. Vitalis in Ravenna wear a vesture which is the forerunner of the surplice, rochet, or alb. But though the thing appears in the sixth century, yet the name hardly makes its appearance before the twelfth.[1] In the late middle ages we find the surplice frequently named as the vesture of clerks. In 1229 the sixth Constitution of W. de Bloys directs that he who serves at mass shall wear a surplice.[2] By Winchelsey's *Ut parochiani* three surplices and one rochet had to be found; and Lyndwood glosses this order, saying that the three surplices are for the priest, deacon, and subdeacon, while the rochet is for the clerk.[3] But there are directions of Archbishop Walter's

[1] D. Wilkins, *Concilia*, Lond. 1737. t. i. p. 624.

[2] The surplice is incidentally alluded to by William of Malmesbury in a work finished by 1125. (*Gesta Pontificum*, lib. i. cap. 44. Rolls Series, 1870. p. 71. "canonicos cappis et superpellitiis ornaverat"), and in the laws of Edward the Confessor, a collection which may have been in existence before 1125 if it be spoken of by Henry I. (B. Thorpe, *Ancient Laws . . . England*, 1840. p. 199. Law xxxvi. "clericis in suppelliciis.") If it could be proved that the surplice is mentioned in the third canon of the Council of Cayaca, A.D. 1050, as Messrs. Addis and Arnold maintain (*Catholic Dictionary*, London, 1884, *sub voce* surplice: and again in the edition of 1897.) the first appearance of the word would be sent back more than half a century; but I cannot find it in the editions of these canons by Labbe, or Mansi, or Saenz. Lyndwood seems to suggest that the word surplice has not the right to exist, because he cannot remember to have found it in the civil or canon law, nor in holy cripture. (*Provinciale*, lib. i. tit. *de off. Archi.* cap. *Sint Ecclesiarum*, verb. *altari.* Oxon. 1679. p. 53.) It may be an example of the frequent antagonism between the canonist and the ritualist. However usual the word may be in liturgy, yet it ought not to be sanctioned unless the canonist have set his seal upon it.

[3] Lyndwood, *Provinciale*, lib. iii. tit. *De ecclesiis aedificandis* cap. *Ut parochiani*, verb. *Tria superpellicia* and *Rochetum*, Oxon. 1679. p. 252. Winchelsey is from 1294 to 1313.

that he who waits at the altar shall be clothed in a surplice,[1] and Lyndwood glosses the second direction which contains the word clerk, by noting that it is the parish clerk. In the same way, in the visitation of the sick, the Constitutions of Alexander, Bishop of Coventry in 1237, direct that the deacon or clerk accompanying the priest who carries the eucharist shall wear a surplice.[2] Under the same circumstances Lyndwood thinks it better that the minister who accompanies the priest should wear a surplice.[3]

Chaucer's parish clerk, the jolly Absolon, wore a surplice:

> I-clad he was ful smal and propurly,
> Al in a kirtel of a fyn wachet
> Schapen with goores in the newe get.
> And therupon he had a gay surplys
> As whyt as is the blosme upon the rys.[4]

And in the clerk's rules we find the clerk is to wear a surplice. At Coventry he collects offerings on Twelfth day for the reparation of his surplice.[5] He wore a surplice when at mass at St. Nicholas, Bristol.[6] At Faversham he wore a rochet.[7] At St. Michael, Cornhill, no minister was to "sitt in quire during divine service without a surplice."[8]

The Churchwardens' accounts and similar documents of the fourteenth, the fifteenth, and the sixteenth centuries show mention of the clerk's surplice or rochet. At St. Michael's, Bath, in 1364, the churchwardens paid for the mending of the parish clerk's surplice.[9] In 1430 they bought a new surplice for him for four shillings and fourpence.[10] In 1455, there was at St. Ewen's, Bristol, "a Rochette for the Clerk."[11] In 1489 the churchwardens at Leicester paid for a "rochet for the clerk and making 2*s.* 1*d.* ob."[12] In 1502–3 at St. Michael's, Bath, they bought linen for a rochet for the parish clerk, two ells and a half for seventeen pence, and paid for the making eightpence.[13]

[1] Lyndwood, lib. i. tit. *de officio Archidi.* cap. *Sint Ecclesiarum*, p. 53. "Qui altari ministrat suppellicio induatur." See also lib. iii. tit. *De celebratione missarum*, cap. *Linteamina* p. 236. "Item nullus clericus permittatur ministrare in officio altaris nisi indutus in superpellicio." Clericus: *supple Parochialis*, adds Lyndwood.

[2] D. Wilkins, *Concilia*, London, 1737. t. i. p. 641.

[3] Lyndwood, lib. iii. tit. *de reliquiis*, cap. *Dignissimum*, verb. *Saltem*, p. 249.

[4] Chaucer, *Miller's tale*, 134, *Poetical Works*, edited by R. Morris, Bell and Daldy, no date, vol. ii. p. 102. The kirtle with gores can hardly have been the clerical cassock that is worn under the surplice. And he was used to let blood (v. 140) forgetting *Ecclesia abhorret a sanguine*. Altogether he was no good clerk.

[5] See below, Appendix I. §§ 18 and 59, pp. 58 and 62.

[6] See below, Appendix III. p. 67, § 18.

[7] See below, Appendix V. p. 76, § 2.

[8] See below, Appendix VI. p. 83, § 11.

[9] C. B. Pearson, *Churchwardens' Accounts . . . of St. Michael without the north gate, Bath*, Somerset Archæological and Natural History Society's Proceedings, vol. xxiii. Taunton, 1878, p. 6.

[10] *Ibid.* p. 41.

[11] Cuthbert Atchley, *Inventories of the Goods of the Parish Church of St. Ewen, Bristol*, p. 6. (Privately printed by G. du Boistel and Co. Bristol, 1900.)

[12] Thomas North, *Accounts of the Churchwardens of St. Martin's, Leicester*, Leicester, 1884, p. 2.

[13] C. P. Pearson, *op. cit.* p. 96.

At St. Margaret's, Westminster, in 1534, they paid for a surplice for the curate; John More, the clerk; Thomas Adams the clerk; and also for the sexton. The curate's cost ten shillings; the others only three. But in 1628, for thirteen ells of holland to make surplices for the two clerks and sextons at 3*s.* 4*d.* the ell they paid £3 16*s.* 8*d.*[1] At Wing in Buckinghamshire in 1562 they "payde for makynge of the Clarkes surplas" at the same time that they also paid "for mendynge of the Curates surples."[2]

In 1568 at Worcester they paid ij*d.* "for mendyng the clark's surples" which they had in 1551.[3] Also in 1572 at Bristol they had two surplices for the priest, two surplices for the clerk, as well as two long houseling towels, and six old albes.[4]

The instances of the wearing of the surplice or rochet by the clerk in the sixteenth century are numerous, and it does not seem necessary to give here all that are known.

From the records of the Parish Clerks' Company in London Mr. Christie is able to cite a rule made in 1610 that the clerks are to appear at their special evensong at Guildhall Chapel in a fair white surplice, under a penalty. But in 1640 the rule is altered: "he shall sit or stand in decent manner in his gowne."[5] This is doubtless the result of the prevailing Puritanism of the time.

The visitation articles of the diocese of Exeter in 1638 inquire if the clerk usually wear a surplice or rochet in the time of divine service.[6]

About thirty years later, in the visitation articles of Dr. John Cosin, Bishop of Durham, in 1662, it is inquired if the parish clerk wear a gown and a surplice over it, if the custom have been such.[7] The gown, doubtless, means some variety of the cassock, such as vergers still wear in cathedral churches.

The surplice or rochet for the clerk seems to have been in use even at the end of the eighteenth century. In the parish church of Bledlow, Buckinghamshire, an inventory was taken in 1783, and one of the items is this:

A surplice without Sleeves, intended for the Clerk.[8]

Also Fosbroke says of the clerks that "in some churches they still wear a surplice without sleeves."[9]

Of the survival of the surplice as part of the vesture of the clerk into the first half of the nineteenth century I have one other solitary

[1] John Nicholls, *Illustrations of the Manners*, etc. London, 1797, pp. 10 and 37.
[2] *Archaeologia*, 1855, vol. xxxvi. p. 235.
[3] John Amphlett, *Churchwardens' Accounts of St. Michael's in Bedwardine, Worcester*, Oxford, 1896, pp. 28 and 63. Here they paid in 1545 "for a peare of gloues for the clerke's ease ij.d." (p. 14) I presume to keep his hands warm.
[4] J. F. Nichols and John Taylor, *Bristol past and present*, 1881, vol. ii. p. 37.
[5] James Christie, *Some account of parish clerks*, 1893, privately printed by James Vincent, p. 175.
[6] See below, Appendix XI. p. 99.
[7] See below, Appendix XI. p. 100.
[8] This inventory will shortly appear in the *Transactions of St. Paul's Ecclesiological Society*.
[9] T. D. Fosbroke, *Encyclopædia of Antiquities*, London, 1825, vol. ii. p. 680.

witness.[1] After the rise of the Cambridge Ecclesiological movement a clerk wearing a surplice may often be found; but this is a restoration, not a survival of old custom.

AGE.—Saint Cyprian tells us of one whom he had ordained reader that he was *illustris adolescens* and therefore it will be seen of no great age.[2] And an early notice that we have of clerks supposes that they will be boys, before the age of puberty and incapable of marriage, for it allows them to marry after they have grown up.[3] There are traces of ordination even in the period of infancy.[4]

We all remember the lines in Chaucer:

> Among these children was a widow sone
> A litel clergeoun, that seve yer was of age.[5]

He was already a little clergyman, though only seven years of age.

Justinian forbad readers to be ordained before the age of 18,[6] and there may be some reminiscence of this in the ninety-first canon of 1603, which orders that the parish clerk shall be at least twenty years of age[7]; and accordingly in the visitation articles of the seventeenth century we find inquiries whether the clerk be of the age of twenty at the least.

MARRIAGE.—St. Gregory, answering one of the questions put to him by St. Augustine of Canterbury, replies that clerks who are not in holy orders may marry and receive their stipends from without.[8] Innocent II. in a Council held at Rhemes in 1131, orders that all who had entered the subdiaconate and upwards and yet retained their wives should be

[1] Dr. F. G. Lee, *Notes and Queries*, May, 1880, 6th Series, vol. i. p. 522.

[2] Cyprian, *Epistolae* xxxiii. Migne, *Patrologia*, t. 4. col. 317.

[3] Canon. 1. Concilium Vasense A.D. 529.

Hoc enim placuit, ut omnes presbyteri, qui sunt in parochiis constituti, secundum consuetudinem, quam per totam Italiam satis salubriter teneri cognovimus, iuniores lectores quantoscumque sine uxore habuerint, secum in domo, ubi ipsi habitare videntur, recipiant: et eos quomodo boni patres spiritaliter nutrientes, psalmos parare, divinis lectionibus insistere, et in lege domini erudire contendant: ut et sibi dignos successores provideant, et a domino praemia aeterna recipiant. Cum vero ad aetatem perfectam pervenerint, si aliquis eorum pro carnis fragilitate uxorem habere voluerit, potestas ei ducendi coniugium non negetur.

(Labbe and Cossart, *Sacrosancta Concilia*, Venetiis, 1728, t. v. col. 821.)

[4] Eugenius [654-657] natione Romanus de regione prima Aventinense, clericus a cunabulis. (L. Duchesne, *Liber Pontificalis*, Paris, 1886, t. i. p. 341.) Other instances among the popes may be found in P. Batiffol, *History of the Roman Breviary*, Ch. ii. § i. London, 1898, p. 55.) Inter quos quam plurimi erant lectores infantuli. (Victor Vitensis, *de persecutione Vandalica*, Lib. v. cap. ix. Migne, *Patrologia*, t. 58. col. 246.) The rule of St. Benedict (capp. lix. and lxx.) encourages the offering of children and infants to a monastery.

[5] Chaucer, *Prioresses Tale*, line 50. (ed. R. Morris, iii. 123.)

[6] *Novellae constitutiones Dn. Iustininiani*, Antv. 1567, p. 224. (thus, for 324) Novel. 123, *Clericos autem.*

[7] *Constitutions and Canons Ecclesiasticall*, London, Robert Barker, 1604, No. xci.

[8] St. Gregory the Great, *Epistolae*, lib. xi. 64. (studio et labore Monachorum O.S.B. Venetiis, 1771, t. viii. p. 297.)

put from their benefices. It may be inferred from this that clerks below the subdiaconate might marry, and yet not lose their benefices.[1]

Lyndwood deals with the marriage of clerks in two glosses.[2] He declares that married clerks, especially if they be twice married, are nothing better than laymen, and that if they do not wear the clerical dress and tonsure they enjoy no clerical privilege. The married clerk is not to sit or stand among the clerks, but among the layfolk. But as is the custom of canonists, what he takes away with one hand, he immediately restores with the other, and he adds at once that when unmarried clerks are not to be had, married clerks may perform duty, provided they have not been twice married and retain the tonsure and clerical dress. A passage from the Decretals of Gregory IX. favours this:

> Clericus, si tonsura dimissa uxorem acceperit, qui quidem sit sine gradu, nec monasterio a parentibus traditus, uxorem permittatur habere, et iterum tondeatur, nec in vita sua uxorem dimittere audeat.[3]

There can be no doubt that married clerks abounded in England. Amongst other instances there are these: John Brian parish clerk of the church of St. Mary Aldermanbury left to Alice his wife his tenements and to the priory of St. Mary de Elsyngspitull his books on the canon law.[4] At St. Mary Bishophill York in 1416 it is complained that the parish clerk and his wife were hindered from entering their house on Sundays with the holy water according to the custom of the city.[5] In the same year the accounts of St. Michael's Bath, twice make mention of payments made *clerico et uxori*.[6] In 1378 the wife of the parish clerk of St. Peter the less in the city of London was successful in her suit for the release of her husband who had spoken disrespectfully of John of Gaunt.[7] In 1514 John Huyk parish clerk of Hull was to be buried beside his wife in the wedding porch of the church.[8]

Exceeding Duties.—In the first years of Elizabeth we meet with an inquiry from the Puritan Bishop of Norwich, Parkhurst, if the reader be exceeding his duties:

> § 27. Whether that any reader being admitted but to reade: taketh vpon him to baptize, to marie, to celebrate the Lords supper or to distribute the Lords cup.[9]

[1] Concilium Remense, anno Domini 1131, Canon IV. (Labbe, *Sacrosancta Concilia*, Venetiis, 1730, t. xii. col. 1463.) See also 3rd Canon of first Lateran Council under Calixtus II. in 1123. (*ibid.* col. 1333.)

[2] W. Lyndwode, *Provinciale*, Lib. iii. tit. *de clericis coniugatis* cap. *cum ex eo* verb. *vestigia canonum*, and tit. *de concessione praebendae*, cap. *a nostris maioribus*, verb. *clericis*, Oxon. 1679, pp. 129, and 142.

[3] *Decreta Gregorii IX.* lib. iii. tit. i. cap. vi. in Æ. L. Richter, *Corpus Iuris Canonici*, Lipsiae, 1839, pars ii. col. 433.

[4] Reginald R. Sharpe, *Calendar of Wills . . . Court of Husting London*, 1890, part ii. p. 24 under year 1361. See also part i. pp. 243, 253, 378, 396, 467, 509, 667, 694, part ii. 18, 77, 228.

[5] *Fabric Rolls of York Minster*, Surtees Society, 1859, p. 248.

[6] C. B. Pearson, *Churchwardens' Accounts . . . of St. Michael without the north gate, Bath*, Somersetshire Archæological and Natural History Society's Proceedings, vol. xxiii. Taunton, 1878, p. 24.

[7] H. T. Riley, *Memorials of London*, 1868, p. 425.

[8] *Testamenta Eboracensia*, Surtees Society, 1884. Vol. v. p. 49.

[9] *Interrogatories*, in *Iniunctions exhibited by John by gods sufferance Bishop of Norwich*, London [1561] B. i. *b*.

In the visitation articles of Matthew Parker,[1] issued in 1569, it is asked "whether their churche or chappell be served with any readers." Apparently in the answer to this question we find more than one instance of the parish clerk intruding into the duties of the parson. At Westbere it is presented:

> That when the Parson is absent the parish clerk readeth the service.

And at Waltham they present:

> That our parish is served by our clerk for the most part, for that our Vicar cometh seldom there.

And at Tenterden:

> John Hopton readeth divine service, having received no orders, neither tolerated to that effect.

While at Fairfield they complain:

> That their church is served with a Reder.[2]

Two years later in 1571, Grindal as Archbishop of York puts out as the first of his injunctions to the laity:

> 1. First, We do enjoin and straightly command, that from henceforth no parish clerk, nor any other person not being ordered, at the least, for a deacon, shall presume to solemnize Matrimony, or to minister the sacrament of Baptism, or to deliver to the communicants the Lord's cup at the celebration of the holy Communion. And that no person, not being a minister, deacon, or, at the least, tolerated by the ordinary in writing, do attempt to supply the office of a minister in saying of divine service openly in any church or chapel.[3]

Sandys also when Bishop of London is said to have issued injunctions in the visitation of his new diocese, of which the last was as follows:

> 6. That parish clerks intrude not into the priests' duty, as before they had sometimes done.[4]

But I have looked through the Articles of his visitation of 1571 and cannot find any inquiry as to exceeding their duty by the parish clerks.[5]

Also in the diocese of Lincoln in 1574 it was inquired:—

> 6. Whether sithens the last visitation, your parish Clerke, or any other not being minister or deacon, or not being licensed by the Ordinarie, haue taken vppon them to begin or say seruice, or minister any sacraments, or distribute the Lords Cup, or read the Homely in your parish, what they be and what be their names.[6]

[1] Edward Cardwell, *Documentary Annals of the Reformed Church of England*, Oxford, 1839, vol. i. p. 322, § vii.

[2] *Home Counties Magazine*, 1903, vol. v. pp. 9, 14, 209, 288.

[3] *Injunctions . . . Metropoliticall Visitation of the Province of Yorke . . . Anno Domini* 1571, printed in the *Remains of Edmund Grindal*, Parker Society, 1843, p. 132.

[4] *Sermons of Edwin Sandys*, edited by John Ayre, Parker Society, 1841. p. xx.

[5] *Articles . . . visitation of the Dioces of London by the Reuerende Father in God Edwyn . . .* London, William Seres, 1571.

[6] *Articles . . . diocese of Lincolne . . . Thomas* [Cowper] London, Rafe Newbery, 1574. A. ii. *b*.

And in 1588 in the same diocese it is inquired:

> Whether the Clarke be . . . suffered to reade anything in the Church, saue the one Lesson, and the Epistle.[1]

But this intrusion into the office of clerks in holy orders must have gone on; and in some cases it was authorised by the bishop. For in 1625–26 in the parish of Stepney, at the request of the vicar, the bishop did grant a licence to empower Robinson, the parish clerk, to bury parishioners and to church their wives, using the prayer book forms. The reason given is that there was more than the curate could do single handed, the mortality from the plague being so great.[2] These two acts, saying the burial service and churching women, are not so exclusively sacerdotal that their performance by a parish clerk might not be winked at in cases of great necessity. But it touches upon the scandalous when the parish clerk is allowed to baptize as well as read prayers, bury, marry, and church. In 1634 in the diocese of Winchester it was answered:

> Touching the Parish Clerk and Sexton all is well only our clerk doth sometimes to ease our Minister, read prayers, church women, christen, bury, and marry, being allowed so to do.[3]

It may be that the following inquiry is not wholly unconnected with this reply:

> *Touching the Parish Clerke, and Sexton.*
>
> * * * * * *
>
> 2. Whether doth your Clerke meddle with anything above his Office, as churching of women, burying of the dead, reading of Prayers, or such like?[4]

After 1630 the Bishop of Lincoln inquires:

> Whether doth the Clerk or any person not authorized meddle above his place, as to read prayers, bury the dead, church women, and such like?[5]

In 1639 the Bishop of Winchester makes the same inquiry.[4]

So also the Bishop of Exeter in 1638,[6] the Archdeacon of Chichester in 1640.[7]

After the Restoration the "meddling above his place" would seem to have been less frequent, if we may judge from its disappearance in the visitation articles after that revival of discipline.

Another sort of meddling above his place may be detected in the giving out of notices; a practice glanced at by the rubric contained in

1 *Articles . . . Diocesse of Lincoln*, London, 1588, § 41.

2 G. W. Hill and W. H. Frere, *Memorials of Stepney Parish*, Guildford, 1890–91, p. xvi. See below, Appendix XII. p. 104, in which the draft of a licence to the parish clerk is given.

3 E. Greatorex. *Reliquary*, 1894, vol. viii. new series, p. 157.

4 Visitation Articles of Walter [Curll] Bishop of Winchester, London, John Norton, 1639. A. iv. *b*.

5 *Appendix E. to the Second Report of the Royal Commission on Ritual, &c.*, 1868, p. 520, tit. 5, § 6.

6 See below, Appendix XI. p. 99.

7 See below, Appendix XI. p. 100.

the book of common prayer after the Nicene creed, which was inserted at the last revision in 1662 it may be to stop such practices. We find it inquired into in an archidiaconal visitation in 1630.

Proclamations of lay-businesses made in the Church [*in m.*]

8. Whether hath your Parish Clerk, or any other in Prayers time, or before Prayers or Sermon ended, before the people departed, made proclamation in your Church touching any goods strayed away or wanting, or of any Leet court to be held, or of common-dayes-works to be made, or touching any other thing which is not meerly ecclesiasticall, or a Church-businesse?

Something like this persisted even into the nineteenth century. Sir Walter Scott speaks of a strange custom at Hexham:

It is common for the traders in cattle, which business is carried on to a great extent, to carry all letters received in course of trade to the parish church, where the clerk reads them aloud after service, and answers them according to circumstances."[1]

Also in a parish near Manchester we are told:

After Sunday morning service it was customary in the last generation for the parish clerk to turn bell-man and announce in the churchyard any engagements for the coming week, such as sales by auction, and other worldly matters in which the parish was interested.[2]

So too Mr. Beresford Hope, speaking of the practice known to him of the reign of King George IV. writes as follows:

The clerk, a wizened old fellow, in a brown Welsh wig, repeated the responses in a nasal twang, and with a substitution of "w" for "v" so consistent as not even to spare the Belief; while the local rendering of "briefs, citations, and excommunications," included announcements by this worthy after the Nicene Creed, of meetings at the town inn of "execūtors" of a deceased Duke. . . . During the sermon this zealous servant of the sanctuary would take up his broom and sweep out the middle alley, in order to save himself the fatigue of a week day visit.[3]

Mr. Christopher Wordsworth informs me that his mother could remember hearing the clerk give out, about 1816, invitations to tradesmen to tender for supplying bread for the poor of the parish. Mr. Vaux says that it was the clerk who published all notices both religious and secular during service.[4]

But these instances of notice-giving do not seem so irreverent as the custom described by Sir Walter Scott. In fact they are akin to the notices now printed and affixed to the church doors, such as jury lists, militia service, and the like. And, when reading and writing were not the common accomplishments that they are now, such verbal notices must have been a convenience to the parishioners, and joined together

[1] J. G. Lockhart, *Memoirs . . . of Sir Walter Scott*, Edinburgh, 1837, vol. i. p. 192.

[2] John E. Bailey, *Old Stretford*, Manchester, 1878, p. 49.

[3] A. J. B. Beresford Hope, *Worship in the Church of England*, London, 1875. Sec. ed. p. 8.

[4] J. E. Vaux, *Church Folklore*, London, 1894, Ch. ix, p. 194. There is a story told in *Blackwood's Magazine*, August, 1903, p. 170, of the parish clerk administering baptism in the last century, but the circumstances do not inspire confidence in the accuracy of the report.

the secular and ecclesiastical aspects of the parish. Nowadays, every effort is made to put the civil and the church notices into strictly separated divisions, so that the life of the parish as a whole is somewhat obscured.

NUMBER.—St. Augustine, it would seem, was accompanied into Britain by more clerks than one. They were part of his train. But the clerk, who was the later companion of the parish priest, who assisted him in all his duties, might be but one, according to Leo IV. Hincmar, and the decretals of Gregory IX.[1] To take the place of the deacon and subdeacon in churches which had no large income, it was allowed by a bishop of Durham in the middle of the thirteenth century that there should be but one clerk.[2] And doubtless this was the rule in most country parishes where the population was but small. But in London there may have been more often two. Brewster gives six instances in fourteenth century.[3]

At the end of the middle ages every considerable church might have had two officers in the position of the parish clerk. It is so at York,[4] Coventry,[5] Bristol,[6] and Faversham,[7] as well as in London.[8] Henry VIII. in the indenture between himself and the mayor and citizens of London directs that the new Christchurch Newgate Street shall have two clerks and one sexton, while St. Bartholomew the Less is to have only one clerk and one sexton.[9]

But at Faversham it will be noted that one of the first results of the changes under Edward VI. was the diminution of the number of clerks. Time out of mind there had been two clerks; but as the work of the clerk was diminished so the number was to be diminished too, and there

[1] See above, p. xviii.

[2] Ad augendum vero divini cultus obsequium ordinamus et disponimus; ut in singulis ecclesiis, quarum facultates ad hoc sufficiunt, sint diaconi et subdiaconi, sicut decet, Deo ministrantes. In aliis vero ecclesiis saltem unus clericus idoneus, et honestus, qui in tonsura decenti congruo habitu deserviat sacerdoti, ne ecclesiae debitis officiis defraudentur; ita quod idem clericus nullatenus uxoratus existat, nec deserviat in altari.

(Constitutiones Walteri de Kirkham, episcopi Dunelm. A.D. 1255, in D. Wilkins, *Concilia*, London, 1737, t. i. p. 707. Cf. Constitutions of Norwich, 1257, *ibid.* p. 733. Acts of the Synod of Ely, 1364, *ibid.* vol. iii. p. 61, where these rules are repeated in substance.)

[3] Samuel Brewster, *Collectanea Ecclesiastica*, London, 1752, p. 405. In an Essay concerning the Office and Duties of Parish Clerks.

[4] See *Testamenta Eboracensia*, vol. v. Surtees Society, 1884, p. 13. In 1509 a bequest is made to every parish clerk and underclerk in the city of York and its suburbs.

[5] See Appendix I. pp. 57 and 61.

[6] See T. P. Wadley, *Notes or abstracts of the Wills . . . at Bristol*, Bristol and Gloucestershire Society, 1886, pp. 9, 11, 42, 137.

[7] See Appendix V. p. 75.

[8] See Appendix VIII. p. 91.

In the early sixteenth century the Founders' Company paid iiij*d.* to the ij parish clerks. (*Archaeological Journal*, 1886, vol. xliii. p. 170.) Money was also paid to the sexton for keeping their light and for ringing.

[9] William Trollope, *A History of the Royal Foundation of Christ's Hospital*, London, 1834. Appendix I. p. viii.

was to be only one clerk and one sexton. The money thus saved by the decrease of the divine service was given to the scavenger.[1]

Occasionally we find a larger number. At the visitation of the college of Maidstone in 1511 by William Warham, Archbishop of Canterbury, it is presented that they lack two clerks, "which were wont to be there of old season." To this the churchwardens answer that they were not bound to provide two more clerks besides those already there.

At another church it was complained that laymen are wont to come into the choir, not putting on their due garments, against the disposition of the law. The four offenders appeared and were enjoined by the commissary under pain of excommunication not to enter the chancel except in surplices and there to chant or sing psalms.[2]

I have not yet come across any decisive evidence to show whether two officers, the clerk and under clerk, became separated into the two whom we now call sexton and clerk, or whether the clerk and under-clerk had always an inferior officer under them, the sexton. In Henry VIII.'s new foundation of Christchurch Newgate Street, at Faversham in 1506, and at St. Stephen's Coleman Street in 1542, there were two clerks and one sexton. In 1506 to the sexton were committed divers menial offices, the keeping clean of the church, the ringing of bells, the lighting of candles, the opening of the church doors; while in London, he had to dig the graves, for which last office he is now best known.

In the seventeenth century Christopher Hervey, the follower of George Herbert, thus divides the duties of the sexton and those of his fellow, the parish clerk. It may be noticed that the sexton has assumed several of the duties which in the middle ages were assigned to the clerk; bellringing, making the church clean, opening and shutting the door.

The Sexton.

The Churches key-keeper opens the door,
  And shuts it, sweeps the floor,
Rings bells, digs graves, and fills them up again;
  All Emblems unto men,
Openly owning Christianity
To mark and learn many good lessons by.

* * * * * *

The Clerk.

The Churches Bible-Clerk attends
  Her Utensils, and ends
  Her prayers with Amen,
Tunes Psalms, and to the Sacraments
  Brings in the Elements,
  And takes them out again;
Is humble minded, and industrious handed,
Doth nothing of himself, but as commanded.[3]

Here the clerk certainly enjoys a better position as to the duties assigned to him, than the sexton. The reading, singing, and responses,

[1] See below, Appendix V. p. 80.
[2] *British Magazine*, 1847, vol. xxxii. pp. 41 and 47.
[3] Christopher Harvey, *The Synagogue*, London, 1679, pp. 24 and 25. These are not in the edition of 1640.

with the preparation of the elements for the sacraments point out a higher office than that of the sexton. But both seem to have been taken from the same class; and the sexton was promoted to be clerk as a vacancy occurred; for the proverb runs: the clerk forgets that ever he was sexton.[1] It may be that to the clerk were assigned the older duties, of singing, reading the lesson and epistle, and helping in the ministration of the sacraments; while to the sexton were given the more menial duties, of ringing the bells, keeping the church clean, opening and shutting the church, and such like.

After 1628 I have not found mention of more than one parish clerk attached to a church.[2] And John Johnson says of them that "now there is but one in a Parish."[3] But the rubrics of the Book of Common Prayer of 1662 retain the word *clerks* in the plural at morning and evening prayer, at Matrimony, and the Burial of the dead, and the Commination service.

RIGHT OF APPOINTMENT.—It may well be imagined that the rector of a parish would take a considerable interest in the appointment of an officer so closely attached to his person as the mediaeval parish clerk. Should the parson have to find the wages or board of the clerk, he might naturally claim the appointment as a right. But if the parishioners had to supply the offerings they might also expect the right to elect. Thus in the thirteenth century we already find a diversity of practice recommended by authority. Peckham in 1280 desires that two clerks who are to carry the holy water, that is the parish clerks, who are usually known by the name of *aquaebaiuli*, are to be elected by the parishioners by whose offerings they are to live.[4] While, on the other hand, it is said that Boniface, Archbishop of Canterbury from 1245 to 1273, or Winchelsey, Archbishop of the same see from 1294 to 1313, made a canon in which it is declared that strife as to the appointment of the parish clerk having broken out between the Rectors and Vicars and their parishioners, the Rectors or their Vicars, knowing best who are the proper persons, are to prefer such to this benefice, and the parishioners are threatened with punishment if they dare to withdraw from the clerk the accustomed wages.[5]

Writing much about the same time, John of Athon speaks of a case then recent in which the clerk appointed by the parishioners disputed the right of the clerk appointed by the rector, even to the effusion of blood and at the altar itself.[6]

[1] S. Brewster, *op. cit.* p. 403.
[2] St. Margaret's Westminster. (John Nichols, *Illustrations* etc. London, 1797, p. 37.)
[3] John Johnson, *Clergy-man's Vade-mecum*, London, 1709, Ch. xxii., vol. i. p. 204.
[4] W. Dugdale, *Monasticon*, ed. Caley, Ellis, and Bandinel, London, 1830, vol. vi. part iii. p. 1246.
[5] Lyndwood, *Provinciale*, Lib. iii. tit. *de concessione praebendae*, cap. *a nostris maioribus*, Oxon. 1679, p. 142. The glosses of Lyndwood should be consulted.
[6] John of Athon, Constitutio Othoboni, *De residentia archiepiscoporum*, cap. *Pastor bonus*, verb. *sanctae obedientiae.* Appendix to Lyndwood, *Provinciale*, Oxon. 1679, p. 119. In the *Dictionary of National Biography* (*sub voce* John Acton) he is stated positively to have died in 1350.

Lyndwood, glossing the chapter *a nostris maioribus*, mentioned above, notes upon the words *Rectores et Vicarii* that in a church where there are a Rector and a Vicar it is more desirable that the Vicar appoint the clerk. Lyndwood has said previously that the parishioners might be claiming the appointment against the Rector or Vicar. But this custom of the parishioners did not die out though condemned; for later, in the time of Henry VII. Sir William Catton, a canon of Newburgh, asks of Sir Robert Plumpton to use his influence that "my brother, your trew servant, myght have that service of the clarkship, trustyng to God he should please the parishioners according to his dutie."[1] The patronage seems to have been in the parishioners of Cukeswald (Coxwold) and the other candidates to have been two sons of the clerk late deceased.

Also in 1527 at Hawkhurst in Kent there was a dispute between the parson and the parishioners, which was settled by a compromise arranged by the Archbishop of Canterbury. It is curious that the parson who agrees to pay the clerk's wages (forty shillings a year, no unusual sum in those days) yet resigns to the parishioners his right of appointing the clerk.

> Memorandum That in the yere of our Lorde m v c xxvij. mr. Drien beynge person, ther arose a contencion betwene the said person and the parochyans aboute the Fyndynge of a surples, wher as the said person would [have] forced the parishe to Fynde for hym or the curate a surples with sleves the whiche the parish denyed beynge before accustomed to Fynde but onely a Rochett, wherupon the said person denyed the Fyndynge of the Clerck. This matter beynge brought before the bisshoppe Warrame dyde then determen and with the said person and parochyans the bysshope decreed that from thence forth the parishe should ever after fynd the curate or person one Sleved Surplys, and the person to Fynde continewally every yere for clerks wages fortie shyllyngs an alwayes the parishe to choose the Clerck. Present at Knoll at this conclusion takyn these persons folowynge
>
> [Here follow the names of 13 parishioners.][2]

In the diocese of London in 1540 we find the parishioners neglecting to elect a parish clerk, and the parson choosing the clerk in default of such election.

> [1540] *Tolleshunt militis.* The sexte day of October presented at Witham, before Mr. Officiall ther sittyng, thes articles following bi me, Richard Baldwyer, parson of Tolleshunt Knyghtis.
>
> * * * * *
>
> Also wher for lacke of a parishe [clerk ?] lawfully chosen by the parishe, and admytted bi the ordinary, I was constrayned to chose me one George Ponde, whiche hathe ben admitted bi you, and hathe helpid me this xviii weeks past, to ministre sacramentis and sacramentallis, with all other devyne service notwithstanding the[y] will note through the meanes of Laurence pay him his wagis.[3]

[1] *Plumpton Correspondence*, edited by Thomas Stapleton, Camden Society, 1839, p. 66.

[2] Churchwardens' accounts of Hawkhurst, edited by W. J. Lightfoot, *Archaeologia Cantiana*, 1863, vol. v. p. 78.

[3] W. H. Hale, *Series of Precedents . . . Ecclesiastical Courts in the Diocese of London*, London, 1847, p. 113. Laurence had met the parson on the King's high way, and there smote him and strake him sondry and diversely.

In the reign of Elizabeth[1] there are enquiries about the appointment of the parish clerk in the visitation articles which show that the appointment had not yet become wholly the right of the parson. Grindal in his metropolitical visitation of the province of York in 1571 enjoins:

> that no parishe Clarke be appoynted agaynst the good will, or without the consent of the person, vicar, or curate, in any Parishe.[2]

Matthew Parker enquires in 1575 at a metropolitical visitation of the province of Canterbury.

> Whether the parishe clarkes be admitted without the consent of the Parson or Vicar.[3]

But Grindal making a visitation of the same province in 1576 merely inquires "whether the parish Clerk be appointed according to the ancient custom of the parish."[4] So does Aylmer Bishop of London in the next year.[5] And there is some evidence that in the city of London especially the parishioners claimed the right of electing the parish clerk. The example set by Grindal is also followed at Lincoln in 1585[6] and 1598.[7] But after 1603 there is a great change; for in this year it was ordered by the 91st Canon that parish clerks should be chosen by the Parson or Vicar; and this choice was to be signified to the parishioners the next Sunday following during the time of divine service.[8] This was the only recognition that remained of the claim of the parishioners to appoint: and there are traces of an inclination to withstand the alteration.

Before the passing of the canon it is noted at Salehurst "in Aprill 1597" "Item the minister hathe ever chosen the parish Clarke and one of the Churchwardens and bothe the Sydemen." And later on a note that James Prichard was appointed Clark in 1614 solely "by my father's [that is, the vicar's] power."[9] There must have been some movement in the parish which caused the insertion of this note. There is an account of the appointment of the parish clerk by the vestry against

[1] It is sometimes said that according to the canons of 1571 the parish clerks were appointed by the parishioners. I cannot help thinking that this is due to a mistranslation of the word *Aedituus* as parish clerk, an error into which John Ayliffe himself has fallen. (*Parergon*, London, 1726, p. 409. "By a Book of Canons in Queen *Elizabeth's* Reign [A.D. 1571. Parish-Clerks are in *Latin* termed Æditui.") But the contemporary translation of these canons, lately reprinted for the first time since 1571 (W. E. Collins, *Canons of* 1571 *in English and Latin*, S.P.C.K. 1899, p. 60) gives *aeditui* as *churchwardens*; and this is clearly enough the meaning of the word, as the context shows.

[2] § 21. *Appendix E. to Second Report of the Royal Commission on Ritual*, 1868, p. 415.

[3] *Ibid.* § 32, p. 417.

[4] *Remains of Edmund Grindal*, Parker Society, 1843, p. 168, § 39.

[5] *Report . . . Ritual Commission*, § 31, p. 420.

[6] *Articles to be enquired . . . within the Dieocsse*† *of Lincoln*, London, John Windet, 1585, § 24, signature B. j. verso.

[7] *Articles to be enquired of, within the Diocesse of Lincolne*, Cambridge, John Legat, 1598, § 33, p. 10. See notes by Whitgift on the appointment of parish clerks. (John Strype, *Annals of the Reformation*, Oxford, 1824, vol. iv. p. 63.)

[8] See below, Appendix XI. p. 99.

[9] *Sussex Archaeological Collections*, 1873, vol. xxv. pp. 155 and 157.

the nomination of the parson in the registers of St. Bartholomew Exchange in 1630.[1]

John Godolphin, writing in the seventeenth century, says that "if custom prevail for vestry to elect this is better than a canon because custom in temporals can only be taken away by Act of Parliament, a clerk being a mere layman."[2] This extraordinary statement appears to have been a dictum of the Court of King's Bench, contradictory as such an opinion may seem to the meaning of the word clerk. I have heard another impossible expression, a lay deacon, because the deacon followed a secular employment. Possibly the judges only intended to state that a parish clerk need not necessarily be in holy orders, and might follow a trade or other business.

With the desuetude into which the office fell in the nineteenth century there would be naturally in our time very few or no disputes as to the right of electing the parish clerk. But in the Act of 1844 it is provided that where the appointment is by others than the parson, it is to be subject to the approval of the parson.[3]

The fact that a parish clerk cannot be dismissed from his office at the mere nod of the parson and churchwardens is some evidence of the importance of his office. A mere menial servant would not have had this privilege. He claimed a freehold, and consequently it was a hard matter to dislodge him from his office of parish clerk, whatever his conduct might be.[4] But the act of 1844 made it possible to prosecute him before the Archdeacon, and to eject him from any premises occupied by him as parish clerk.[5]

WAGES.—Under this heading may be pursued still further the duties of the clerk, especially those duties for which he received particular remuneration. The sources of these wages or rewards of the clerk are many; and it will be convenient to consider them under several heads.

1. *The carrying round of holy water.* From this office the clerk derives his name of *aquaebaiulus.* The constitutions of Alexander, Bishop of Coventry in 1237, speak of this. The poor scholar is to take round the holy water in country places; but no clerk who serves in the church is to live of the fees thus received.

De aqua benedicta.[6]

Ad hec. Quia oportet in ecclesia dei esse pastores et doctores⁄ nec est diuisio inter pastores et doctores cum alia diuidat apostolus. Dicit enim. Ipse

[1] *Vestry Minute Books of the Parish of St. Bartholomew Exchange*, edited by Dr. Edwin Freshfield, London, Rixon and Arnold, 1890, p. 99.

[2] See Appendix XIII. p. 107. A quotation from John Godolphin, *Repertorium Canonicum*, cap. xvii. § 15. London, 1687. Third ed. p. 193.

[3] 7 and 8 Victoria, Cap. 59, § 3.

[4] "The Ordinary cannot deprive the *Parish-Clerk*, tho' he may Censure, and Excommunicate him for any Fault; but they only, who put him in, can deprive him." (J. Johnson, *Clergy-man's Vade-Mecum*, London, 1709, vol. i. p. 204, ch. xxiii.)

[5] See below, Appendix XI. p. 103. See §6 of the Act.

[6] British Museum, Vesp. E. iii. fo. 142. *b.* formerly 132. *b.* See D. Wilkins, *Concilia*, Lond. 1737, t. i. p. 641.

quidem dedit alios quidem apostolos et euangelistas, alios pastores et doctores. Hic nullam fecit diuisionem. Precipimus igitur ut illi quorum interest videant ut in singulis locis ubi est regimen scolarum: sint tales qui sciant alios doctrina instruere et uelint eos exemplo bone vite informare, Sed quia plerique scolares carent necessariis quorum scientia multi per gratiam dei poterunt edificari: uolumus ut scolares ferant aquam benedictam. per villas rurales. si sint qui postulent et indigeant.

* * * * *

Item. precipimus sub pena suspensionis ut nullus clericus qui seruit in ecclesia viuat de aqua benedicta.

The eleventh constitution of W. de Bloys in 1229 also directs that this office is only to be given to the poor scholars.[1] So also a constitution attributed to Boniface or Robert Winchelsey directed that the profits of carrying round the holy water should be assigned to the poorer clerks. Much to the same effect is a constitution of John Peckham in 1280.

Volumus insuper ibidem esse duos clericos scolasticos per parochianorum de quorum habeat vivere elemosinis industriam eligendos, qui aquam benedictam circumferant in parochia et capellis diebus dominicis et festivis in divinis ministrantes officiis, et profestis diebus disciplinis scolasticis indulgentes.[2]

How poor these *aquaebaiuli* were, and how unsparing in their exactions were the officers of the Roman court, the following story from Matthew Paris teaches us. It was written in the same century as the foregoing constitutions. The scene is laid in France.

Harum quoque in Francia factarum extorsionum unam, quia turpissimam, duximus memorandam. Contigit ut memoratus papalis exactor obvium haberet unum clericulum de villa venientem, aquam in vasculo cum aspersorio et frusta panis, data sibi pro aspersione aquae benedictae, baiulantem. Cui Romanus insidiator ait, "Ad quantum pretium ascendit beneficium hoc tibi ab ecclesia concessum per annum?" Cui clericus, laqueorum ignarus Romanorum, respondit, "Ad viginti, ut aestimo, solidorum." Cui Romanus iam se manifestans, ait, "Hic ergo assurgunt ad fisci commodum per annum viginti et quatuor denarii, scilicet duo solidi." Et suffocavit ipsum pauperem ostiatim mendicantem, dicens, "Redde domino regi quod debes." Unde pro illa substantiola persolvenda cogebatur ille pauperculus, multis diebus scolas exercens, venditis in parvisio libellis, vitam famelicam et codrinam protelare. Talibus igitur omissis sermocinationibus collateralibus, ad materiam redeamus principalem.[3]

By Lyndwood's time, the right of the parish clerk to the benefit of holy water was well established. He could claim something from every

[1] Constitutiones . . . W. de Bloys, Worcester, Wilkins, *op. cit.* p. 624.

[2] W. Dugdale, *Monasticon*, ed. Caley, Ellis, and Bandinel, Lond. 1830, vol. vi. part iii. p. 1246.

[3] Matthew Paris, *Chronica Maiora*, Rolls Series, 1880, ed. H. R. Luard, vol. v. p. 172. [A.D. 1250.] Mr. J. A. Herbert of the British Museum has been kind enough to give me the following transcript which shows the carrying of holy water to have been a custom of the Gallican Church very similar to that in England:

Audivi de quodam milite qui morabatur in quadam villa in dyocesi Parisiensi sita. Quidam autem pauper et religiosus scolaris diebus dominicis portabat aquam benedictam in parrochia illa secundum consuetudinem Gallicanam. (MS. Harl. 463, fo. 6. *b*; a 14th century MS. of the *Exempla* of Jacques de Vitry, Bishop of Acre, afterwards Cardinal Bishop of Tusculum, ob. 1240. The above passage is printed from a Paris MS. in Crane's edition of the *Exempla of J. de Vitry*, Folk Lore Soc. 1890, p. 47.)

householder.[1] At Coventry the senior clerk had every Sunday to bear holy water to every house in his ward, and to have his duty of every man after his degree quarterly. Also every Sunday he and his fellow brought their holy water stock with water to be blessed.[2] So also at St. Nicholas, Bristol, the clerk had to take the holy water to every house, abiding so convenient a space that every man might receive his holy water.[3] And at Faversham[4] and St. Stephen's, Coleman Street,[5] the clerk was to bear holy water every Sunday in the year.

At the conclusion of the great dispute at Morebath in 1536 one of the points agreed upon as to the dues to be given to the clerk was this: that he should go about the parish with his holy water when men have shorn their sheep, to gather wool to make him a coat to go in the livery of the parish.[6]

Other things connected with the holy water had to be seen to by the clerks. At St. Stephen's, Coleman Street, for example, after mattins on Sunday they had to make ready the water and salt to be blessed.[7] At St. Nicholas, Bristol, the suffragan had to see that fresh water was in the holy water stocks; the clerk had to provide the bunches of twigs for sprinkling holy water, not only for the church, but for him that went about with the holy water.[8] At Faversham the clerks had to keep clean the holy water stoops of laten.[9] At St. Stephen's, Coleman Street, the clerks had to cleanse the font and fill it again with clean water at Easter and Whitsuntide and oftener if need require[10]; and at Coventry at these two feasts, the first clerk was to see that water was brought to the church for the blessing of the fonts, and also a barrel of water prepared on Maundy Thursday for the washing of the altars.[11]

Closely connected with the holy water is the holy loaf. The holy loaf was blessed after the holy water on Sundays,[12] and the delivery of it was the cause of a demand by the parish church clerk for a reward, the holy loaf halfpenny.

At Stillington in 1472 they complained that the vicar demanded a tithe of beer, contrary to custom; and also every Sunday the parish clerk's halfpenny called the *haly bred halfpeny*.[13]

At Coventry the first clerk had to see the holy loaf cut every Sunday according to every man's degree, and he gave it to those on

[1] Unusquisque Paterfamilias die quolibet Dominico Clerico deferenti aquam Benedictam aliquid secundum exigentiam Status sui tribuat. (*Provinciale*, Lib. iii. tit. *de concessione prebendae* cap. *a nostris maioribus* ad verb. *Compellantur*. Oxon. 1679. p. 143.)

[2] See below, Appendix I. p. 58, §§ 14, 17, p. 63, § 78.

[3] See below, Appendix III. p. 68, § 21.

[4] See below, Appendix V. p. 77, § 12.

[5] See below, Appendix VIII. p. 91, § 18.

[6] See below, Appendix VII. p. 88, § 13.

[7] See below, Appendix VIII. p. 92, § 28.

[8] See below, Appendix III. p. 66, § 3, and p. 68, § 21.

[9] See below, Appendix V. p. 78, § 14.

[10] See below, Appendix VIII. p. 91, § 2.

[11] See below, Appendix I. p. 58, § 20, p. 62, § 64.

[12] *Missal . . . Sarum*, ed. F. H. Dickinson, Burntisland, 1861–1883, Col. 33**

[13] *Fabric Rolls of York Minster*, Surtees Society, 1859, p. 254.

the north side of the church. The second clerk dealt the holy bread to those on the south side.[1] At St. Stephen's, Coleman Street, the clerks every Sunday after mattins had to prepare water and salt for holy water and to cut the holy loaf.[2]

But the giving of holy bread, together with the giving of holy water, did not survive the changes of the sixteenth century. In 1543 a man is enjoined penance for giving his dog holy bread in contempt of the ceremony of holy bread.[3] And the first years of Edward VI. saw the ceremony of taking holy bread made voluntary,[4] so that it becomes dubious if the directions at Doncaster were issued by commissioners appointed by the Protector Somerset. Both holy water and holy bread were then ordered, but it is said that the parish clerk is not hereafter to go about the parish with holy water; but nevertheless, instead of that labour, he is to accompany the churchwardens and register the names of the persons that give and the sums given to the poor.[5]

And in the first prayer book of Edward VI. it appears to be understood that the holy loaf has disappeared, and in its place its value was to be given at the time of the offertory towards defraying the expenses of the bread and wine for the communion.[6] Consequently we find in the fifth year of Edward VI. anno Domini 1551, that there was a fresh arrangement made as to the wages of the clerk at Reading.

> At this day it was concludid and aggreid that from hensforthe euery inhabitant of the parisshe shall bere and pay euery Sonday in the yere v*d.* for euery tenement as of old tyme the Holy Lofe was used to be paid and be received by the parisshe clark wekely, the said clark to have euery Sonday for his paynes i*d.* And iiij*d.* residewe to be paied and delyuered euery Sonday to the churchewardens to be employed for bred and wyne for the communyon.[7]

Yet the holy loaf returns under Mary, as the very curious and interesting document from Stanford in the Vale shows us.[8] The disuse of holy bread is said to have begun as early as 1547, the "second" year of Edward VI. The money collected for the holy bread was devoted to the supplying of bread and wine for the communion, and with this is an enumeration of the houses wont to give the holy loaf.

Though after Mary the holy loaf may be found here and there in parish registers, yet it had ceased to be a direct source of profit to the clerk.

[1] See below, Appendix I. p. 58, § 18, p. 62, § 59.
[2] See below, Appendix VIII. p. 92, § 28.
[3] W. H. Hale, *A series of Precedents*, London, 1847, p. 124.
[4] Edward Cardwell, *Documentary Annals of the Reformed Church of England*, Oxford, 1839, vol. i. p. 35.
[5] See below, Appendix IX. p. 95.
[6] See the third and fifth rubrics at the end of the Communion Service in Edward VI.'s first book. (Grafton, 1549, fo. cxxxiii. *b.*)
[7] Charles Kerry, *A history . . . St. Lawrence, Reading*, Reading, 1883, p. 48.
[8] See below, Appendix X. p. 96. See the contemporary explanation of holy bread, holy water and the pax in Edm. Bonner's *Articles to be enquired &c.*, 1554. Signature C. i.

2. *Cakes, Eggs, and Sheaves.* Lyndwood tells us that besides the claim the parish clerk could make upon every householder for the holy water brought every Sunday, he had the right to demand from every household one loaf at Christmas, eggs at Easter, and sheaves in the Harvest.[1]

In the settlement of the great dispute at Morebath it was agreed that the clerk should have "a steche of clene corne to euery howsseholde"[2]· and there are directions how it should be compounded for.

Traces of the right to cakes and eggs last into the following century. I am indebted to the Rev. J. R. Hughes, Rector of Rempstone, for a transcript from his registers of 1629 which shows the custom of giving eggs at Easter to the clerk to have persisted to that year, but by courtesy. So also a peck of barley for every yardland, but the time of paying this had been postponed from harvest to the weeks between Christmas and Lady Day.

22nd November, 1629.

The wages of the Clarke of the Parish Church of Rempston.

At Easter yearely he is to have of every Husbandman one pennie for every yard land[3] he hath in occupation. And of every Cottager two pence.

Furthermore he is to have for every yard land one peche of Barley of the husbandmen yearely.

Egges at Easter by Courtesie.

For every marriage two pence. And at the churching of a woman his dinner.

The said Barley is to be payed between Christmasse and the feast of the Annunciation of the Blessed Virgin Marie.

This is signed by the Clerk, an Ex-clerk, the Rector, and several parishioners.

At Houghton le Spring 1658 the buns at Christmas and the eggs at Easter were still paid.

That the Clerk's wages of this parish is ix*d.* upon a plow, iiij*d.* upon a cottager to be paid yearely at Easter time. Also for a Christning j*d.* a Buriall 4*d.* a marriage 4*d.* and asking the banes 2*d.*

That the Sexton's wages is 2*d.* a plow, each cottage a *ob.* a Christning 2*d.* for a grave in the Quire vj*d.* in the Church iiij*d.* in the yard ij*d.* And buns at Xtmas and egs at Easter yearely.[4]

Robert Story, who was himself a parish clerk, has left some lines describing his emoluments. It would seem that the egg which he claimed at Easter had already developed into the chicken:

Learn, next, that I am Parish Clerk
A noble office, by St. Mark!
It brings me in six guineas clear
Besides *et cetcras*, every year.

* * *

[1] Et quod in Natali Domini habeat a singulis Domiciliis unum Panem, et etiam certa Ova ad Pascha, et in Autumno certas garbas. (*Provinciale*, Lib. iii. *de concessione praebendae* cap. *a nostris maioribus*, ad verb. *compellantur*, Oxon. 1679, p. 143.)

[2] See below, Appendix VII. pp. 85 and 88, §§ 4 and 8.

[3] A yardland varies in amount. It may be as much as 25 or 40 acres.

[4] *Churchwardens' accounts of Pittington*, Surtees Society, 1888, p. 318. The number of acres in a ploughland is uncertain, but it is rated at £50 a year.

Nor less the sport, when Easter sees
The daisy spring to deck the leas ;
Then, claimed as dues by Mother Church,
I pluck the cackler from the perch ;
Or, in its place, the shilling clasp
From grumbling Dame's slow opening grasp.[1]

3. *Glebe and House.* The clerk sometimes had a house and also a glebe. About 1411 it is complained at St. Michael le Belfrey in York that the parish chaplain and parish clerk have no house assigned to them.[2] In 1590 they payd "for mendyng the clark's house"[3] at St. Michael's Worcester.

In 1653 at St. Edmund's, Salisbury, there must have been a clerk's house and garden, for both are spoken of, and the clerk was to have forty shillings "by the yeare in lewe of his house."[4] I owe this reference to the kindness of Mr. Christopher Wordsworth, who has besides given me several other instances drawn from his own observation in country parishes as well as from the Charity Commissioners' Reports.

Mr. Vaux speaks of a clerk's glebe at Barton Turf, Norfolk, where the rent of three acres known as "dog whippers land" is paid to him.[5]

A cottage and garden formerly belonged to the parish clerk of Saltwood, Kent, but it has lately been sold.

In the Act of 1844 it is expressly enacted that the parish clerk when suspended from his office may be ejected from the premises which he holds as parish clerk.[6]

4. *Fees.* These again have varied sources. The present rubric in the marriage service directs that the accustomed duty to the priest and clerk shall be laid upon the book at a certain moment in the service. Other fees seem due by custom ; at funerals, for ringing the bell, churchings, baptisms. In Beaumont and Fletcher's play, the Spanish curate talks thus with his sexton :

Let weddings, christ'nings, churchings, funerals,
And merry gossipings, go round, go round still ;
Round as a pig that we may find the profit.[7]

These occasions probably represent the chief sources of the clerk's fees. The amount varies very considerably, and most likely the variations have always followed the position and wealth of the persons whom the parish clerk thus assists. A table of the fees at St. Margaret's,

[1] Robert Story, *Poetical Works*, London, 1857, p. 109. In a "Reply to an Epistle from Mr. Gourley, 1828."

[2] *Fabric Rolls of York Minster*, Surtees Society, 1859, p. 250.

[3] John Amphlett, *Churchwardens' Accounts of St. Michael's in Bedwardine, Worcester*, Oxford, 1896, p. 100.

[4] H. J. F. Swayne, *Churchwardens' Accounts of S. Edmund and S. Thomas, Sarum*, Wilts Record Society, 1896, p. 230, last lines. In the same volume, p. 310, a sexton's house is spoken of under the year 1620.

[5] J. E. Vaux, *Church Folklore*, London, 1894, p. 199.

[6] 7 and 8 Victoria, Cap. 59, § 6.

[7] Beaumont and Fletcher, *The Spanish Curate*, III. ii. The merry gossipings are perhaps the ales.

Lothbury, in 1571, is given below,[1] and it may be compared in some respects with the fees allowed in a country parish in Sussex much about the same time.

April 18 1597.

Memorandum that the dutyes for Churchinge of women in the parishe of Salehurst is vnto the minister jx*d.* ob. and vnto the Clarke ij*d.*

Item the due vnto the minister for a marriadge is xxj*d.* And vnto the Clarke ij*d.* the Banes, and iiij*d.* the marriadge.

Item due for burialls as followeth

To the minister in the Chancell	xiij*s.* iiij*d.*
To the Clarke in the Chancell	vj*s.* viij*d.*
To the parish in the Church	vj*s.* viij*d.*
To the Clarke in the Church	v*s.* o*d.*
To the Clarke in the Churchyard for great Coffins	ij*s.* vj*d.*
for great Corses vncoffined	ij*s.* o
for Chrisomers and such like Coffined	j*s.* iiij*d.*
and vncoffined	o xij*d.*
for tolling the passing bell an houre	j*s.*
for ringing the sermon bell an houre	j*s.* o*d.*
To the Clarke for Carying the beere	o iiij*d.*
if it be fetched	o ij*d.*

Item at funeralls the minister is to haue the mourning pullpit Cloth, and the Clarke the herst Cloth

Item the minister hathe ever chosen the parishe Clarke and one of the Churchwardens and bothe the Sydemen

Item if they bring a beere or poles with the Corps the Clarke is to haue them

If any Corps goe out of the parish they are to pay double dutyes and to haue leaue

If any Corps come out of an other parish to be buryed here, they are to pay double dutyes besides breakinge the ground ; which is xiij*s.* 4*d.* in the Church and 6*s.* viij*d.* in the Churchyard

For marryage by licence double fees both to the minister and clerke[2]

5. *Clerks' Ales.* These were part of the Wakes or Revels, which are known under the generic termination of ale, as Church ale, bride ale, Whitsun ale, bid ale. The clerk's ale was for the benefit of the parish clerk, and was commonly held at Easter.[3] At Morebath it was agreed that the clerk should have his "hyre mette at ester of euery howse holder"; but as Easter had passed in the year of the great contention without a clerk's ale, it was agreed that it should be upon Trinity Sunday that year only.[4]

But unfortunately for the Ales they were commonly celebrated on

[1] See Appendix IV. p. 72. Appendix VII. p. 88, §§ 10, 11, Appendix XIV. p. 110, § 10. See also above, p. lv. for Houghton le Spring. See also a table made in 1630 for St. Bartholomew Exchange. (*Vestry Minute Books*, edited by Dr. Edwin Freshfield, London, printed by Rixon and Arnold, 1890, p. 106.)

[2] From Salehurst Parish Books, *Sussex Archaeological Collections*, 1873, vol. xxv. p. 154.

[3] There may be notes of the clerk's ale about 1457 in the *Transactions of the Bristol and Gloucestershire Archaeological Society*, 1890-91, vol. xv. pp. 166, 167, 169.

[4] See below, Appendix VII. pp. 85 and 88, §§ 3 and 14.

the Sunday,[1] and the rise of Puritanism, with its insistence upon the Jewish keeping of the "Sabaoth," proved fatal to them. The judges ordered them to be discontinued as early as 1594 according to Prynne, who prints the documents at length[2]; but about 1633, the judges in the west again forbad wakes and revels. This coming to the ears of Dr. Laud, just elected Archbishop of Canterbury, he asked his suffragan, Dr. William Pierce, Bishop of Bath and Wells, to make some enquiry how these had been managed of late. The answer as to clerks' ales is as follows:

> Touching Clerke-ales (which are lesser Church-ales) for the better maintenance of Parish-Clerks, they have bin used (untill of late) in divers places, and there was great reason for them; for in poore Countrey Parishes, where the wages of the Clerke is very small, the people thinking it unfit that the Clerke should duly attend at Church, and lose by his office, were wont to send him in Provision, and then feast with him, and give him more liberality then their quarterly payments would amount unto in many years. And since these have bin put down, some Ministers have complained unto me, that they are afrayd they shall have no Parish Clerks for want of maintenance for them.[3]

Dr. Pierce's answer was not forgotten by the Parliamentarians. The Commons accused him in 1642, and the fifth article of impeachment asserts that he "both by precept and example most prophanely opposed the sanctification of the Lords day, by approving and allowing of prophane Wakes and Revels on that day": and the articles end with the discovery of "what a desperately prophane, impious, turbulent Pilate the Bishop is."[4]

The more sober-minded and reasonable people seem to have found no great harm in these ales. John Aubrey speaks well of them[5] and White Kennett, with regret, says they were abolished by the "nice Puritans."[6]

6. *Salary*. The churchwardens' accounts give us abundant information as to the amount of wages paid to the parish clerk by these officers; but only a few instances may be here given from these and other sources. The French clerk spoken of by Matthew Paris in the thirteenth century had only 20 sous a year.[7] At the end of the

[1] The prejudice against these ales, or indeed against any manner of recreation on a Sunday, is plain in Philip Stubbes' *Anatomie of Abuses*, 1583 (edited for the New Shakspere Society, 1877-79, pp. 137 and 150.) "Some spend the Sabaoth day (for the most part) in frequenting . . . May-games, Church-ales, feasts, and wakeesses: . . . In foot-ball playing, and such other deuilish pastimes."

[2] It is from these that P. Heylin (*Cyprianus Anglicus*, Part ii. Lib. iv. A.D. 1633, London, 1771, p. 242) and D. Neal, *History of the Puritans*, vol. ii. chap. v. London, 1733, vol. ii. p. 246) seem to have drawn their accounts of this affair.

[3] William Prynne, *Canterburies Doome*, London, 1646, p. 151, Signature V. 2. The pagination of this work is irregular.

[4] *Articles of Accusation and Impeachment of the House of Commons . . . against William Pierce*, London, 1642, pp. 4 and 8.

[5] *Topographical Collections of John Aubrey*, ed. J. E. Jackson, Wiltshire Archaeological and Natural History Society, Devizes, 1862, p. 10. See also notes to Appendix X.

[6] White Kennett, *Parochial Antiquities*, Oxford, 1818, vol. ii. p. 309.

[7] See above, p. lii.

fifteenth century at Craffield, the sexton or clerk had 4*s.* 4*d.* a year.[1] At St. Giles, Reading, about 1520, they paid the clerk for his year's wages 26*s.* 8*d.*[2]

In the middle of the sixteenth century the clerk's wages, as might be expected from the decrease in the value of money, rose considerably. In Henry VIII.'s new foundation of Christ Church, Newgate Street, the two parish clerks had £6, and the sexton £4 yearly. It was to be the same as St. Bartholomew the Less.[3] At St. Michael's, Cornhill, in 1556, the year's wages were £6 6*s.* 8*d.*[4] In the country the clerk's yearly wages were not far off from those in London. At Bishop's Stortford in 1546 they were £4.[5] It will thus be seen that the clerk's wages in the middle of the sixteenth century were in London as high as those recorded by the clerk poet, Robert Story, in the first half of the nineteenth century.[6] But at the end of the seventeenth century the priest who served the office of parish clerk at St. James', Westminster, was to have £30 a year,[7] the highest salary from anything like an endowment that I have yet met with.

But in some parishes they seem to have been extraordinarily low. The churchwardens' accounts of Came in Dorsetshire from 1696 to 1780 show that ten shillings a year was the usual amount paid the clerk during this time; and where it is said he was paid twelve shillings it is very likely that the two extra shillings were for the washing of the surplice.[8] The churchwardens' accounts for the eighteenth century at Bledlow, in Buckinghamshire, have lately been under my notice, and the annual charge for the clerk's wages is only ten shillings.

The quarterage, a sum paid every quarter to the clerk, is spoken of by Lyndwood[9] amongst other of the clerk's dues, and it may be found as late as the seventeenth century. At Morebath it was agreed that the clerk should have a penny a quarter of every householder.[10] I am not as yet confident that it was the same as the duty paid for the holy water.

The collecting of the clerk's wages or fees led to trouble, and proceedings in the ecclesiastical courts. In 1465, Thomas Walynger refused payment towards the light on the beam and the salary of the parish

[1] W. Holland and J. J. Raven, *Cratfield*, London, 1895, pp. 22 and 30. The church ales abound in these churchwardens' accounts.

[2] W. L. Nash, *Church-wardens' Account Book . . . St. Giles Reading*, 1881. p. 10.

[3] William Trollope, *A history of the Royal Foundation of Christ's Hospital*, London, 1834. Appendix I. p. viii.

[4] *Accounts of the Churchwardens . . . Saint Michael, Cornhill*, ed. Overall and Waterlow, privately printed about 1871. p. 129.

[5] J. L. Glas-cock, *Records of St. Michael's Parish Church, Bishops Stortford*, London, 1882, p. 46.

[6] See above, p. lv.

[7] See below, Appendix XI. p. 102.

[8] My son has given me these notes from Came, and he has also helped me with the papers from Morebath, printed as Appendix VII.

[9] *Provinciale*, Lib. iii. *de concessione praebendae*, cap. *a nostris maioribus*, ad verb. *compellantur*, Oxon. 1679. p. 143. See also Appendix IV. p. 71.

[10] See below, Appendix VII. pp. 85 and 88. §§ 2 and 9.

clerk. A little later on Peter Cornel would not give the clerk his fee at marriage, and one declined the clerk's wages.[1] Much about the same time, by rules made between 1455 and 1469, we find at All Saints', Bristol, that refusal of communion was to follow refusal to content the clerk.[2] The disturbance at Morebath in 1531 and 1536 was owing to the objection of some parishioners to pay the accustomed dues.[3] Excommunication was threatened in Warham's time with satisfactory results :

> In the Visitation of Archbishop *Warham*,[4] a little before the Reformation, one Inhabitant was enjoyn'd, *Quod solvat ad Salarium Aquaebaiuli ibidem cessionem suam*; and two others, *Sub poena 'Excommunicationis, ad solvend' salarium Aquaebaiuli ibidem, ut alii Parochiani solvunt*; and, in another place,[5] it is noted as follows, *Iconomi dixerunt, quod omnes subtrahentes Salarium* Aquaebaiuli, *satisfecerunt et composuerunt.*[6]

A well known antiquary, whose acquaintance with the parish records of the city of London is very great, thinks that it is quite likely that hereafter it will be proved that the money collected for the clerk was the source of the church rate of modern times, abolished some years ago, by making the payment voluntary. The sum collected under the name of the clerk's wages was, he tells me, applied to all sorts of church purposes.

MISCELLANEOUS.—The clerk in former times had his seat close by the parson, below him or at his side. It was his practice to precede the parson from the vestry to the reading desk at the beginning of divine service. There is evidence that the clerk had a seat to himself in the quire in mediaeval times, for at the visitation St. Maurice at York it is complained that the desks on both sides of the quire, where the parish chaplain and the parish clerk used to sit, need repair.[7]

As this was in 1416 it seems hardly possible that the first pew erected for a clerk was in 1627.[8] And in the visitation articles of the diocese of Norwich in 1620 it is inquired whether there be a seat for the clerk near the parson.[9]

Some instances have been brought forward of women having served the office of parish clerk, and that decisions have been given in the courts in favour of the practice.[10] Certainly strange notions have been entertained in Westminster Hall as to the character of the parish clerk ; but they hardly agree with the facts taught by the history of the

[1] W. H. Hale, *Series of Precedents and Proceedings . . . from Act books of the Ecclesiastical Courts in the Diocese of London*, London, 1847. pp. 2, 3, 14.

[2] See below, Appendix II. p. 64.

[3] See below, Appendix VII. p. 84.

[4] Reg. Warh. f. 60. a f. 62, 6, [*in m.*]

[5] f. 68. a. [*in m.*]

[6] Edm. Gibson, *Codex Iuris Ecclesiastici Anglicani*, tit. ix. cap. xiv. Oxford, 1761. t. i. p. 214, note d.

[7] *Fabric Rolls of York Minster*, Surtees Society, 1859, p. 248.

[8] See *All the Year Round*, 1880, vol. xxvi. (new series) November 6, p. 54. *n.*

[9] *Articles . . . diocese of Norwich*, London, 1620, sign. B. 3, § 4.

[10] *All the Year Round*, 1880, vol. xxvi. (new series) p. 83.

parish clerk. If parish clerks be in an inferior degree of orders, no woman can possibly be a parish clerk, for she is incapable of receiving orders. She may in some degree perform part of the menial duties of a parish clerk, which consist in keeping the church clean, or opening the doors and the like; but the higher duties such as reading in the church, singing, and attending at the altar, cannot be performed by a woman.

Instances of the office having passed from father to son through several generations have been quoted as something extraordinary. But in a village with a small population, and indeed elsewhere, offices often tend to become hereditary in a family.

The parish clerks of London have been a company since the year 1422, and they were granted a charter by Henry VI. in 1442, and the company still exists.[1] There was a guild of clerks at Lincoln in 1381, but it is uncertain if they were parish clerks. It was apparently dissolved about 1549.[2]

It may be worth while to give here an instance of a penance inflicted upon a parish clerk for misbehaviour, at the end of the eighteenth century, when discipline was not, it is commonly said, at its highest in the Church of England.

In January, 1799, the Dean of Middleham cited the parish clerk into his court and pronounced the following sentence:

> That Thomas Ibbotson should be suspended from the office of parish clerk, without forfeiting the wages, until after the 10th day of February then next, being the first Sunday in Lent; that he do not apprcach the Sacrament of the Lord's Supper on that day, that, by the prayers of Lent, he might be fitted for it at the festival of Easter; and, lastly, that, on the first Sunday of the ensuing Lent, he should stand during service until the Nicene creed was read, before the font under the gallery, and then depart to a private seat, after having read distinctly the following acknowledgement, viz.
>
> "I, Thomas Ibbotson, do acknowledge that, on the day of the Feast of Circumcision, I behaved very irreverently in the House of God: that I interrupted the divine service, and conducted myself in such a manner, both in the church and out of it, as to give just cause of offence to the congregation then present: that I was led to this misconduct by resentment, and not being perfectly sober at the time, for which I beg pardon of Almighty God, and do promise to order myself with greater sobriety and decency for the time to come."[3]

There are many allusions to the parish clerk in general English literature. We all of us remember the description that Crabbe gives of the parish clerk of a hundred years ago; of his fall from a proud austerity of life to the practice of stealing the money collected at the offertory. Probably also a good view is given incidentally of what manner of man the parish clerk then was.[4] Another aspect is given of the clerk of that same period by Dr. Johnson, who hearing a wish that

[1] James Christie, *Some account of Parish Clerks*, 1893, privately printed by the Company, p. 25.

[2] Christopher Wordsworth, *Notes on Mediaeval Services in England*, London, 1898, p. 149.

[3] *Documents relating to . . . Middleham*, Camden Society, 1847, p. 42.

[4] See the *Borough*, Letter xix.

better provision were made for parish clerks, said, "Yes, sir, a parish clerk should be a man who is able to make a will, or write a letter for anybody in the parish."[1] He could see that unless the clerk were adequately paid his education was not likely to be as high as his duties demanded; and that his office has been, since the great rebellion, much degraded, there seems good evidence to show, while there are many wishes expressed in the literature of the eighteenth century for a restoration of the office to better things. The activities of the nineteenth century, so often misplaced, appear to have done hardly anything to improve the parish clerk. This introduction may be ended by an extract from the preface of a little work written by a parish clerk for parish clerks at the end of the seventeenth century, and thus coming from the period between 1660 and 1730, which has not unjustly been described as the golden age of the Church of England.

To the Reader.

The *Parish Clerk* is an Officer to be chosen by the Minister of the Parish (unless Custom prevail to the contrary) . . . . A *Parish Clerk* then is not so mean and contemptible an office as some people render it. He is more than a Door-Keeper in the House of God, he is *Servus in Sacris*, conversant in all the Holy Offices of the Church; whose Life and Conversation ought to be such, that he be Habitually prepared at all times to Communicate with the Sick, &c. The Clerk is to take care about the Elements proper to be used in the Holy Sacraments; of the Holy Vestments, that they be decently kept to the Honor of God, and the Reputation of that particular Church he hath the honour to serve. In a word, the *Parish-Clerk* ought to be an exact Pattern of Conformity in all the respective Offices of the Church, by whose good example the congregation may be excited to Reverence and Devotion, *viz.* Kneeling at Prayer, standing up at the Creed, bowing at the name of Jesus, &c.[2]

[1] J. Boswell, *Life of Samuel Johnson*, June 3. 1781.

[2] *The Parish Clerks Vade-Mecum*, by B. P. Parish Clerk. London, Benj. Motte, 1694.

THE

CLERK'S BOOK

OF

1549.

/ ¶ The Psalter [✠. i.

or Psalmes of Dauid, cor-

rected and poyncted, as

thei shalbe song in Churches

after the translacion

of the greate

Bible.

¶ Hereunto is added, diuerse thyn-

ges as maie appere on the next

side, where is expressed

the contentes of

this boke.

A°. Domini. M.D.XLIX.

Mense Augustij.†

/ The contentes of this boke. [✠ 1. *v.*

I. First, the ordre how the Psalter shalbe red.

II. The table for the ordre of the Psalmes.

III. The Kalender for the ordre of common praier.

IIII. The ordre for Mattyns and Euensong the whole yere.

V. The Letanie and Suffrages.

VI. All that shall apperteigne to the clerkes to saie or syng, at the ministracion of the Communion and when there is no Communion.

At Matrimonie.

The visitacion of the Sicke.

At Buriall of the dedde.

At the Purificacion of women.

And the first daie of Lent.

Here is to bee noted, that throughout this boke of the Psalter, ye shall find ouer the hed of euery leaf. Moneth. First. ii. iii. iiii. daie. &c. Which signifieth, that forasmuche as the Psalter is appoyncted to bee redde ouer euery .xxx. daies, ye shall nede no more, but turne to the daie of the Moneth, titled ouer the hedde of the leafe, and there ye shall finde bothe where Mattins for that daie beginneth, and also Euensong.

/ ¶ The ordre how the Psalter is appoyncted [✠. 2. to be redde.

THe Psalter shalbe red through once euery Moneth, and because that some Monethes, be longer then some other be: it is thought good, to make them euen by this meanes.

To euery Moneth, as concernyng this purpose, shalbe appoyncted iust .xxx. daies.

And because Ianuary and Marche hath one daie, aboue thesaied nombre, and February whiche is placed betwene them bothe, hath onely xxviii. daies, February shall borowe of either of the Monethes, of Ianuary and Marche one daie, and so the Psalter whiche shalbee redde in February, muste bee begon the last daie of Ianuary, and ended the firste daie of Marche.

And where as Maie, Iuly, August, October, and December, hath xxxi. daies a pece, it is ordered that thesame Psalmes, shalbee red the last daie of thesaied Moneth, whiche were redde the daie before, so that the Psalter maie be begon again the first daie of the next Monethes ensuyng.

Now to knowe what Psalmes shalbe redde euery daie, looke in the Kalendar the nombre that is appoyncted for the Psalmes, and then find thesame nombre in this table, and vpon that nombre shall you see, what Psalmes shalbe saied at Mattins, and Euensong.

And where the .C.xix. Psalme is deuided into .xxii. porcions, and is ouer long to be red at one tyme: it is so ordered, that at one tyme shall not bee red aboue foure or fiue of thesaied porcions, as you shall perceiue to bee noted in this table.

And here is also to bee noted, that in this table, and in all other partes of the seruice, where any Psalmes are appoyncted, the nombre is expressed after the greate Englishe Bible, whiche from the .ix. Psalme, vnto the .C.xlviii. Psalme (folowyng the diuision of the Ebrues) doth vary in nombres from the common Latin translacion.

This is also to be noted, that whensoeuer there bee any propre psalmes or lessons, appoyncted for any feast, moueable or vnmoueable, then the Psalmes and Lessons appoyncted in the Kalender, shalbee omitted for that tyme.

¶ A table for the ordre of the Psalmes, to be said at Mattins and Euensong. [✠. 2. v.

	¶ Mattins.	¶ Euensong.
1	1. 2. 3. 4. 5	6. 7. 8.
2	9. 10. 11.	12. 13. 14.
3	15. 16. 17.	18.
4	19. 20. 21.	22. 23.
5	24. 25. 26.	27. 28. 29.
6	30. 31.	32. 33. 34.
7	35. 36.	37.
8	38. 39. 40.	41. 42. 43.
9	44. 45. 46.	47. 48. 49.
10	50. 51. 52	53. 54. 55.
11	56. 57. 58.	59. 60. 61.
12	62. 63. 64.	65. 66. 67.
13	68.	69. 70.
14	71. 72.	73. 74.
15	75. 76. 77.	78.
16	79. 80. 81.	82. 83. 84. 85.
17	86. 87. 88.	89.
18	90. 91. 92.	93. 94.
19	95. 96. 97.	98. 99. 100. 101.
20	102. 103.	104.
21	105.	106.
22	107.	108. 109.
23	110. 111. 112. 113.	114. 115.
24	116. 117. 118.	119. Inde. 4.
25	Inde. 5.	Inde. 4.
26	Inde. 5.	Inde. 4.
27	120. 121. 122. 123. 124. 125.	126. 127. 128. 129. 130. 131.
28	132. 133. 134. 135.	136. 137. 138.
29	139. 140. 141.	142. 143.
30	144. 145. 146.	147. 148. 149. 150.

ℂ IANUARY.					Mattins.		Euensong.	
				ℂ Psalmes	1. Lesson.	2. Lesson.	1. Lesson.	2. Lesson.
A	Kalend.	1	Circumcisio.	1	Gene. 17	Roma. 2	Deut. 10	Collos. 2
b	4. No.	2		2	Gene. 1	Math 1	Gene. 2	Roma. 1
c	3. No.	3		3	3	2	4	2
d	Prid. No.	4		4	5	3	6	3
e	Nonas	5		5	7	4	8	4
f	8. Id.	6	Epiphania.	6	Esay. 60	Luke 3	Esay 49	Ihon. 2
g	7. Id.	7		7	Gene. 9	Math. 5	Gene. 11	Roma. 5
A	6. Id.	8		8	12	6	13	6
b	5. Id.	9		9	14	7	15	7
c	4. Id.	10		10	16	8	17	8
d	3. Id.	11		11	18	9	19	9
e	Prid. Id.	12		12	20	10	21	10
f	Idus.	13		13	22	11	23	11
g	19. kl.	14		14	24	12	25	12
A	18. kl.	15		15	26	13	27	13
b	17. kl.	16		16	28	14	29	14
c	16. kl.	17		17	30	15	31	15
d	15. kl.	18		18	32	16	33	16
e	14. kl.	19		19	34	17	35	1. Cor. 1
f	13. kl.	20		20	36	18	37	2
g	12. kl.	21		21	38	19	39	3
A	11. kl.	22		22	40	20	41	4
b	10. kl.	23		23	42	21	43	5
c	9. kl.	24		24	44	22	45	6
d	8. kl.	25	Con. Paule.	25	46	Actes. 22	47	Actes 26
e	7. kl.	26		26	48	Math. 23	49	1. Cor. 7
f	6. kl.	27		27	50	24	Exodi. 1	8
g	5 kl.	28		28	Exodi 2	25	3	9
A	4. kl.	29		29	4	26	5	10
b	3. kl.	30		30	6	27	7	11
c	Prid. kl.	31		1	8	28	9	12[1]

[1] The signature ✠ 3 appears within the last rule below the line for the last day of the month.

ℂ February.					Mattins.		Euensong.	
				ℂ Psalmes.	1. Lesson	2. Lesson	1. Lesson	2. Lesson
d	Kalend.	1		2	Exodi. 10	Marke 1	Exod. 11	1. Cor. 13
e	2. No.	2	Purif. Mari	3	12	2	13	14
f	1 No.	3		4	14	3	15	15
g	Prid. No	4		5	16	4	17	16
A	Nonas	5		6	18	5	19	2. Cor. 1
b	8. Id.	6		7	20	6	21	2
c	7. Id.	7		8	22	7	23	3
d	6 Id.	8		9	24	8	32	4
e	5. Id.	9		10	33	9	34	5
f	4. Id.	10		11	35	10	40	6
g	3. Id.	11		12	Leuit. 18	11	Leuit. 19	7
A	Prid Id.	12		13	20	12	Num. 10	8
b	Idus	13		14	Nume. 11	13	12	9
c	16 kl.	14		15	13	14	14	10
d	15 kl.	15		16	15	15	16	11
e	14 kl.	16		17	17	16	18	12
f	13 kl.	17		18	19	Luk. di. 1.	20	13
g	12 kl	18		19	21	di. 1	22	Gala. 1
A	11. kl	19		20	23	2	24	2
b	10. kl.	20		21	25	3	26	3
c	9 kl.	21		22	27	4	28	4
d	8 kl.	22		23	29	5	30	5
e	7. kl.	23		24	31	6	32	6
f	6. kl.	24	Mathias.	25	33	7	34	Ephe. 1
g	5 kl.	25		26	35	8	36	2
A	4 kl	26		27	Deut. 1	9	Deut. 2	3
b	3 kl.	27		28	3	10	4	4
c	Prid. kl.	28		29	5	11	6	5

ℂ Marche.					Mattins.		Euensong.	
				ℂ Psalmes.	1. Lesson	2. Lesson	1. Lesson.	2. Lesson
d	Kalend.	1		30	Deut. 7	Luke 12	Deut. 8	Ephe. 4
e	6. No.	2		1	9	13	10	Philip. 1
f	5. No.	3		2	11	14	12	2
g	4. No.	4		3	13	15	14	3
A	3. No.	5		4	15	16	16	4
b	Prid No	6		5	17	17	18	Collos. 1
c	Nonas.	7		6	19	18	20	2
d	8. Id.	8		7	21	19	22	3
e	7 Id.	9		8	23	20	24	4
f	6. Id.	10		9	25	21	26	1. Tessa. 1
g	5. Id.	11		10	27	22	28	2
A	4. Id.	12		11	29	23	30	3
b	3. Id.	13		12	31	24	32	4
c	Prid. Id.	14		13	33	Ihon. 1	34	5
d	Idus.	15		14	Iosue 1	2	Iosue 1	2. Tess. 1
e	17. kl.	16		15	3	3	4	2
f	16. kl.	17		16	5	4	6	3
g	15. kl.	18		17	7	5	8	1. Tim. 1
A	14. kl.	19		18	9	6	10	2. 3
b	13 kl.	20		19	11	7	12	4
c	12. kl.	21		20	13	8	14	5
d	11. kl.	22		21	15	9	16	6
e	10 kl.	23		22	17	10	18	2. Tim. 1
f	9. kl.	24		23	19	11	20	1†
g	8 kl.	25	Annunciacio.†	24	21	12	22	3
A	7. kl.	26		25	23	13	24	4
b	6. kl.	27		26	Iudic. 1	14	Iudic. 2	Tit. 1
c	5. kl.	28		27	3	15	4	2. 3
d	4. kl.	29		28	5	16	6	Phile. 1
e	3 kl.	30		29	7	17	8	Hebre. 1
f	Prid. kl.	31		30	9	18	10	2[1]

[1] Below this but within the rule is the signature mark ✠ .4.

ℂ Aprill.					Mattins.		Euensong.	
				ℂ Psalmes	1. Lesson	2. Lesson	1. Lesson.	2. Lesson.
g	Kale[n]d	1		1	Iudic. 11	Ihon. 19	Iudic. 12	Hebre. 3
A	4 No.	2		2	13	20	14	4
b	3 No.	3		3	15	21	16	5
c	Prid. No.	4		4	17	Actes. 1	18	6
d	Nonas.	5		5	19	2	20	7
e	8. Id.	6		6	21	3	Ruth. 1	8
f	7. Id.	7		7	Ruth. 2	4	3	9
g	6. Id.	8		8	4	5	1. Regum. 1	10
A	5. Id.	9		9	1. Regum. 2	6	3	11
b	4. Id.	10		10	4	7	5	12
c	3. Id.	11		11	6	8	7	13
d	Prid. Id.	12		12	8	9	9	Iacob. 1
e	Idus.	13		13	10	10	11	2
f	18 kl.	14		14	12	11	13	3
g	17. kl.	15		15	14	12	15	4
A	16 kl.	16		16	16	13	17	5
b	15 kl.	17		17	18	14	19	1. Peter. 1
c	14 kl.	18		18	20	15	21	2
d	13 kl.	19		19	22	16	23	3
e	12. kl	20		20	24	17	25	4
f	11 kl.	21		21	26	18	27	5
g	10 kl.	22		22	28	19	29	2. Peter 1
A	9 kl.	23		23	30	20	31	2
b	8 kl.	24		24	2. Regum 1	21	2. Regum 1	3
c	7. kl.	25	Marke Eua.	25	3	22	4	1. Ihon. 1
d	6. kl.	26		26	5	23	6	2
e	5. kl	27		27	7	24	8	3
f	4. kl.	28		28	9	25	10	4
g	3. kl.	29		29	11	26	12	5
A	Prid. kl.	30		30	13	27	14	2. 3 Ihon.

¶ Maie.					Mattins.		Euensong.	
				¶ Psalmes	1. Lesson	2. Lesson	1. Lesson	2. Lesson
b	Kalend.	1	Phi. & Iames	1	2. Reg. 15	Actes. 8	2 Reg. 16	Iudas. 1
c	6 No.	2		2	17	28	18	Roma 1
d	5. No.	3		3	19	Math. 1	20	2
e	4. No.	4		4	21	2	21	3
f	3. No.	5		5	23	3	24	4
g	Prid. No	6		6	3. Regum. 1	4	3. Regum 2	5
A	Nonas	7		7	3	5	4	6
b	8. Idus	8		8	5	6	6	7
c	7. Id.	9		9	7	7	8	8
d	6. Id.	10		10	9	8	10	9
e	5. Id	11		11	11	9	12	10
f	4. Id.	12		12	13	10	14	11
g	3. Id.	13		13	15	11	16	12
A	Prid. Id.	14		14	17	12	18	13
b	Idus	15		15	19	13	20	14
c	17 kl.	16		16	21	14	22	15
d	16 kl.	17		17	4. Regum 1	15	4 Reg. 2	16
e	15 kl.	18		18	3	16	4	1. Cor. 1
f	14 kl.	19		19	5	17	6	2
g	13 kl.	20		20	7	18	8	3
A	12 kl.	21		21	9	19	10	4
b	11 kl.	22		22	11	20	12	5
c	10 kl.	23		23	13	21	14	6
d	9 kl.	24		24	15	22	16	7
e	8 kl.	25		25	17	23	18	8
f	7 kl.	26		26	19	24	20	9
g	6 kl.	27		27	21	25	22	10
A	5 kl.	28		28	23	26	24	11
b	4 kl.	29		29	25	27	1. Esdre. 1	12
c	3 kl.	30		30	1. Esdr. 2	28	3	13
d	Prid kl	31		30	4	Marke 1	5	14[1]

[1] Below this but within the rule is the signature mark ✠ .5.

ℂ Iune.					Mattins.		Euensong.	
				ℂ Psalmes.	1. Lesson.	2. Lesson	1. Lesson	2. Lesson
e	Kalend.	1		1	1. Esdr. 6	Marke 2	1. Esdr. 7	1. Cor. 15
f	4. No.	2		2	8	3	9	16
g	3. No.	3		3	10	4	2. Esdr. 1	2. Cor. 1
A	Prid No	4		4	2. Esdr. 2	5	3	2
b	Nonas.	5		5	4	6	5	3
c	8. Id.	6		6	6	7	7	4
d	7. Id.	7		7	8	8	9	5
e	6. Id.	8		8	10	9	11	6
f	5. Id.	9		9	12	10	13	7
g	4 Id.	10		10	Hester. 1	11	Hester. 2	8
A	3 Id.	11	Barnabe Ap.	11	3	Actes 14	4	Actes 15
b	Prid. Id	12		12	5	Mar. 12	6	2. Cor. 9
c	Idus	13		13	7	13	8	10
d	18 kl.	14		14	9	14	Iob. 1	11
e	17. kl.	15		15	Iob. 2	15	3	12
f	16. kl.	16		16	4	16	5	13
g	15. kl.	17		17	6	Luke. 1	7	Galla. 1
A	14. kl.	18		18	8	2	9	2
b	13. kl.	19		19	10	3	11	3
c	12. kl.	20		20	12	4	13	4
d	11. kl.	21		21	14	5	15	5
e	10. kl.	22		22	16	6	17. 18	6
f	9. kl.	23		23	19	7	20	Ephe. 1
g	8 kl.	24	Nat. Ihon. ba.	24	Mala. 3	Matth. 3	Mala. 4	Mat. 14
A	7. kl.	25		25	Iob. 21	Luke. 8	Iob. 22	Ephe. 2
b	6 kl.	26		26	23	9	24. 25	3
c	5 kl.	27		27	26. 27	10	28	4
d	4 kl.	28		28	29	11	30	5
e	3. kl.	29	S. Peter.	29	31	Actes. 3	32	Actes. 4
f	Prid.	30		30	33	Luke. 12	34	Ephe. 6

ℂ Iuly.					Mattins.		Euensong.	
				ℂ Psalmes	1. Lesson	2. Lesson	1. Lesson	2. Lesson
g	Kalend.	1		1	Iob. 35	Luke .13	Iob. 36	Philip. 1
A	6. No.	2		2	37	14	38	2
b	5 No.	3		3	39	15	40	3
c	4. No.	4		4	41	16	42	4
d	3. No.	5		5	Prou. 1	17	Pro. 2	Coll. 1
e	Prid No.	6		6	3	18	4	2
f	Nonas	7		7	5	19	6	3
g	8. Id.	8		8	7	20	8	4
A	7. Id.	9		9	9	21	10	1. Tes. 1
b	6. Id.	10		10	11	22	12	2
c	5. Id.	11		11	13	23	14	3
d	4. Id.	12		12	15	24	16	4
e	3. Id.	13		13	17	Ihon 1	18	5
f	Prid. Id	14		14	19	2	20	2. Tes. 1
g	Idus.	15		15	21	3	22	2
A	17. kl.	16		16	23	4	24	3
b	16. kl.	17		17	25	5	26	1. Tim. 1
c	15. kl.	18		18	27	6	28	2. 3
d	14 kl.	19		19	29	7	30	4
e	13. kl.	20		20	31	8	Eccles. 1	5
f	12 kl.	21		21	Eccls. 2	9	3	6
g	11. kl.	22	Magdalen.	22	4	10	5	2. Tim. 1
A	10 kl.	23		23	6	11	7	2
b	9 kl.	24		24	8	12	9	3
c	8 kl.	25	Iames apost.	25	10	13	11	4
d	7 kl.	26		26	12	14	Ierem. 1	Tit. 1
e	6 kl.	27		27	Iere. 2	15	3	2. 3
f	5 kl.	28		28	4	16	5	Phile.
g	4. kl	29		29	6	17	7	Hebre. 1
A	3 kl	30		30	8	18	9	2
b	Prid. kl.	31		30	10	19	11	3

ℂ August					Mattins.		Euensong.	
				ℂ Psalmes	1. Lesson.	2. Lesson	1. Lesson	2. Lesson
c	Kalend.	1		1	Ierem. 12	Ihon. 20	Iere. 13	Hebre. 4
d	4. No.	2		2	14	21	15	5
e	3 No.	3		3	16	Actes 1	17	6
f	Prid No	4		4	18	2	19	7
g	Nonas.	5		5	20	3	21	8
A	8. Id	6		6	22	4	23	9
b	7. Id.	7		7	24	5	25	10
c	6. Id.	8		8	26	6	27	11
d	5. Id.	9		9	28	7	29	12
e	4. Id.	10		10	30	8	31	13
f	3. Id.	11		11	32	9	33	Iacob. 1
g	Prid. Id	12		12	34	10	35	2
A	Idus.	13		13	36	11	37	3
b	19. kl.	14		14	38	12	39	4
c	18. kl.	15		15	40	13	41	5
d	17. kl.	16		16	42	14	43	1. Peter 1.
e	16. kl.	17		17	44	15	45. 46	2
f	15. kl.	18		18	47	16	48	3
g	14. kl.	19		19	49	17	50	4
A	13. kl.	20		20	51	18	52	5
b	12. kl.	21		21	Lamen. 1	19	Lamen. 2	2. Pete. 1
c	11. kl.	22		22	3	20	4	2
d	10. kl.	23		23	5	21	Ezechi. 2	3
e	9. kl.	24	Bart. Apostle.	24	Ezechi. 3	22	6	1. Ihon 1
f	8. kl	25		25	7	23	13	2
g	7. kl	26		26	[1] 4	24	18	3
A	6. kl.	27		27	33	25	34	4
b	5. kl.	28		28	Daniel. 1	26	Daniel. 2	5
c	4 kl.	29		29	3	27	4	2. 3. Ihon
d	3 kl.	30		30	5	28	6	Iude 1
[e]	Prid. kl.	31		30	7	Math. 1	8	Roma. 1

ℂ September.					Mattins.		Euensong.	
				ℂ Psalmes	1. Lesson	2. Lesson	1. Lesson	2. Lesson
f	Kalend.	1		1	Dani. 9	Math. 2	Dani. 10	Roma. 2
g	4. No.	2		2	11	3	12	3
A	3. No.	3		3	13	4	14	4
b	Prid. No	4		4	Ose. 1	5	Ose. 2. 3	5
c	Nonas	5		5	4	6	5. 6	6
d	8. Id.	6		6	7	7	8	7
e	7. Id.	7		7	9	8	10	8
f	6 Id.	8		8	11	9	12	9
g	5. Id.	9		9	13	10	14	10
A	4. Id.	10		10	Ioel. 1	11	Ioel. 2	11
b	3. Id.	11		11	3	12	Amos. 1	12
c	Prid. Id.	12		12	Amos. 2	13	3	13
d	Idus.	13		13	4	14	5	14
e	18. kl.	14		14	6	15	7	15
f	17. kl.	15		15	8	16	9	16
g	16. kl.	16		16	Abdias. 1.	17	Ionas. 1	1. Cor. 1
A	15. kl.	17		17	Ihon. 2. 3.	18	4	2
b	14 kl	18		18	Miche. 1	19	Miche. 2	3
c	13. kl	19		19	3	20	4	4
d	12. kl.	20		20	5	21	6	5
e	11. kl.	21	Maethewe.†	21	7	22	Naum. 1	6
f	10 kl.	22		22	Naum 2	23	3	7
g	9. kl.	23		23	Abacuc 1	24	Abacuc 2	8
A	8. kl.	24		24	3	25	Soph. 1	9
b	7. kl.	25		25	Soph. 2	26	3	10
c	6. kl.	26		26	Agge. 1	27	Agge 2	11
d	5. kl.	27		27	Zacha. 1	28	Zach. 2. 3	12
e	4. kl.	28		28	4. 5.	Marke 1	6	13
f	3. kl.	29	Michaell	29	7	2	8	14
g	Prid. kl	30		30	9	3	10	15

ℂ Octobbr.					Mattins.		Euensong.	
				ℂ Psalmes.	1. Lesson.	2. Lesson	1. Lesson.	2. Lesson.
A	Kalend.	1		1	Zach. 1[1]	Mark. 4	Zach. 12	1. Cor. 16
b	6. No.	2		2	13	5	14	2. Cor. 1
c	5. No.	3		3	Mal. 1	6	Mal. 2	2
d	4. No.	4		4	3	7	4	3
e	3. No.	5		5	Toby. 1	8	Toby. 2	4
f	Prid No	6		6	3	9	4	5
g	Nonas.	7		7	5	10	6	6
A	8. Id.	8		8	7	11	8	7
b	7. Id.	9		9	9	12	10	8
c	6. Id.	10		10	11	13	12	9
d	5. Id.	11		11	13	14	14	10
e	4. Id.	12		12	Iudit. 1	15	Iudith. 2	11
f	3. Id.	13		13	3	16	4	12
g	Prid. Id.	14		14	5	Luk. di. 1	6	13
A	Idus.	15		15	7	di. 1	8	Gala. 1
b	17. kl.	16		16	9	2	10	2
c	16. kl.	17		17	11	3	12	3
d	15. kl.	18	Luke Euang.	18	13	4	14	4
e	14. kl.	19		19	15	5	16	5
f	13. kl.	20		20	Sap. 1	6	Sap. 2	6
g	12 kl.	21		21	3	7	4	Ephe. 1
A	11. kl	22		22	5	8	6	2
b	10. kl.	23		23	7	9	8	3
c	9. kl.	24		24	9	10	10	4
d	8. kl.	25		25	11	11	12	5
e	7. kl.	26		26	13	12	14	6
f	6. kl.	27		27	15	13	16	Philip. 1
g	5. kl.	28	Simon & Iu.	28	17	14	18	2
A	4. kl.	29		29	19	15	Eccls. 1	3
b	3. kl.	30		30	Eccls. 2	16	3	4
c	Prid. kl.	31		30	4	17	5	Collos. 1

ℂ Nouember.					Mattins.		Euensong.	
				ℂ Psalmes.	1. Lesson	2. Lesson	1. Lesson	2. Lesson
d	Kalend.	1	All sainctes.	1	Sapi. 3	He. 11. 12	Sapi. 5	Apo. 19
e	4. No.	2		2	Eccl. 6	Luke. 18	Eccl. 7	Collos. 2
f	3. No.	3		3	8	19	9	3
g	Prid. No.	4		4	10	20	11	4
A	Nonas.	5		5	12	21	13	1. Tes. 1
b	8. Id.	6		6	14	22	15	2
c	7. Id.	7		7	16	23	17	3
d	6. Id.	8		8	18	24	19	4
e	5. Id.	9		9	20	Ihon 1	21	5
f	4 Id.	10		10	22	2	23	2. Tes. 1
g	3. Id.	11		11	24	3	25	2
A	Prid. Id.	12		12	26	4	27	3
b	Idus.	13		13	28	5	29	1. Tim. 1
c	18. kl	14		14	30	6	31	2. 3
d	17. kl.	15		15	32	7	33	4
e	16. kl.	16		16	34	8	35	5
f	15. kl.	17		17	36	9	37	6
g	14. kl.	18		18	38	10	39	2. Tim. 1
A	13. kl.	19		19	40	11	41	2
b	12. kl.	20		20	42	12	43	3
c	11. kl.	21		21	44	13	45	4
d	10. kl.	22		22	46	14	47	Tit. 1
e	9. kl.	23		23	48	15	49	2. 3
f	8. kl.	24		24	50	16	51	Phile. 1
g	7. kl.	25		25	Baruc. 1	17	Baruc. 2	Hebre. 1
A	6. kl.	26		26	3	18	4	2
b	5 kl.	27		27	5	19	6	3
c	4 kl.	28		28	Esaie. 1	20	Esaie 2	4
d	3. kl.	29		29	3	21	4	5
e	Prid. kl.	30	Andrew Apo.	30	5	Actes. 1	6	6

ℭ December.					Mattins.		Euensong.	
				ℭ Psalmes	1. Lesson.	2. Lesson	1. Lesson	2. Lesson.
f	Kalend.	1		1	Esaie 7	Actes. 2	Esaie 8	Hebre. 7
g	4. No.	2		2	9	3	10	8
A	3. N.	3		3	11	4	12	9
b	Prid No	4		4	13	5	14	10
c	Nonas.	5		5	15	6	16	11
d	8. Id.	6		6	17	di. 7	18	12
e	7. Id.	7		7	19	di. 7	20. 21	13
f	6. Id.	8		8	22	8	23	Iacob. 1
g	5. Id.	9		9	24	9	25	2
A	4. Id.	10		10	26	10	27	3
b	3. Id.	11		11	28	11	29	4
c	Prid. Id	12		12	30	12	31	5
d	Idus	13		13	32	13	33	1. Pet. 1
e	19. kl.	14		14	34	14	35	2
f	18. kl.	15		15	36	15	37	3
g	17. kl.	16		16	38	16	39	4
A	16. kl.	17		17	40	17	41	5
b	15. kl.	18		18	42	18	43	2. Pet. 1
c	14 kl.	19		19	44	19	45	2
d	13. kl.	20		20	46	20	47	3
e	12 kl.	21	Thomas apo.	21	48	21	49	1. Ihon. 1
f	11. kl.	22		22	50	22	51	2
g	10 kl.	23		23	52	23	53	3
A	9. kl.	24		24	54	24	55	4
b	8. kl.	25	Nati. domini	25	Esaie 9	Math. 1	Esaie 7	Tit. 3
c	7. kl.	26	Stephen.	26	56	Acte. 6. 7	57	Actes. 7
d	6. kl.	27	Ihon Euan.	27	58	Apoca. 1	59	Apoc. 22
e	5. kl.	28	Innocentes.	28	Iere. 31	Actes. 25	60	1. Ihon. 5
f	4 kl.	29		29	Esaie. 61	26	62	2. Ihon. 1
g	3 kl.	30		30	63	27	64	3. Ihon 1.
A	Prid. kl.	31		30	65	28	66.	Iude. 1

¶ An ordre for Mattyns daily through the yere. [a.i.

☞ The priest beeyng in the quier, shall begin with a loude voyce, the Lordes praier, called the *Pater noster.*

OUR father whiche art in heauen, hallowed bee thy name. Thy Kyngdome come. Thy will bee doen in yearth as it is in heauen. Geue vs this day our daily bread. And forgeue vs our trespasses, as we forgeue them that trespasse against vs. And leade vs not into temptacion. But deliuer vs from euill. Amen.

Then likewise he shall saie.

O lorde open thou my lippes.

Answere.

And my mouthe shall shewe furth thy praise.

Priest.

O God make good spede to saue me.

Answere.

O lorde make hast to helpe me.

/Priest. [a. i. *v.*

Glory be to the father, and to the sonne: and to the holy ghoste.

As it was in the beginnyng, is now, and euer shalbe: worlde without ende. Amen.

Praise ye the Lorde.

¶ And from Easter to Trinitie Sondaie.

Alleluya.

☞ Then shalbe saied or song without any Inuitatory this Psalme, *Venite exultemus. &c.* in Englishe, as foloweth.

O Come, lette vs syng vnto the lorde: let vs hartely reioyce in the strength of our saluacion.

Let vs come before his presence with thankesgeuyng: and shew ourself glad in hym with Psalmes.

For the Lorde is a greate God: and a greate kyng aboue all Goddes.

In his hande are all the corners of the yearth: And the strength of the hilles is his also.

The sea is his and he made it: and his handes prepared the drie lande.

O come, let vs worship and fal doune: and knele before the lorde our maker.

/For he is (the lorde) our God: And we are the [a. ii. people of his pasture, and the shepe of his handes.

To daie if ye wil heare his voyce, harden not your hartes: As in the prouocacion, and as in the daie of temptacion in the wildernesse.

When your fathers tempted me: proued me, and sawe my workes.

Fortie yeres long was I greued with this generacion, and saied: it is a people that do erre in their hartes, for thei haue not knowen my waies.

Unto whom I sware in my wrathe: that thei should not entre into my rest.

Glory be to the father, and to the. &c.

As it was in the beginnyng. &c. Amen

❧ Then shall folowe certain Psalmes in ordre, as thei been appoyncted in a Table made for that purpose, excepte there bee propre Psalmes appoyncted for that daie. And at thend of euery psalme through out the yere, and likewise in the ende of *Benedictus*, *Benedicite*, *Magnificat*, and *Nunc dimittis*, shalbe repeated.

Glory be to the father, and to the. &c.

¶ Then shalbe red .ii. lessons distinctly with a loude voyce, that the people maie heare. The first of thold /testament, [a. ii. *v.* the seconde of the newe. Like as thei bee appoyncted by the Kalendar, except there be proper Lessons assigned for that day: the minister that readeth the Lesson, standyng and turnyng him so as he mai best bee heard of all suche as bee present. And before euery lesson, the minister shall saie thus. The firste, second, third .iiii. Chapiter of Genesis, or Exodus, Matthewe, Marke, or other like as is appoincted in the Kalendar. And in the ende of euery Chapiter he shall saie.

Here endeth suche a Chapiter of suche a booke.

❧ And (to thende the people maie the better heare) in suche places where thei dooe syng, there shall the Lessons bee song in a plain tune, after the maner of distinct readyng: and likewise the Epistle and Gospel.

❧ After the first Lesson shall folowe *Te deum* in Englishe, daily throughout the yere, except in Lent, all the whiche tyme in the place of *Te deum* shalbee vsed *Benedicite omnia opera domini domino*, in Englishe as foloweth.

Te deum.

WE praise thee, O GOD, wee knowlege thee to be the lorde.

Al the yearth doth worship thee, the father euerlastyng.

To thee all Angelles crie a loude, the heauens and all the powers therein.

To thee Cherubyn, and Seraphyn, /continually do crie. [a. iii.

Holy, holy, holy, lorde God of Sabaoth.

Heauen and yearth are full of the maiestie of thy glory.

The glorious compaignie of the Apostles praise thee.

The goodly felowship of the Prophetes, praise thee.

The noble armie of Martyrs, praise thee.

The holy Churche throughout al the worlde doth knowlege thee.

The father of an infinite Maiestie.

Thy honorable, true, and onely sonne.

Also the holy ghost the comforter.

Thou art the kyng of glory, O Christ.

Thou arte the euerlastyng sonne of the father.

When thou tookest vpon thee to deliuer manne, thou diddest not abhorre the Virgins wombe.

When thou haddest ouercomed† the sharpenesse of death: thou didest open the kyngdome of heauen to all beleuers.

Thou sittest on the right of God, in the /glory of the [a. iii. *v.* father.

We beleue that thou shalt come to be our Judge.

We therefore praie thee, helpe thy seruauntes whom thou hast redemed with thy precious bloud.

Make theim† to bee nombred with thy sainctes, in glory euerlastyng.

O Lorde saue thy people: And blesse thyne heritage.

Gouerne them and lift them vp for euer.

Daie by daie we magnifie thee.

And we worship thy name euer world without ende.

Vouchsafe, O Lorde to kepe vs this daie without synne.

O Lorde haue mercie vpon vs: Haue mercie vpon vs.

O Lorde, let thy mercie lighten vpon vs: as our trust is in thee.

O Lorde, in thee haue I trusted: Let me neuer be confounded.

Benedicite.

O All ye woorkes of the Lorde, speake good of the Lorde: praise hym, and /set hym vp for euer. [a. iiii.

O ye Angels of the lorde, speake good of the Lorde: praise hym, and set hym vp for euer.

O ye heauens speake good of the lorde: praise hym, and set hym vp for euer.

O ye waters that be aboue the firmament, speake good of the lord: praise him and set hym vp for euer.

O all ye powers of the Lorde, speake good of the lorde: praise hym, and set him vp for euer.

O ye Sonne and Moone, speake good of the Lorde: praise hym, and set hym vp for euer.

O ye Starres of heauen, speake good of the Lorde: praise hym, and set hym vp for euer.

O ye showers and dewe, speake good of the Lorde: praise hym, and set hym vp for euer.

O ye wyndes of GOD, speake good of the Lorde: Praise hym, and set hym vp for euer.

O ye fire and heate, praise ye the lord: /praise hym, [a. iiii. *v.*
and set hym vp for euer.

O ye Wynter and Sommer, speake good of the lorde: praise him, and set him vp for euer.

O ye Dewes and frostes, speake good of the lorde: Praise hym, and set hym vp for euer.

O ye frost and cold, speake good of the lorde; praise him, and set him vp for euer.

O ye ise and snowe, speake good of the lorde: praise hym, and set him vp for euer.

O ye nightes and Daies, speake good of the Lorde: praise hym, and set hym vp for euer.

O ye Light and Darkenesse, speake good of the Lord: Praise hym, and sette hym vp for euer.

O ye lightnynges and cloudes, speake good of the lorde: praise hym, and set him vp for euer.

O lette the yearth speake good of the Lorde: yea, let it praise hym, and set hym vp for euer.

O ye Mountaignes and Hilles, speake good of the Lorde:
praise hym, and sette/ hym vp for euer. [a. v.

O al ye grene thynges vpon the yearth, speake good of the Lorde: Praise hym, and set hym vp for euer.

O ye welles, speake good of the lorde: praise hym, and set hym vp for euer.

O ye seas and fluddes, speake good of the lorde: praise him, and set him vp for euer.

O ye whales, and all that moue in the waters, speake good of the lorde: praise hym, and set hym vp for euer.

O all ye Foules of the Ayre, speake good of the lorde: praise hym, and set him vp for euer.

O all ye Beastes and Cattell, speake good of the lorde: praise hym, and set him vp for euer.

O ye children of men, speake good of the lorde: praise hym, and set hym vp for euer.

O let Israell speake good of the lorde: praise hym, and set hym vp for euer.

O ye priestes of the lorde, speake good of the Lorde: praise hym, and set hym vp for euer.

O ye seruauntes of the Lorde, speake /good of the [a. v. *v.* lorde: praise hym, and set him vp for euer.

O ye spirites and soules of the righteous, speake good of the lorde, praise hym and set hym vp for euer.

O ye holy and humble men of harte, speake ye good of the lorde: praise ye him and set hym vp for euer.

O Ananias, Azarias, and Misaell, speake ye good of the lord: praise ye hym, and set hym vp for euer.

Glory be to the father, and to the sonne and to the holy ghost.

As it was in the beginnyng, is nowe, and euer shalbe: worlde with. &c. Amen.

¶ And after the second lesson, throughout the whole yere, shalbe vsed *Benedictus*, in Engilshe† as foloweth.

BLessed bee the lorde God of Israell: for he hath visited and redemed his people.

And hath lifted vp an horne of saluacion to vs: in the house of his seruaunt Dauid.

As he spake by the mouth of his holy /Prophetes: [a. vi. whiche hath been sence† the worlde began.

That wee should bee saued from our enemies: and from the handes of all that hate vs.

To perfourme the mercie promised to our fathers: and to remembre his holy couenaunt.

To performe the othe whiche he sware to our father Abraham: that he would geue vs.

That wee beeyng deliuered out of the handes of our enemies: might serue him without feare.

In holinesse and righteousnesse before hym: all the daies of our life.

And thou child, shalt be called the prophete of the hiest: for thou shalt go before the face of the lorde, to prepare his waies.

To geue knowlege of saluacion vnto his people: For the remission of their synnes.

Through the tendre mercie of oure God: whereby the daie spryng from an high hath visited vs.

To geue lighte to theim that sitte in /darknesse, and [a. vi. *v.* in the shadowe of death: and to guyde our feete into the waie of peace.

Glory be to the father, and to the. &c.
As it was in the beginnyng. &c. Amen.

Then shalbe saied daily through the yere, these praiers folowyng, aswell at Euensong as at Mattins, all deuoutly knelyng with a loude voyce. &c.

Lorde haue mercie vpon vs.
Christ haue mercie vpon vs.
Lorde haue mercie vpon vs.

Then the minister shall saie the Crede, and the Lordes praier in Englishe.

Answere.

But deliuer vs from euill. Amen.

Priest.

O lorde shewe thy mercie vpon vs.

Answere.

And graunt vs thy saluacion.

Priest.

O lorde saue the Kyng.

Answere

And mercifully heare vs when we call vpon thee.

Priest.

Indue thy ministers with righteousnes

Answere.

And make thy chosen people ioyfull.

/Priest. [a. vii.

O lorde saue thy people.

Answere.

And blesse thyne inheritaunce.

Priest.

Geue peace in our tyme, O lorde.

Answere.

Because there is none other that fighteth for vs, but onely thou, O God.

Priest.

O God, make cleane our hartes within vs.

Answere.

And take not thyne holy spirit from vs.

Priest.

The Lorde bee with you.

Answere.

And with thy spirite.

¶ Then shall daily folowe three Collectes. The firste of the daie, whiche shalbee thesame that is appoyncted at the Communion. The second for peace. The thirde for grace to liue well. And the twoo last Collectes shall neuer alter, but daily bee saied at Mattins, throughout al the yere, as foloweth. The priest standyng vp and saiyng.

¶ Let vs praie.

Then the Collect of the daie.

The second Collect for peace.

O GOD, whiche art aucthor of peace, and louer of [a. vii. *v.* concorde, in knowlege of whom standeth our eternall life, whose seruice is perfecte fredome: defende vs thy humble seruauntes, in al assaultes of our enemies, that wee surely trustyng in thy defence, maie not feare the power of any aduersaries: Through the might of Iesu Christ our lorde. Amen.

¶ The third Collect: for grace.

O Lorde oure heauenly father, almightie and euerliuyng GOD, whiche hast safely brought vs to the beginnyng of this daie: defende vs in the same, with thy mightie power, and graunt that this daie we fall not into sin, neither runne into any kynd of daunger, but that al our doynges, maie be ordred by thy gouernaunce, to do alwaies that is righteous in thy sight: through Iesus Christ our lorde. Amen.

/An ordre for Euensong throughout the yere. [a. viii.

¶ The priest shall saie.

Our Father. &c.

Then likewise he shall saie.

O God make spede to saue me.

Answere.

O Lord make hast to helpe me.

Priest.

Glory be to the father, and to the. &c.
As it was in the beginnyng. &c. Amen.
Praise ye the Lorde.

¶ And from Easter to Trinitie Sondaie.

Alleluya.

¶ As before is appoincted at Mattins.

Then Psalmes in ordre, as thei bee appoyncted in the Table for Psalmes, excepte there bee propre Psalmes appoyncted for that daie. Then a Lesson of the olde Testament, as is appoyncted likewise in the Kalendar, excepte there bee propre Lessons appoyncted for that daie. After that (*Magnificat*) in Englishe, as foloweth.

/*Magnificat.* [a. viii. *v.*

My soule doth magnifie the lord.
And my spirit hath reioysed in God my sauior.
For he hath regarded the lowlinesse, of his handmaiden.
For behold from hencefurthe all generacions shall call me blessed.
For he that is mightie, hath magnified me: and holy is his name.
And his mercie is on theim that feare hym, throughout all generacions.
He hath shewed strength with his arme he hath scattered the proude in the imaginacion of their hartes.
He hath put doune the mightie from their seate, and hath exalted the humble and meke.
He hath filled the hungery with good thynges, and the riche he hath sent emptie awaie.

He remembryng his mercie, hath holpen his seruaunt Israell: As he promised to our fathers, Abraham and his sede for euer.

Glory be to. &c. As it was. &c. Amen.

/ Then a Lesson of the Newe testament. And after that [b. i. (*Nunc dimittis*) in Englishe, as foloweth.

Nunc dimittis Luke. ij. [in m.]

LOrde, now lettest thou thy seruaunt depart in peace Accordyng to thy woorde.

For mine iyes haue seen : thy saluacion.

Whiche thou hast prepared : before the face of all people.

To be a light to lighten the Gentiles: and to be the glory of thy people Israell.

Glory be to the father, and to the. &c.

As it was in the begin. &c. Amen.

Then the Suffrages before assigned at Mattins, the Clerkes kneelyng likewise, with three Collectes. Firste of the daie: Seconde of peace : Thirde for aide against all perilles, as here foloweth. Whiche twoo last Collectes shalbe daily saied at Euensong, withoue alteracion.

¶ The second Collect at Euensong.

O God, from whom al holy desires, all good counsailes, and all iuste woorkes doo procede: geue vnto thy seruauntes that peace, whiche the worlde cannot geue, that both our hear/tes maie be so set to obeye thy commaundementes, [b. i. *v.* and also that by thee, wee beyng defended from the feare of oure enemies, maie passe oure tyme in reste and quietnesse: Through the merites of Iesu Christ our sauior. Amen.

¶ The third Collect for aide against al perils.

LIghten our darkenes we beseche thee, O lorde, and by thy greate mercie, defende vs from al perils and daungers of this night, for the loue of thy onely sonne our sauior Iesu Christ. Amen.

¶ In the feastes of Christmas, Thepiphanie, Easter, the Assencion, Pentecost, and vpon Trinitie Sondaie, shalbe song or saied immediatly after *Benedictus*, this confession of our Christian faithe.

Quicunque uult. [in m.]

WHosoeuer will be saued : before all thynges it is necessary that he hold the catholike faithe.

Whiche faithe, except euery one do kepe holy and vndefiled : without doubt he shall perishe euerlastyngly.

And the catholike faithe is this : that wee worship one God in Trinitie, and /Trinitie in vnitie. [b. ii.

Neither confoundyng the persones : nor deuidyng the substaunce.

For there is one persone of the father, another of the sonne, and another of the holy ghost.

But the Godhed of the father, of the sonne, and of the holy ghoste, is all one : the glory equall, the maiestie coeternall.

Suche as the Father is, suche is the sonne : and suche is the holy ghost.

The father vncreate, the sonne vncreate : and the holy ghost vncreate.

The father incomprehensible, the sonne incomprehensible : and the holy ghost incomprehensible.

The Father eternal, the Sonne eternall : and the holy ghost eternall.

And yet thei are not three eternalles : but one eternall.

As also there bee not three incomprehensibles, nor three vncreated : But one vncreated, and one incomprehensible.

So likewise the father is almightie : the sonne almightie, and the holy ghost /almightie [b. ii. *v.*

And yet are thei not three almighties : but one almightie.

So the father is God, the sonne is god : and the holy ghost is God.

And yet are thei not thre Goddes : but one God.

So likewise the Father is Lorde, the sonne lorde : and the holy ghost lorde.

And yet not thre lordes : but one lorde.

For like as wee bee compelled by the Christian veritie : To acknowlege euery persone by hymself to be God and lorde.

So are we forbidden by the catholike religion : to saie there be three Goddes or three Lordes.

The father is made of none : Neither created nor begotten.

The sonne is of the father alone : Not made nor created, but begotten.

The holy ghost is of the father, and of the sonne: neither made nor created, nor begotten, but procedyng.

So there is one father, not thre fathers one sonne, not thre sonnes: one holy ghost, /not three holy ghostes [b. iii.

And in this Trinitie, none is afore or after other: none is greater nor lesse then other.

But the whole three persones: be coeternall together and coequall.

So that in all thynges, as is afore said: the vnitie in Trinitie, and the Trinitie in vnitie, is to be worshipped.

He therefore that will be saued: muste thus thynke of the Trinitie.

Furthermore it is necessary to euerlastyng saluacion: that he also beleue rightly in the incarnacion of our Lorde Iesu Christe.

For the right faithe is that we beleue and confesse: that our lorde Iesus Christ the sonne of God, is God and man.

God of the substaunce of the father, begotten before the worldes: and manne of the substaunce of his mother, borne in the worlde.

Perfect God and perfect man: of a reasonable soule, and humain fleshe subsistyng.

Equall to the father as touchyng his /Godhed: And [b. iii. *v.* inferior to the father, touchyng his manhode.

Who although he bee God and man: yet he is not twoo, but one Christ.

One, not by conuersion of the Godhede into fleshe: but by takyng of the manhod into God.

One altogether, not by confusion of substaunce: but by vnitie of persone.

For as the reasonable soule and fleshe is one man: so God and man is one Christ.

Who suffered for our saluacion: descended into hell, rose again the thirde daie from the dedde.

He ascended into heauen, he sitteth on the right hande of the father, GOD almightie: From whence he shall come to iudge the quicke and the dedde.

At whose commyng all men shall rise again with their bodies: And shall geue accompt of their awne workes.

And thei that haue dooen good, shall go into life euerlasting: and thei haue doen euill into euerlastyng fire.

This is the Catholike faithe: whiche / except a man [b. iiii. beleue faithfully, he cannot be saued.

Glory be to the father, and to the. &c.

As it was in the beginnyng. &c. Amen.

¶ The Letanie and Suffrages.

O God the father of heauen : haue mercie vpon vs miserable synners.

O God the father of heauen : haue mercie vpon vs miserable synners.

O God the sonne, redemer of the worlde : haue mercie vpon vs miserable synners.

O God the sonne, redemer of the worlde : haue mercie vpon vs miserable synners.

O God, the holy ghoste, procedyng from the father and the sonne : haue mercie vpon vs miserable synners.

O God the holy ghost, procedyng from the father and the sonne : haue mercie vpon vs miserable synners.

O holy, blessed, and glorious Trinitie, three persones and one God : haue mercie vpon vs miserable synners.

/O holy, blessed, and glorious Trinitie, thre persones and [b. iiii. *v.* one God : haue mercie vpon vs miserable synners.

Remembre not Lorde, our offences, nor the offences of our forefathers, neither take thou vengeaunce of our synnes : spare vs good lorde spare thy people whom thou haste redemed with thy moste precious bloud, and bee not angrie with vs for euer.

Spare vs good Lorde.

From al euil and mischief, from synne, from the craftes and assautes of the Deuill, from thy wrathe, and from euerlastyng dampnacion :

Good Lorde deliuer vs.

☞ From blindnes of hart, from pride, vainglory, and hypocrisy, from enuie, hatred, and malice, and all vncharitablenesse :

Good Lorde deliuer vs.

From fornicacion, and all other dedly sinne, and from all the deceiptes of the worlde, the fleshe, and the deuill :

Good Lorde deliuer vs.

From Lightnyng and Tempest, from plague, pestilence, and famine, from battaill, and murder, and from sodain death :

/Good Lorde deliuer vs. [b. v.

From all sedicion and priuie conspiracie, from the tyranny of the bishop of Rome and all his detestable enormities, from all false doctryne and heresy, from hardenesse of harte and contempt of thy worde and commaundement :

Good Lorde deliuer vs.

By the misterie of thy holy incarnacion, by thy holy natiuitie and circumcision, by thy baptisme, fastyng, and temptacion :

Good Lorde deliuer vs.

By thyne agonye and bloudy sweate, by thy Crosse and Passion, by thy precious death and buriall, by thy glorious resurreccion, and ascencion, by the commyng of the holy ghost :

Good Lorde deliuer vs.

In all tyme of our tribulacion, in al tyme of our wealthe, in the houre of death, in the daie of Iudgement :

Good Lorde deliuer vs.

We synners do beseche thee to heare vs, O Lorde GOD, and that it maie please thee to rule and gouerne thy holy Churche vniuersall in the right waie :

/We beseche thee to heare vs good Lorde. [b. v. *v.*

That it maie please thee to kepe Edward the .vi. thy seruaunt our kyng and gouernor :

We beseche thee to heare vs good Lorde.

That it maie please thee to rule his hart in thy faithe, feare and loue, that he maie alwaies haue affiaunce in thee, and euer seke thy honor and glory.

We beseche thee to heare vs good Lorde.

That it maie please thee to be his defender, and keper, geuyng hym the victorie ouer all his euemies.†

We beseche thee to heare vs good Lorde.

That it maie please thee to illuminate all Bishoppes, Pastours, and Ministers of the Churche, with true knowlege and vnderstandyng of thy woorde, and that bothe by their Preachyng and liuyng, thei maie sette it furthe, and shewe it accordyngly :

We beseche thee to heare vs good Lorde.

That it maie please thee to endue the lordes of the Counsaill, and all the nobilitie with grace, wisedom, and vnderstandyng :

We beseche thee to heare vs good Lorde.

That it maie please thee to blesse and kepe /the magis- [b. vi. trates, geuyng them grace to execute iustice, and to maintein truthe:

We beseche thee to heare vs good Lorde.

That it maie please thee to blesse and kepe all thy people:

We beseche thee to heare vs good Lorde.

That it maie please thee to geue to al nacions, vnitie, peace, and concord:

We beseche thee to heare vs good Lorde.

That it maie please thee to geue vs an harte to loue, and dread thee, and diligently to liue after thy commaundementes:

We beseche thee to heare vs good Lorde.

That it maie please thee to geue all thy people increase of grace, to heare mekely thy worde: and receiue it with pure affeccion, and to bryng furth the fruites of the spirite:

We beseche thee to heare vs good Lorde.

That it maie please thee to bryng into the waie of truthe, all suche as haue erred, and are deceiued:

We beseche thee to heare vs good Lorde.

That it maie please thee to strengthen suche as do stande, and comfort and helpe the weake harted, and to raise vp theim /that fall, and finally to beate doune Sathan vnder our [b. vi. *v.* fete:

We beseche thee to heare vs good Lorde.

That it maie please the to succour, helpe and comfort all that bee in daunger, necessitie and tribulacion:

We beseche thee to heare vs good Lorde.

That it maie please thee to preserue all that trauaill by lande or by water, all women laboryng of child, all sicke persones and young children, and to shewe thy pitie vpon all prisoners and captiues:

We beseche thee to heare vs good Lorde.

That it maie please thee to defende and prouide for the fatherlesse children and widdowes, and all that bee desolate and oppressed:

We beseche thee to heare vs good Lorde.

That it maie please thee to haue mercie vpon all men:

We beseche thee to heare vs good Lorde.

That it maie please thee to forgeue oure enemies, persecutours and slaunderors, and to turne their hartes:

We beseche thee to heare vs good Lorde.

That it maie please thee to geue and pre/serue to our [b. vii. vse the kyndly fruites of the yearth, so as in due tyme we maie enioye theim:

We beseche thee to heare vs good Lorde.

That it maie please thee to geue us true repentaunce, to forgeue us all our sinnes negligences, and ignoraunces, and to endue vs with the grace of thy holy spirite, to amende our liues accordyng to thy holy worde:

We beseche thee to heare vs good Lorde.

Sonne of God: we beseche thee to heare vs.

Sonne of God: we beseche thee to heare vs.

O Lambe of God, that takest awaie the synnes of the worlde:

Graunt vs thy peace.

O Lambe of God that takest awaie the synnes of the worlde:

Haue mercie vpon vs.

O Christ heare vs:

O Christ heare vs.

Lorde haue mercie vpon vs.

Lorde haue mercie vpon vs.

Christ haue mercie vpon vs.

Christ haue mercie vpon vs.

/Lorde haue mercie vpon vs. [b. vii. *v.*

Lorde haue mercie vpon vs.

Our father whiche art in heauen. &c.
And lede vs not into temptacion.

But deliuer vs from euill. Amen.

The versicle.

O Lorde deale not with vs after our synnes.

Answere.

Neither reward vs after our iniquities.

¶ Let us praie.

O God, mercifull father that despisest not the sighyng of a contrite harte, nor the desire of suche as be sorowfull, mercifully assist oure praiers, that we make before the in al our troubles and aduersities, whensoeuer thei oppresse vs: And graciously heare vs, that those euilles whiche the craft and subteltie of the deuill or man worketh against vs, be brought to naught, and by the prouidence of thy goodnesse thei maie bee dispersed, that we thy seruauntes beeyng hurte by no persecucions, maie euermore geue thankes vnto thee, in thy holy Churche: thorowe Iesus Christ our Lorde.

/O Lorde arise, helpe vs, and deliuer vs for thy name sake. [b. viii.

O God wee haue heard with our eares, and our fathers haue declared vnto vs, the noble woorkes that thou diddest in their daies, and in the old tyme before them.

O Lorde arise, help vs, and deliuer vs for thine honor.

Glory be to the father, the sonne, and the holy ghost: as it was in the beginnyng, is now, and euer shalbe world without ende.

Amen.

From our enemies defende vs, O Christ:

Graciously loke vpon our affliccions.

Pitifully behold the sorowes of our hart:

Mercifully forgeue the synnes of thy people.

Fauorably with mercie heare our praiers

O sonne of Dauid haue mercie vpon vs.

Bothe now and euer vouchsafe to heare vs Christ:

Graciously heare vs, O Christ, graciously heare vs, O Lorde Christ.

The versicle.

O lorde, let thy mercy be shewed vpon vs:

The answere.

As we do put our truste in thee.

¶ Let us praie.

/WE humbly beseche thee, O father, mercifully to [b. viii. *v.* looke vpon our infirmities, and for the glory of thy name sake, turne from vs those euils, that we most righteously haue deserued: and graunt that in al our troubles wee maie put our whole truste and confidence in thy mercie, and euermore serue thee in purenesse of liuyng, to thy honor and glory: Through our onely mediator and aduocate Iesus Christe our lorde. Amen.

ALmightie God, whiche haste geuen vs grace at this tyme with one accorde to make our common supplicacions vnto thee and dooest promise, that when twoo or three be gathered in thy name, thou will graunt their requestes: Fulfill nowe, O lorde, the desires and peticions of thy seruauntes, as maie be moste expedient for them: grauntyng vs in this worlde, knowlege of thy truth, and in the worlde to come, life euerlasting. Amen.

/¶ All that appertein to the clerkes to say or syng [c. i.

at the ministracion of the Communion, and when there is no Communion.
At Confirmacion.
At Matrimonie.
The visitacion of the sicke.
At buriall of the dedde.
At the purificacion of women.
And the first daie of Lent.

At the Communion.

Clerke.

First the Psalme appoyncted for the Introite.

Priest.

Almightie God. &c.

Answere.

iii. Lorde haue mercie vpon vs.
iii. Christ haue mercie vpon vs.
iii. Lorde haue mercie vpon vs.

Priest.

Glory to God on high.

Answere.

And in yearth peace, good wil towardes menne.

Wee praise thee, wee blesse thee, wee worship thee, wee glorifie thee, we geue thankes to thee, for thy greate glory, O /Lorde God heauenly Kyng, God the father almightie. [c. i. *v.*

O Lorde the onely begotten sonne Iesus Christ, O Lorde God, lambe of God, sonne of the father, that takest awaie the synnes of the worlde, haue mercie vpon vs: thou that takest awaie the synnes of the worlde, receiue our praier.

Thou that sittest at the right hande of God the father, haue mercie vpon vs: for thou onely art holy: Thou onely art the Lorde. Thou onely (O Christe) with the holy ghost, art moste high in the glory of God the father. Amen.

Priest.

The Lorde be with you.

Answere.

And with thy spirite.

Priest.

¶ Let us praie.

Almightie God, &c.

Priest or Clerke.

The Epistle.

Priest.

The holy Gospell written. &c.

Answere.

/Glory bee to thee O lorde. [c. ii.

Priest.

I beleue in one God.

Answere.

The father almightie, maker of heauen and yearth, and of al thynges visible, and inuisible: And in one Lorde Iesu Christ, the onely begotten sonne of God, begotten of his father, before al worldes, God of God, light of light, verie God of verie God, begotten not made, beeyng of one substaunce with the father, by whom all thynges were made, who for vs men, and for our saluacion, came doune from heauen, and was incarnate by the holy ghost, of the virgin Mari, and was made man, and was Crucified also for vs, vnder Poncius Pilate, he suffered and was buried, and the thirde daie he rose again accordyng to the scriptures, and ascended into heauen, and sitteth at the right hand of the father: And he shall come again with glory to iudge bothe the quicke and the ded[1]

[1] Here the Creed ends abruptly, at the bottom of the page, but not at the end of a line.

/☙ The Offertorie. [c. ii. *v.*

Clerke.

Matth. v. [in m.]

Let your light so shine before menne, that thei maie se your good workes, and glorifie your father whiche is in heauen.

Matth. vi. [in m.]

Laie not vp for your selfes treasure vpon the yearth, where ruste and Mothe dooth corrupt, and where theues breake through and steale: But laie vp for your selfes treasure in heauen, where neither rust nor Mothe doth corrupt, and where theues do not breake through nor steale.

Math. vij. [in m.]

Whatsoeuer ye would, that menne should do vnto you, euen so do you vnto them, for this is the lawe of† the Prophetes.

Mate. vij. [in m.]

Not euery one that saieth vnto me, Lorde, Lorde, shall entre into the kyngdome of heauen, but he that doth the wil of my father whiche is in heauen.

Luke. xix. [in m.]

Zache stode furthe, and saied vnto the Lorde, behold lorde, the halfe of my goodes I geue to the poore, and if I haue doen any wrong vnto any man, I restore foure /folde. [c. iii.

i. Cor. ix. [in m.]

Who goeth a warfare at any tyme at his awne cost? who planteth a vineyard, and eateth not of the fruite thereof? Or who fedeth a flocke, and eateth not of the milke of the flocke.

i. Cor. ix. [in m.]

If we haue sowen vnto you spirituall thynges, is it a greate matter, if we shall reape your worldly thynges?

i. Cor. ix. [in m.]

Dooe ye not knowe, that thei whiche minister aboute holy thynges, liue of the sacrifice. Thei whiche waite of the altar are partakers with the Aultar, euen so hath the Lorde also ordeigned: that thei whiche preache the Gospell, should liue of the Gospell.

ij. Cor. ix. [in m.]

Thei whiche soweth litle, shall reape litle, and he that soweth plenteously shal reape plenteously. Let euery man do accordyng as he is disposed in his hart, not grudgyngly, or of necessitie, for God loueth a cherefull geuer.

Gala vi. [in m.]

Let hym that is taught in the woorde, Minister vnto hym that teacheth in all good thynges. Bee not deceiued, God is /not mocked. For whatsoeuer a man soweth, that shall [c. iii. *v.* he reape.

Gala vi. [in m.]

While we haue tyme, let vs doo good vnto all menne, and specially vnto them, whiche are of the houshold of faithe.

i. Timo. vi [in m.]

Godlinesse is great riches, if a manne bee contented with that he hath : for wee brought nothyng into the world, neither maie we cary any thyng out.

i. Timo vi. [in m.]

Charge theim whiche are riche in this worlde, that thei bee ready to geue, and glad to distribute, laiyng vp in store for theimselfes a good foundacion, against the tyme to come, that thei maie attain eternall life.

Hebre. vi. [in m.]

God is not vnrighteous, that he will forget your workes, and labor that procedeth of loue, whiche loue ye haue shewed for his names sake, which haue ministered to the sainctes, and yet do minister.

Hebre. xiij. [in m.]

To do good and to distribute, forget not, for with suche sacrifices God is pleased.

i. Iohn iii. [in m.]

Whoso hath this worldes good, and seeth his brother haue nede, and shutteth /vp his compassion from hym, how [c. iiii. dwelleth the loue of God in hym.

Toby. iiij. [in m.]

Geue almose of thy goodes, and turne neuer thy face from any poore man, and then the face of the lorde shall not be turned awaie from thee.

Toby. iiij. [in m.]

Be mercifull after thy power : If thou haste muche, geue plenteously, if thou hast litle, doo thy diligence gladly to geue of that litle, for so gatherest thou thy self a good reward, in the daie of necessitie.

Prouer. xix. [in m.]

He that hath pitie vpon the poore, lendeth vnto the Lorde, and looke what he laieth out: it shalbe paied again.

Psal. xli. [in m.]

Blessed be the man that prouideth for the sicke and nedy: the lorde shall deliuer hym, in the tyme of trouble.

Priest.

The Lorde be with you.

Answere.

And with thy spirite.

Priest.

Lift vp your hartes.

Answere.

We lift them vp vnto the Lorde.

Priest.

/Let vs geue thankes to our lorde God. [c. iiii. *v.*

Answere.

It is mete and right so to do.

Priest.

It is very mete, right and our bounden. &c.

Clerke.

Holy, holy, holy, Lorde God of hostes, heauen and yearth are full of thy glorie: Osanna in the highest. Blessed is he that commeth in the name of the lorde: ¿Glory to thee in the highest.

Priest.

Let vs praie for the whole state of Christes Churche.
Almightie and euerliuyng God. &c.
And leade vs not into temptacion.

Answere.

But deliuer vs from euill. Amen.

Priest.

The peace of the Lorde bee alwaie with you.

Answere.

And with thy spirite.

Clerke in the Communion tyme shall saie or syng.

ii. O Lambe of God that takest awaie the synnes of the worlde: have mercie v/pon vs [c. v.

O lambe of God that takest awaie the synnes of the worlde: graunt vs thy peace.

Sentences to be saied or song, euery daie one after the holy Communion.

Math. xvi. [in m.]
If any manne will folowe me, let hym forsake hymself, and take vp his Crosse and folowe me.

Marke xiij. [in m.]
Whosoeuer shall indure vnto thende, he shalbe saued.

Luke. i. [in m.]
Praised be the lorde God of Israel, for he hath visited and redemed his people: therefore let vs serue hym all the daies of our life, in holinesse and righteousnesse accepted before hym.

Luc. xij. [in m.]
Happie are those seruauntes, whom the lorde (when he commeth) shall find wakyng.

Luc. xij. [in m.]
Be ye ready for the sonne of man will come, at an houre when ye thynke not.

Luc. xij. [in m.]
The seruaunt that knoweth his Masters wil, and hath not prepared hymself neither hath doen accordyng to his will, shalbe beaten with many stripes.

Iohn. iiij. [in m.]
The houre commeth and nowe it is, /when true [c. v *v.* worshippers shall worship the father in spirite and truthe.

.v. nohI† [in m.]
Beholde, thou art made whole, synne no more, least any worse thyng happen vnto thee.

Ihon. viij. [in m.]
If ye shall continue in my worde, then are ye my very disciples, and ye shall know the truth, and the truth shall make you fre.

Ihon. xij. [in m.]
Whyle ye haue light, beleue on the light, that ye may be the children of light.

Ihon xiiij. [in m.]
He that hath my commaundementes and kepeth theim, thesame is he that loueth me.

Iohn xiiij. [in m.]
If any man loue me, he will kepe my worde, and my father will loue hym, and we will come vnto hym, and dwell with hym.

Ihon. xv. [in m.]
If ye shall bide in me, and my woorde shall abide in you, ye shall aske what ye will, and it shalbe doen to you.

Ihon. xv. [in m.]
Herein is my father glorified, that ye beare muche fruite, and become my Disciples.

Ihon. xv. [in m.]
This is my commaundement, that you loue together, as I have loued you.

Roma. viij. [in m.]
/If God bee on our side, who can bee against vs? [c. vi.
whiche did not spare his awne sonne, but gaue him for vs all.

Roma. viij. [in m.]
Who shal laie any thing to the charge of Gods chosen? It is God that iustifieth who is that can condempne?

Roma. xiij. [in m.]
The night is passed, and the daie is at hande, let vs therefore cast awaie the deedes of darkenesse, and put on the armour of light.

i. Cor. i. [in m.]
Christ Iesus is made of God, vnto vs wisedome, and righteousnesse, and sanctifiying, and redempcion, that (accordyng as it is written) he whiche reioyseth should reioyse in the lorde.

i. Cor. iij. [in m.]
Knowe ye not that ye are the temple of God, and that the spirite of God dwelleth in you? If any man defile the temple of God, hym shall God destroye.

i. Cor. vj. [in m.]
Ye are derely bought, therefore glorify God in your bodies, and in your spirites, for thei belong to God.

Ephe. v. [in m.]
Be you folowers of God as dere children, and walke in loue euen as Christe loued vs, and gave himself for vs, an of/feryng and a Sacrifice of a swete sauor to God. [c. vi. *v.*

Priest.

The lorde be with you

Answere.

And with thy spirite.

Priest.

¶ Let vs praie.

Almightie and euerliuyng. &c.

Answere

Amen.

ℂ At Matrimonie.

The Clerke shall saie or syng with the priest, this Psalme.

Beati omnes. Psal. Cxxviij. [in m.]

BLessed are al thei that feare the lorde: and walke in his waies. &c.

Or els this Psalme.

Deus miseria[*tur*].† *Psal. lxvij.* [in m.]

God be mercifull vnto vs and blesse. &c.

Priest.

Lorde haue mercie vpon vs.

Answere

Christ haue mercie vpon vs.

Priest.

Lorde haue mercie vpon vs.

Answere.†

/Priest. [c. vij.

Our father whiche art in heauen. &c.
And leade vs not into temptacion.

Answere.

But deliuer vs from euill. Amen.

Priest.

O lorde saue thy seruaunt and thy handmaide.

Answere.

Whiche put their trust in thee.

Priest.

O Lorde, sende them helpe from thy holy place.

Answere.

And euermore defende them.

Priest.

Be vnto them a tower of strength.

Answere.

From the face of their enemie.

Priest.

O lorde heare my praier.

Answere.

And let my crie come to thee.

Priest.

Let us praie.

O God of Abraham. &c.

/The visitacion of the Sicke. [c. vii. *v.*

Priest.

Peace be within this house. &c.

Domine exaudi. Psal. Cxliij. [in m.]

Heare my praier. Psal. Cxliii.

Antheme.

REmembre not Lorde our iniquities nor the iniquities of our forefathers spare vs good lord, spare thy people whom thou hast redeemed with thy moste precious bloud, and bee not angrie with vs for euer.

Priest.

Lorde haue mercie vpon vs.

Answere.

Christ haue mercie vpon vs.

Priest.

Lord haue mercie vpon vs.
Our father whiche art in heauen. &c.
And leade vs not into temptacion.

Answere.

But deliuer vs from euil. Amen.

Priest.

O lorde saue thy seruaunt.

Answere.

Whiche putteth his trust in thee.

/Priest. [c. viii.

Sende hym helpe from thy holy place.

Answere.

And euermore mightely defende hym.

Priest.

Let the enemie haue none aduauntage of hym.

Answere.

Nor the wicked approche to hurt him.

Priest.

Be vnto hym, O lorde, a strong tower.

Answere.

From the face of his enemie.

Priest.

Lorde heare my praier.

Answere.

And let my crye come vnto thee.

Priest.

Let vs praie.

O lorde loke doune. &c.
Heare vs almightie. &c.
Derely beloued. &c.
Our lorde Jesus Christ. &c.
O moste mercifull God. &c.

Then this Psalme.

In te domine. Psal. lxxiij.† [in m.]

In thee O lorde. &c.

Antheme.

/O Sauior of the worlde saue vs, whiche by thy crosse [c. viii. *v.* and precious bloud hast redemed vs, helpe vs we beseche thee O God.

Priest.

The almightie lorde. &c.
As with this visible oyle. &c.

Then this psalme.

How long wilt thou forget me. &c.

The Communion of the sicke.

Psal. C.xvii. [in. m.]

O Praise the Lorde, all ye nacions, laude hym all ye people: For his mercifull kyndnesse is confirmed toward vs, and the truthe of the lorde endureth for euer.

Glory be to the father, and to the. &c.
As it was in the begin. &c. Amen.

Priest.

The lorde be with you.

Answere.

And with thy spirite.

Priest.

Let vs praie.

/Almightie euerlastyng God. &c. [d. i.

The Epistle.

Hebre. xi. [in. m.]

My sonne, despise not the correccion of the lorde, neither faint when thou art rebuked of him: for whom the Lorde loueth, hym he correcteth, yea and he skourgeth euery sonne, whom he receiueth.

The Gospell.

Verely, verely. &c.

The Preface.

The lorde be with you,

Answere.

And with thy spirite.

Priest.

Lift vp your. &c, vnto the ende of the Canon.

☙ When the sicke persone is visited, and receiueth the holy Communion, all at one tyme, then the priest for more expedicion, shall vse this ordre at the visitacion.

The antheme.

Remembre not lorde. &c.
Lorde haue mercie vpon vs.
Christ haue mercie vpon vs.
Lorde haue mercie vpon vs.
Our father whiche art in heauen. &c.
/And lede vs not into temptacion. [d. i. *v*.

Answere.

But deliuer vs from euill. Amen.

Let vs praie.

O lorde loke doune. &c.

With the firste parte of the exhortacion, and all other thynges vnto the psalme.

In te domine spe[*raui*]. *Psal. xxxi.* [in. m.

In the lorde haue I put my trust. &c.

And if the sicke desire to be annoynted, then shall the priest vse the appoyncted praier, without any psalme.

¶ At the buriall of the dedde.

Priest or clerk shall saie or syng.

Iohn xi. [in. m.]

I Am the resurreccion and the life (saith the lorde) he that beleueth in me, yea, though he were dedde, yet shall he liue. And whosoeuer liueth and beleueth in me shall not dye for euer.

Iob. xix. [in. m.]

I Knowe that my redemer liueth, and that I shall rise out of the yearth, in the last daie, and shalbe couered again in my skynne, and shall se God in my fleshe: yea, and my self shall beholde hym, not /with other, but with these same iyes. [d. ii.

i. Timo. vi. Iob i. [in m.]

VVee broughte nothyng into this worlde, neither maie wee cary any thyng out of this worlde. The lorde geueth, and the Lorde taketh awaie. Euen as it pleaseth the lorde, so commeth thynges to passe: Blessed bee the name of the Lorde.

At the graue the priest or clerke shall saie or syng.

Iob. xiiii. [in m.]

MAn that is borne of a woman, hath but a shorte tyme to liue, and is full of misery: He commeth vp and is cut doune like a floure, he flieth as it wer a shadow and neuer continueth in one staie.

In the middest of life, wee be in death, of whom maie we seke for succour but of thee, O lorde, whiche for our synnes iustely art moued: yet O lorde God moste holy, O lorde moste mightie, O holy and most merciful sauior, deliuer vs not into the bitter paines of eternall death. Thou knowest lorde, the secretes of our hartes, shut not vp thy mercifull iyes to our prayers: But spare vs Lorde moste holy, O /God moste mightie, O [d. ii. *v.* holy and mercifull sauior, thou moste worthy iudge eternall, suffre vs not at our laste houre, for any paines of death, to fall from thee.

The priest castyng yearth vpon the corps, shall saie.

I commende thy soule to God the father almightie. &c.

The priest or clerke shall saie or syng.

Apoca. xiiij. [in m.]

I Heard a voyce from heauen, saiyng vnto me, write: Blessed are the dedde whiche die in the lorde. Euen so saith the spirite, that thei rest from their labours.

Priest.

Let vs praie.

We commende into thy handes. &c.

The priest or clerke shall saie or syng these Psalmes.

Dilexi quoni[*am*]. *Psal. C.xvi.* [in m.]

I Am well pleased: that the Lorde hath heard the voyce of my. &c.

Domine probasti. Psal. Cxxxix. [in m.]

O Lorde thou haste searched me out and knowen me. &c.

Lauda anima. Psal. Cxlvi. [in m.]

PRaise the lorde (O my soule) while I liue I will praise the Lorde: yea, as long as I haue any beyng, I will. &c.

/The priest or clerke shall reade this lesson. [d. iii.

i. Cor. xv. [in m.]

CHrist is risen from the dedde, and become the firste fruites of theim that slepte. For by a manne came death, and by a man came the resurreccion of the dedde. For as by Adam all dye: Euen so by Christ shall all bee made aliue, but euery man in his awne ordre. The first is Christ, then thei that are Christes at his commyng. Then commeth thende when he hath deliuered vp the kyngdom to God the father, when he hath put doune all rule, and all aucthoritie and power. For he must reigne, till he hath put al his enemies vnder his fete. The last enemie that shalbee destroyed, is death: For he hath put all thynges vnder his fete. But when he saith, all thynges are put vnder hym, it is manifest that he is excepted, whiche did put all thynges vnder hym: when all thynges are subdued vnto hym that putte all thynges vnder hym, that God maie be all in all. Els what do thei, whiche are Baptized ouer the dedde, if the ded rise not at all? Why are they /then baptized ouer theim? yea, and why stande we alwaie in [d. iii. *v.* ieoperdy? By our reioysyng whiche I haue in Christe Iesu our lord, I die daily. That I haue fought with beastes at Ephesus after the maner of menne, what auauntageth it me, if the dedde rise not again? Lette vs eate and drynke, for to morowe we shall dye. Bee not ye deceiued: Euill woordes corrupte good maners. Awake truly out of slepe, and synne not, for some haue not the knowlege of God: I speake this to your shame But some menne will saie: how arise the dedde? With what body shall thei come? Thou foole, that whiche thou sowest, is not quickened excepte it dye. And what sowest thou? Thou sowest not the body that shalbe: but bare corne as of wheate, or of some other, but God geueth it a body at his pleasure, to euery sede his awne body. All fleshe is not one maner of flesh: but there is one maner of fleshe of men, another maner of fleshe of beastes, another of Fishes, another of birdes. There are also celestiall bodies, and there are bodies terrestriall. But the glory of the /celestial is one, and the glory of the terrestrial is [d. iiii. another. There is one maner glory of the Sonne, and another glorye of the Mone, and another glorye of the Starres. For as one starre differeth from another in glory: so is the resurreccion of the dedde. It is sowen in corrupcion, it riseth again in incorrupcion. It is sowen in dishonour, it riseth again in honour. It is sowen in weakenesse, it riseth again in power. It is sowen a naturall body, it riseth again a spiritual body. There is a naturall body, and there is a spirituall body: as it is also written, the firste man was made a liuyng soule, and the laste Adam was made a quickenyng spirit. Howbeit, that is not first that is spirituall: but that whiche is naturall, and then that whiche is spirituall. The first man is of the yearth yearthy: The seconde man is the Lorde, from heauen heauenly. As is the heauenly, suche are thei that are heauenly. And as wee haue borne the Image of the yearthy, so shall we beare the image of the heauenly. This saie I brethren, that fleshe and bloud /cannot inherite the Kyngdome of God, nither [d. iiii. *v.* doth corrupcion inherit vncorrupcion. Behold, I shewe you a mistery, we shall not all slepe: But wee shall all bee chaunged, and that in a moment, in the twinkelyng of an iye, by the last trompe. For the trompe shall blowe, and the ded shall rise incorruptible: and wee shalbee chaunged. For this corruptible must put on incorrupcion: and this mortall muste put on immortalitie. When this corruptible, hath put on incorrupcion, and this mortall hath put on immortalitie: Then shalbe brought to passe, the saiyng that is written: death is swallowed vp in victory. Death where is thy styng? Hell where is thy victory? The styng of death is syn: and the strength of synne is the Lawe. But thankes be vnto God, whiche hath geven vs victory, through our lorde Iesus Christ. Therefore my dere brethren, bee ye stedfast and vnmoueable, alwaies riche in the woorke of the Lorde, forasmuche as ye know, how that your labor is not in vain in the lorde.

/ The lesson ended the priest shall saie. [d. v.

Lorde haue mercie vpon vs.
Christ haue mercie vpon vs.
Lorde haue mercie vpon vs.

Our father whiche art in heauen. &c.
And leade vs not into temptacion.

Answere.

But deliuer vs from euill. Amen.

Priest.

Entre not (O Lorde) into Iudgement with thy seruaunt.

Answere.

For in thy sighte no liuyng creature shalbe iustified.

Priest.

From the gates of hell.

Answere.

Deliuer their soules O lorde.

Priest.

I beleue to se the goodnesse of the lorde.

Answere.

In the lande of the liuyng.

Priest.

O lorde graciously heare my praier.

Answere.

And let my crie come vnto thee.

Priest

/ ¶ Let vs praie. [d. v. *v.*

O lorde, with whom do liue. &c.

At the Communion when there is a Buriall

The introit.

Quemadmodum. Psal. xlii. [in m.]

LIke as the Harte desireth the waterbrokes: so longeth my soule after. &c.

The Epistle.

i. Thessa. iiii. [in m.]

I Would not brethren, that ye should be ignoraunt concerning them whiche are fallen a slepe, that ye sorowe not as other do, whiche haue no hope. For if wee beleue that Iesus died, and rose again: Euen so them also which slepe by Iesus, wil God bryng again with hym. For this saie we vnto you in the worde of the lorde: that wee whiche shall liue, and shall remain in the commyng of the Lorde, shall not come ere thei whiche slepe. For the lorde hymself shall descende from heauen, with a shout, and the voyce of the Archangel /and [d. vi. *v.* trompe of GOD. And the dedde in Christ shall rise firste: then wee whiche shall liue (euen we whiche shall remain) shalbe caught vp with theim also in the Cloudes, to mete the Lorde in the aire. And so shall we euer bee with the lorde: wherefore comfort yourselfes one another with these wordes.

The Gospell.

Ihon. vi. [in m.]

Iesus said to his disciples. &c.

ℂ At the Purificacion of women.

This Psalme.

Leuaui oculos. Psal. Cxxi. [in m.]

I Haue lifted vp mine iyes vnto the hilles: from whence commeth my. &c.

Lorde haue mercie vpon vs.
Christ haue mercie vpon vs.
Lorde haue mercie vpon vs.
Our father whiche art in heauen. &c.
And leade vs not into temptacion.

Answere

But deliuer vs from euill. Amen.

/Priest. [d. vi *v.*

O lorde saue this woman thy seruaunt.

Answere.

Whiche putteth her trust in thee.

Priest.

Be thou to her a strong tower.

Answere.

From the face of her enemie.

Priest.

Lorde hare† my praier.

Answere.

And let my crie come to thee.

Priest.

Let vs praie.

O almightie God. &c.

The first daie of Lent, commonly called Ashwednesdaie.

After the cursses ended, the Clerke with the priest shall saie this psalme.

Miserere mei Psal. li. [in m.]

HAue mercie vpon me (O God) after thy great goodnesse, accordyng vnto the multitude of thy mercies, do away myne offences. &c.

/Priest. [d. vii.

Lorde haue mercie vpon vs.

Answere.

Christ haue mercie vpon vs.

Priest.

Lorde haue mercie vpon vs.
Our father whiche art in heauen. &c.
And leade vs not into temptacion.

Answere.

But deliuer vs from euill. Amen.

Priest.

O lorde saue thy seruauntes.

Answere.

Whiche put their trust in thee.

Priest.

Sende vnto them helpe from aboue.

Answere.

And euermore mightely defend them.

Priest.

Helpe vs O God our sauior.

Answere.

And for the glory of thy names sake deliuer vs.
And be mercifull vnto vs synners for thy names sake.

Priest.

O lorde heare my praier.

/Answere. [d. vii. *v.*

And let my crie come to thee.

Priest.

Let vs praie.

O lorde we beseche thee. &c.

Clerke or Minister to saie or syng this Antheme.

TVrne thou vs, O good lorde, and so shall we be turned : be fauorable (O lorde) be fauorable to thy people, whiche turne to thee in wepyng, Fastyng, and praiyng : for thou art a mercifull God, ful of compassion, long sufferyng, and of a greate pitie. Thou sparest when we deserue punishement, and in thy wrathe thynkest vpon mercie, spare thy people, good lorde, spare theim, and let not thy heritage be brought to confusion: heare vs (O lorde) for thy mercie is great and after the multitude of thy mercies looke vpon vs.

APPENDIX I.

THE CONSTITUTIONS OF THE PARISH CLERKS AT TRINITY CHURCH COVENTRY MADE IN 1462.

[The constitutions were printed by Thomas Sharp in his *Illustrations of the History . . . Holy Trinity Church Coventry*, published at the Coventry in 1818. They were also reprinted in the *British Magazine*, 1834, vol. vi. p. 262. By the kind offices of the Rev. F. M. Beaumont, Vicar of Holy Trinity, Coventry, and Hon. Canon of Worcester, the manuscript was deposited at the British Museum for the purposes of transcription and editing. It consists of two leaves of paper; on the first, recto and verso, are written the duties of the first deacon; on the second, those of the second deacon, both sides of the paper being written upon.

The leaves measure 12 inches by $8\frac{1}{4}$ or $\frac{3}{8}$. They are now fastened into a large folio book with other memoranda, many of which were edited by Thomas Sharp in his *History*.

The writing is of the common hand of the middle of the fifteenth century.]

Memorandum that these be the constitucions off the offesse off the dekyn off the trinite churche made in the yere off owr lorde a Mccccl x and ij yer

[1.] In primis the dekyn schall euery day hopyn the churche durrs at vj off the clok and delyuer to the pryste that syngythe the trinite masse a boke and a chales and a vestment and wan masse ys don to se the sayd boke and chales and vestment be leyd vp in the vestre.

[2.] Item the sayd dekyn schall ryng all in to matens with hys Felo at euery comemoracion and ix lessons.

[3.] Item the sayd dekyn schall beyr Forthe the bokes [1]for matens and masse[1] belongyng to the sowthe syde off the quere and wan matens ys don to beyr them in to the vestre A gayne.

[4.] Item the sayd dekyn schall ryng with ys Fellow to hye masse and syng in the quere at the masse and wan masse ys don to se that the chales and the bokes be lokkyd sur in the vestre

[1]—[1] *Written over*, on the *struck out*.

[5.] Item the sayd dekyn schall be at the churche a gayn be iij off cloke to help to ryng all in to Evynsong yff yt be a commemoracion or a Feste off ix lessones or dowbull Feste.

[6.] Item the sayd dekyn schall syng evynsong on the sowthe syde in the quer and yff that yt be wolyday or dowbull Feste the sayd dekyn schalbe rectur in the quer For the sowthe syde off the quer.

[7.] Item wan evynsong ys don the sayd dekyn schall make sur the vestre and se that all the boks be in.

[8.] Item he schall lokk the churche durrs at a convenyant owr.

[9.] Item the sayd dekyn schall ryng day bell with won bell euery day.

[10.] Item he schall Fynde a dekyn to rede the gospell at hye masse euervery[1] sonday and woly day.

[11.] Item he schall se the [2]florthe off the[2] quere and the florthe off the body off the churche be swepyd euery tyme wan yt hathe nede.

[12.] Item the sayd deken schall se that the leds ovyr the quer and ovyr the body off the churche be made clene euery time wan they haue nede [2]and yff yt be a snowe to voyd the guttars leste they [be] stoppyd[2].

[13.] Item the sayd dekyn schall set a Form at the priory dur on palm sonday For[3] the stacions wen that ys don he schall cawse yt to be set a for the rode for the prest to syng *ave rex*.

[14.] Item the sayd dekyn shall bryng a woly water stoke with water for hys preste euery sonday for the preste to make woly water.

[15.] Also the sayd dekyn schall hyng a towell abowte the Fantt att estur and at wytsontyd.

[16.] Item he schall se that ther be iij copys browght down to the Fant For prysts to syng *rex sanctorum*.

[17.] Item the sayd dekyn schall euery sonday beyr woly watur of hys chyldern to euery howse in hys warde and he to haue ys dewty off euery man affter hys degre quartarly.

[18.] Also the sayd dekyn schall se [that] the woly cake euery sonday be kyte a quordyng for euery manes degre and he shall beyr the woly bred to serve the[4] pepyll in the northe syde off the churche and he to go to them on the xijth day For hys offyrryng to the reparacione off his syrples.

[19.] Item the said dekyn and his felow schall euery[5] princypall feste avat[6] wayte on the Churche wardens at the thryd peell off the fyrste evysong to a ray the hye awter with clothys nessessary For yt.

[20.] [7]Also the sayd dekyn[7] schall worden[8] a barrell on schere thursday and on ester evyn and on wyttson evyn For hys part a gayne the byttar[9] bryng water for the awtars and the fantte.

[1] *Thus, for* every ; *and* day *follows, struck through.*
[2]—[2] *interlined. Read* floor of the quire.
[3] *interlined.*
[4] sates on the northe Folkes : *struck through.*
[5] day : *struck out.*
[6] avat : *struck out.*
[7]—[7] *Repeated.*
[8] ordain, make ready.
[9] See Murray's *New English Dictionary*, under Bitter, one who has charge of a fire bucket : " 1467. *E. E. Giles* 382. That the bitters be redy with hur horses and bittes to brynge water." A bit is a butt or cask.

[21.] Item the sayd dekyn schall at euery snowe be with hys Felowe and voyd the florthe off the stepyll and caste owte the snowe for rotyng the tymber.

[22.] Also he schall se in his quarter that the clapurs off the bells hyng in ordur and to se the bawdryks be sur and yffe they be nott to schewe to the churche wardens that they may[1] be mendyd in sesen and to schewe [2]to them[2] the bell ropps in lyk manner.

[23.] Also he schall se the pallmes be brennyd For the askys that schalbe dawlte on aske wensday.

[24.] Also he schall provyd For palme[3] on palmsonday for his parte.

[25.] Also he schall[4] wache the sepulcur on Astur evyn tyll the resurreccion be don then he and hys Felow schall take downe the lenttyn clothys a bowte the awter and a For the rode.

[26.] Also he schall orden on schere thursday a byrche besom for the pryst that waschythe the awtars.

[27.] Also iij dyssiplyn rodds For hys parte.

[28.] And[5] he schall helpe [6]to sarue[6] the parechschones of bred and alle and theise things at mylbornes derege[7] and master meynleys and other dereges[7] that bye made of the churche cost.

[29.] And[8] hys Fellowe schall gresse the bellys and Fynde greyse ther to wan they haue nede.

[30.] And they schall haue the profetts off the bells wan they ryng for any quorse or obett.

[31.] Also the sayd dekyn and hys Felow schall ryng the bells at the Cummyng off the kyng and the quene and the prince yff they Fawte[9] the dekyn and hys felow to beyr the losse.

[32.] Item the sayd dekyn schall tende the lampe and to Feche oyle and ryschys weyr the church wardens wyll a syne ym.

[33.] Item the sayd dekyn schall kevyr the pylpyt with a pall wan any doctor prechys.

[34.] Also the dekyn[10] schall fynde a dekyn to beyr the crysmatory to the Fantte wan they go a pressession in ester weke.

[35.] Item he schall hyng Forthe the vykars banar[11] on the churche woly day and to take yt downe a gayn the viij th day.

[36.] Item the sayd dekyn schall go with the preste wan he gothe to veset the sek in hys warde or else won in hys stede.

[37.] Item also the sayd dekyn and his Fellow schall euery sonday and hye day Folde vp the albus and vestmentts that be ocupyed that day.

[38.] Item the sayd dekyn and hys Felow schall helpe the churche wardens to cover the awter and[12] the rode [13]in lent[13] with lentyn clothys

[1] *interlined.*
[2]—[2] *interlined.*
[3] agayn : *struck out.*
[4] *interlined.*
[5] any who : *struck out.*
[6] *a word illegible, struck out.*
[7] dirge.
[8] *In the space above is* schall *struck out.*
[9] make default. they *struck out.*
[10] and hys Felowe : *struck through.*
[11] *interlined, over a word struck out and illegible.*
[12] *repeated.*
[13]—[13] *interlined.*

and to hyng the vayle in the quere and the churche wardens schall gyffe them money to drynke.

[39.] Item the sayd dekyn schall ryng the grete bell[1] to complyn every setter day in lentt.

[40.] Also the dekyn [shall] Feche every quors to churche in [2]Hys syrples[2] that dessessythe in hys warde and he to haue For hys labur[3]

[41.] Item the sayd dekyn schall euery setterday and woly evyn be at churche with hys felyschep and ryng noon as the Fest requerythe.

[42.] Item he shall knoll to hy masse sacryng euery sonday and woly day he won quarter and hys Felow a noder and euery pressescion day to knoll the pressescion lyke wysse.

[43.] Item at euery pressescion to brynge Forthe pressescionars a quordyng For hys syde off the quere and to se they be born in to the vestre wan the presscion ys don.

[44.] Item he schall se the durr at the hye[4] awter ende be lokkyd ther as the sacramente standythe and the manewells[5] be brought in at euery wedyng in hys warde[4] wan the weddyng ys don.

[45.] Also he schall haue off euery pardenar that cummyth ij d and the sayd dekyn schall lende to ym a syrples to go with the preste into the pylpyt.

[46.] Also the sayd dekyn schall go on all halowe[6] day at evyn a mong the pepyll in the northe syd off the churche and [7]gedyr money off them for the ryngars that ryng for all crystyn solls.

[47.] Item he schall fynde won to ryng a pressescion euery sonday and his fellow lykewysse.[8]

[1] *a word struck out.*
[2]—[2] *written in margin.*
[3] *There is no space here in the manuscript, but it runs on direct to the next* Item.
[4] *interlined.*
[5] manuals.
[6] euyn : *struck out.*
[7] gedyll : *struck out.*
[8] *end of first leaf.*

[Constitution of the office of Second deacon.]

Memorandum that thes be the constituciens be longyng to the offesse off the seconde dekyn off the trinite churche

[48.] In primis the dekyn schalbe at churche euery woke[1] day alfe owr[2] a For vij a cloke and ryng the second bell a peell to matens yff yt be a feste of ix lessons or a comemoracion yff yt be fowll fest[3] he schall ryng ij belles at the seconde pell.

[49.] Item the sayd deken schalbe at churche and helpe to ryng all in to matens [4]and masse and evynsong[4] with hys Felow yff yt be a Ferry[5] he schall ryng won bell ym selfe a sartayn space as the ordynall spesyffythe.

[50.] Item he schall berr Forthe off the vestre all syche bokes nessessary For the northe syde off the quer for mattens and masse and evynsong and he schall syng in the quer daly serves on the same northe syd and yff yt be sonday or woly day he schalbe[6] rectur and be gyn all the salmys[7] for that syd off the quer and wan sarves ys don he schall beyr all syche bokes as ys ocupyd on that syde and ley theme in ther place wyche ys ordenyd For them [8]in the vestre[8]

[51.] Item he schall do hys dewty at evynsong in lyke maner.

[52.] Item the said dekyn schall ryng Curffew euery nyght at viij off the cloke and wan yt ys don he schall[9] serche the churche all abowte lest ther be any person lyeng in any sete or corner and then lokk the churche dur suire.

[53.] Item the sayd dekyn schall swepe the Florthe off the [10]sowthe syde[10] hyell off the churche euery tyme wan yt athe nede and also make clene the ledes off the same hyell wan yt ys nede and at euery snowe to voyd the guttars off the same hyell lest the pypys be stoppyd.

[54.] Item he schall[11] be subdekyn euery sonday and woly day at pressescion and masse [12]and reade the pystill.[12]

[55.] Item he schall euery woly day help[13] hys felow to folde vp all syche albys and westements that ar ocupyed that day and at[14] euery pressescion bryng forthe pressescionars a cording for hys syd off the quer and wane the pressescion ys don to ley them in ther place a gayne [15]in the vestre.[15]

[1] *interlined. First* woke *was written and afterwards an* r *has been written between* o *and* k, *to make* worke day.

[2] half an hour.

[3] full feast.

[4]—[4] interlined.

[5] feria, a week day.

[6] *a letter here struck out.*

[7] *a word beginning with two* ff *struck out.*

[8]—[8] *interlined.*

[9] *a word beginning with* s *struck through.*

[10]—[10] *interlined, written over* north, *struck through.*

[11] *two letters struck out.*

[12]—[12] *interlined.*

[13] *a* y *and one letter struck out.*

[14] *repeated.*

[15]—[15] *interlined.*

[56.] Item the sayd dekyn schall haue all the weddings that the wemen be in hys warde and he schall kepe the offeryngs at the masse of the sayd weddings and wan masse ys don he schall[1] bryng vp the boke that the preste wedd them with and also the ij tapyrs off the vykars [2]wyche be ocupyed at the masse.[2]

[57.] Item the sayd dekyne schall greyse the belles and fynde gresse ther to he won quartar and hys Fellow the todur and also he schal se in hys quartar that the bawdrykes off the bells be sur [3]and the clapurs off the belles hung in ordur[3] yff they be nott he schall schewe the churche wardens that the bawdrykes may be mendyd in seson.

[58.] Item he schall se the bell ropps in lyke maner also he schall knyll the pressescion euery presescion day and also euery sonday and woly day knyll to hye masse sacrying in his quarter.

[59.] Item he schalse the woly bred be dawlte euery sonday on the sowthe syde off the churche euery man in his degre and he to go among them on twylffe day at evyn song to haue hys reward towards the reparacione of hys syrples.

[60.] also he schall be with hys Felowe and se that the palmes be brennyd For askys a gayne aske wennysday also he schall provyde For palme [4]agayne palme sonday[4] suffyscyant [5]for hys[5] warde.

[61.] Item the said dekyn schall go with the preste wan he gothe with the sacramente to any sek body in hys warde.

[62.] Item he schall feche euery quors in hys warde to churche in hys syrples and he to haue For hys labur[6]

[63.] Item the sayd dekyn schall on ester euyn go to the churche wardens and cawse theme to provyd For collys that the halowd Fyr schal be off and the sayd dekyn schall se the collys be leyd on the sowthe syde off the Font and he to se they be conuenyantly kyndyld a gayne the prestes com to halow the Fyr.

[64.] also he schall provyde for a vessell and hys Fellow a nodur For the byttar[7] wan he schall bryng watur For the Fante.

[65.] Item he schall wache the sepulcur on gode Fryday att nyght also he schall se that the dur at the hye awter ende[8] wer the sacrament standythe and the manewells[9] lythe be euery day lokkyd.

[66.] also he schall euery sonday and woly day ryng the seconde peell to matenes at syche howr as [10]ys wont to be.

[67.] also he schall helpe the[11] hys Fellow to make clene the florthe off stepyll wan yt athe nede and also to caste owte the snowe off the stepyll ywan ther ys any.

[68.] Item he schall orden on scherthe thursday at the waschyng of the awtars a byrche besom[12] and hys Felowe a nodur [13]and iij dysplyng roddes.[13]

[1] by *struck out.*
[2]—[2] *added.*
[3]—[3] *interlined.*
[4]—[4] *interlined.*
[5]—[5] *repeated.*
[6] *Here the manuscript runs on to the next* Item *without a space as in* § [40.] *above.*
[7] *See above, note to* § [20.]
[8] be : *struck out.*
[9] manuals.
[10] hys : *struck out.*
[11] *thus: followed by a* w *struck out.*
[12] For : *struck out.*
[13]—[13] *interlined.*

[69.] Item the sayd dekyn schall se ther be wyn to powr on the crossys off the awters and also a woly water stoke For to beyr the water that schall wasche the awtars and hys Felow anoder.

[70.] Also the sayd dekyn schall go on all hallow day at evyn among the pepyll in the sowthe syde off the churche and gedyr off them money For the ryngars that ryng For all crysten solls.

[71.] Item the sayd dekyn schall hyng the wyrys ovyr the hy awter at crystymas with yve and candyls off the vykars coste.

[72.] also the sayd dekyn schall on the dedycacion day in the mornyng bring Forthe in to the quer syche skonsys for to set in candyls For the quer[1] as be ordenyd ther For the wyntur tym and he schall wan the seson ys don that they be leyd in ther place a gayn that ys in the neydur almery be hynde the hye awter.

[73.] Item he schall delyuer to the churchyng off women a tapur and bred For woly brede.

[74.] Item he schall ryng For quorsyes and obetts and haue alfe the profett off the belles and the todur dekyn the wodur alffe.

[75.] Also he schall ryng a gayne the cummyng off the byschap and off the kyng the quene and the prynce.

[76.] also he schall euery prynsypall Feste at the Ferste evynsong sens [2]the pepill in[2] the sowthe syd off the churche.

[77.] also he schall fynd[3] alffe the ryngars to ryng a pressescion euery sonday and woly day.

[78.] also he schall euery sonday bryng his woly water stoke with water For to be made[4] woly water and hys felow like wyse.

[79.] also he shall ryng to complyn euery feryall day in lentt with the Fyrste bell.

[80.] also he schall euery day make redy the hye awter For the preste to syng hye masse and he schall Feche Forth the masse boke and the chales and se the preste haue bred and wyne and he schall[5] cawse a chylde to a tende to the preste at masse and wan masse ys done he schall beyr vp the boke and the chales in to ther place agayne

[81.] also he schalle help to sarve at euery drenkyng after euery derege done at the coste of the churche.[6]

[1] and : *struck out.*
[2]—[2] *interlined.*
[3] we : *added and struck out.*
[4] *interlined.*
[5] and : *added and struck through.*
[6] *This section is a later aadition.*

APPENDIX II.

CONSTITUTIONS FOR THE PARISH CLERK AT ALL SAINTS BRISTOL BETWEEN 1455 AND 1469.

[I owe the transcript of this document to the kindness of Mr. Cuthbert Atchley, by whom it was taken from a large volume bound in leather, and entitled on the back *Minutes of All Saints Parish in the Reign of Edward IV.* This volume is still in the possession of the parish. The rules for the Clerk occur on p. 4 and they were written between 1455 and 1469.]

Constytucyons and Ordynawnces for the Clerke ys fyndyng

Memorandum hit ys ordeynyd and assygned by the greement of the paryschons that vij of hem to fynde the Clerke ys bord on hole yer and vij another yer and so yerly to be fownd by the Assygnement of the procutores and euery man of the parysche to pay to his wagys qwarterly as they schall be sett and stended by suche iij as schall be chosen by the parysche that ys to sey on of the worschypfull and ij of the mene of the seyd parysche. and he that schall dysobey fro hens-forward to pay and content the Clerke for the tyme beyng aftyr the stenting and settyng of suche iij men so y-chosyn when by the procutores other clerke hit ys axyd of hem. then hit schall be lefull for the procutores to content the Clerke of the Churche money as moche as can not be leveyd vn-to the Fest of Estyr And then they so dysobeyeng and withholdyng a-geynst this ordynawns be compellyd to absteyn hem fro her howsyll vn-tyll suche dewtes afor expressyd be payed and to the Churche restoryd.

The Clerke ys charge

[1.] In primis he to be trewe and profytabyll vn-to the Churche vn-to hys power as yn kepyng and gydyng the vestymentes and Bookes. Jewellys and all other Ornamentes longyng to the seyd Churche and to see that the Churche Doorys be y-openyd and schutte yn dewe tymys and by hym sewrly serchyd other by sum other man of trewe and sadde Dysposycyon.

[2.] Item he to be lovyngly attendant vn-to the vicary yn tyme of Dyvyn seruyce and yn vysytyng of the Seeke and to be obedyent vn-to hym yn all thynges that ys lawfull concernyng the lawde of god and of the Churche and trewly to yelde vn-to the vicar all maner Oblacyons and all maner of thynges that ys loste with-yn the Churche that cum to his hondes that trewe enqwery myght be had to whom hit longyth vn-to.

[3.] mor ouyr that he ber no talys by-twene the vycar and his bretheryn nother by-twene hym and his paryschons nether by-twene Neyghbor and Neyghbor wher-by eny Occasyon of Stryfe or Debate schuld growe yn tyme on.

[4.] All-so to see the Churche y-kept clene yn Rofys. Wyndowys Pylloures Wallys and the grownd Stallys Segys[1] and specyally the Awters.

[1] seats.

APPENDIX III.

DUTIES OF THE CLERKS AT ST. NICHOLAS CHURCH, BRISTOL, IN 1481.

[I owe this again to the kindness of Mr. Cuthbert Atchley, who has published the document in the *Transactions of St. Paul's Ecclesiological Society*, 1902, Vol. V. part ii. p. 107, with many learned notes, of which advantage will hereafter be taken.

The document is transcribed from a volume belonging to St. Nicholas Church, Bristol, which is bound in leather and made up of leaves of vellum, containing inventories, wills, and memoranda of vestry agreements, benefactions. The document printed below begins on fol. 32.]

/Howe the Clerke And the Suffrigann of Seynt Nicholas Churche Aught to do [Fol. 32.]

In the sayde Church After the vse laudable of yeris paste and the Agrement nowe of all the worshypfull of the paryshe the yere of owre lorde M[l] CCCC lxxxj[o]

[1.] The suffygann† Avgh to fastenn the Churche Dorys with a Dewe serche in the sayde Churche for fere of Slepers.

[2.] And at a dewe Seasonn in the mornynge to set Opyn the Dores and the entre-close Dore vndyr payne[1] of such Damage as shal-be leveyde of his s-merites[2]

[3.] The sayde suffrygann to se Oyle in the .ij. lampes. And also that they be brennynge and cleane Water in the holy water Stokkes vnder the payne of ij[d] as ofte as he is fownde fauty in Any of this.

[4.] The sayde suffrygann to Rynge the ffurste Pele to Mateyns of conuenient lenght and to Euensonges. The Clerke the seconde Pele And bothe at the Ryngyng of the laste pele With ij Bellys the payne of the firste euer ij[d]. The seconde iij[d]. And at the thyrde whoo that fayles iiij[d].

[5.] The Satyrday the Clerke and the suffrygann to Ryng None with ij Belles A pele of leyneth Convenient with-owte Any fayle excepte Dowbyll ffestes vndyr payne of iiij[d] to eche that fayles in this same

[1] Pain, *i.e.* penalty.

[2] *The* s *of* his *has been reduplicated and one carried forward to the next word,* merits, *i.e.* deserts, *what is due to him.*

[6.] The sayde suffrygann euery Satorday to spring[1] the churche with water for Resyng of Dowste And so to streke hit vndyr payne of vj[d] tociens quociens as he fayles [notandum *in different ink in the margin*].

[7.] The sayde suffrygann to pare[2] the Crowde[3] the Steyre and the Church Dores and so to be had a-weye as ofte as nedyth [under] payne of iiij[d] tociens quociens

[8.] The Clerke and the suffrygann bothe to leye furthe The Bokes in the quere at the seconde pele both a-fore Mateyns and also A-fore Evensonges and the seruyce so ended and donn to sette the sayde Bokes Clapsed and seurely in there place [under] payne of ij[d] to eche that fayles tociens quociens

[9.] The Clerke and the suffrygan to see in principall fest-is that the Copys to be borne at the sensyng Auters be Redy/ [fol. 32 *verso*] Apon the awtere by-fore the[4] begynnyng of Evensonges And in lyke wyse at Matenys And second Evynsonge And they bothe to se the foldyng vppe vndyr payne of iiij[d] tociens quociens

[10.] The Clerke and the suffrygann to se in pryncipall festes the Avters Dressyd in the Churche above . at there Charge. And to se . Coppeweste[5] avoyded and Duste fro Auters and ymagery . vndur payne of vj[d]. tociens quociens.

[11.] The suffrigann to goo with the Curate and to wayte oponn His koope[6] and sensor . at all his sensynges vndyr payne of j[d] tociens quociens [notandum *in different ink in the margin*].

[12.] The Clerke and suffrygann to Swope the Glasynn wyndowys Churche wallys and Pillars . euery quarter ooneys vndyr payne of iiij[d] to eche of them as ofte as they fayle

[13.] The suffrygan to Rynge Curfew . with onn Bell at . ix . of the Clokke A conuenyent Pele . the Mowntnance of Halfe a quarter of An owre large . vndyr payne of ij[d]

[14.] The Clerke and the suffrygann to Dresse vppe the Bysshopes Sete A-yeniste . Seynte Nicholas Daye vndyr payne of vj[d] a-pece.

[15.] The Clerke and the suffrygann to Dress vppe the sepulcure takyng for a Soper vj[d].

[16.] The Clerke and the suffrygann to se the lyght ouer Estere evynn a-boute the Sepulcure takyng for ther dyner——iiij[d].

[17.] The suffrygann to se dayle . for the hight Awter whenn Matenns ys Donn that there be Redy . A-yenste the hight masse wyne and water and to set onn the Awter bothe Boke and Chalice [under] the payne of ij[d] tociens quociens

[18.] The Clerke and suffrygann in there Surples to Resseve of the Vicary [his] Chiseple . and other of his ornamentys . and they to fold hit when Mas ys donn the workyn-dayes [under] the payne of a j[d]. tociens quociens.

1 sprinkle. 2 prepare, make tidy.
3 crowd is the usual name for what we now call a crypt.
4 byg: *struck out.* 5 cobwebs.
6 cope.

[19.] The Clerke to ordeyne the Sonday . and ffestes the Belles . at the Hight Masse Sacrynge to be Ronge solempnely and euer[y] fferyall day to knoll . to Sacrynge [under] the payne of [iiij^d^. *written over an erasure*] tociens quociens.

[20.] The suffrygann to be charged . with Ryngyng . for Dundoure[1] vndyr payne of vj^d^ tociens quociens Also vpponn the same payne to Rynge to Oowre lady masse in lente seasonn a computante Pele.

[21.] /The Clerke to ordeynn Spryngals[2] for the Churche. [fol. 33.] And for hym . that visiteth the Sondayes . and dewly . to bere his holy water. To euery howse Abydyng soo conuenient a space . that euery mann may Receyue . hys Holy water [under] payne of iiij^d^ tociens quociens.

[22.] And the Suffrygann to weyte vpponn the preeste in visitacionn of seke beryng with hym . the Surples . Boke oile-fate and stole. And in daye-time . in the suffrygans Absence abowte suche sayde occupacionns The Clerke to se for the saue-garde of the Churche.

[23.] The Clerke to synge in Redynge the Epistele Dayly . vndyr . payne of ij^d^ and vpponn the same payne to Ring the complene pele in lente seasonn.

[24.] The suffrygann to vette[3] fire or do to[4] be vette for the Sensores in the fire-plate And not in the sensoure vndyr payne of j^d^.

[25.] The suffrygann to vette oyle for the lampes in the churche above as oftenn-times as nedith . [under] the payne of a . j^d^.

[26.] The suffrygann to se that Awbes Amys Towels[5] And avter Clothis . be had to wesshyng . The procurators[6] payeng there-fore And to be Redye . a-yenste ffestys [under] the payne of ij^d^

[27.] The Clerke to be chargyd with Ryngyng of None . and Curfewe in principall festes And others . Acordyng with a . solempne and a . conuenient pele in lenght . At viij of the Clokke . vndire payne of vj^d^. tociens quociens

[28] The suffrygann to warne the procuratours that the sensours . Candylstykkys And Shippe[7] be Redye sette fourth[8] be-fore the last pele the peyne of a . j^d^. the koope[9] also before euery euynsong whann hit shall be vsid the sayd sofrygann shall se Redy . in the Quere vndyr payne . of . j^d^. tociens quociens

[29.] Hit was so accostemyd . And nowe agreed . of olde that the Clerke shold take for Ryngyng of A parrosshyng[10] there [fore. *struck out*] fro None in-to viij. And a morowe fro viij in-to None with . v. Belles iij^s^. iiij^d^. And no more . from hens-forward . vndyre the payne of vj^s^. viij^d^. tociens quociens.

[30.] Jtem the vndirsofregann[11] whiche at the ordynaunce Here-of His Callyd lymner shall se that . ij Torches . inthe Sondaye be brennyng at the hygh Masse sacryng And for all other /lyghtes [fol. 33 *verso*]

[1] thunder.
[2] bunches of twigs for sprinkling holy water.
[3] fetch.
[4] cause to be fetched.
[5] albs, amices, towels.
[6] churchwardens.
[7] the vessel to hold the incense.
[8] A blank space and erasure here.
[9] cope.
[10] a parishioner.
[11] The under-suffragan.

save the quyre lyghtes a-cordyng to euery feste and in the feriall. Dayes. the suffryganm to be chargid with the same. and with the quere. lyght . at all tymes vpponn the payne of ij^d

[31.] The suffrygann and the Clerke to weyte vpponn the quere Dayly. and The Clerke at Cesonys. accordyng to kepe. the Organs. vndyr payne of $iiij^d$. tociens quociens.

[32.] The Clerke and the suffrygann Aught to vette to Churche the Crosse. as well the poore as the Riche vndire the payne of . ij^d. tociens quociens

[33.] The Clerke aught not to take no Boke oute of the quere. for Childerynn to lerne In with owte lisence of the procu[ra]tours vndyr payne. that the Curate. and the procu[ra]tours Assignn hem

[34.] The Clerke and the suffrygann in seruyce tyme Aught not to absente them from the Quere. with-owte licence of the Curate. or his debite[1] And nether of hem. to be. absent from. ony Euynsong. Masse Mateyns or eny othyr devyne seruice with-owte licence bothe of the Curate and of the procurators vndyr payne of $iiij^d$ tociens quociens.

[35.] The suffrygann to se that there be a torche Redy for the Masses that ys sayde in the Churche. Dayly. And the Torches. to put owte fro all maner Awterys And the quere [under the] payne of a . j^d. tociens quociens

[36.] The Clerke to fynd Ryngars and Ropys for the Bellys with Dewe serche of the Bawderykys and Claperys. at all tymys. And suffyciently to warne the procurators whenn nede ys. to a-mende the sayde Bawderykes. Claperys. or Whelys vndyr such payne as the Curate or His Debite[1]. with the proctors and. ij. or. iij. of the Whorshipfull of the parroche Woll assignn as ofte as nede ys.

[37.] The Clerke and the suffrygann to Ryng Dayly to Hyght Masse at the Custenable owre [under the] payne of ij^d eche of Hem tociens quociens.

[38.] Also the suffrygann to fynde palme. and flourys A-yenste palme-sonday at his Coste. vppon payne of xx^d

[39.] And also the Clerke and the suffrygann to make Clene the segys[2] in the churche whann they be callyd vpponn

[40.] /All othyr thynges longyng to eny of there seruice. [fol. 34.] the Curate or his debite[1]. with the proctors[3] shall certyfye hem whenn eny nede shall Happynn in tyme Comyng

And all theys sayde Paynes oonly to Returne }
To the Wele off Seynte Nicholas Churche. }

DEO GRACIAS. Ricardus [*notarial mark*] Blewet.

[*In a different hand, and in black instead of rusty coloured ink.*]

Thy ben the Caswell Avaylis[4] longgyng to the Clerke & the Suffrygan.

[1] deputy.
[2] seats.
[3] churchwardens.
[4] casual avails, or perquisites.

[1.] In primis the Clerke to haue the vaylys of the bellis the Banys[1] And ofuery Pardoner for the Surplyse &c.

[2.] Also the Clerke to haue the vaylys on Seynt Nicholas nyghth goenge wyth *Sospitati*

[3.] Also the Clerk to haue the herse cloth when Any such fall that is kept vppon the graue Durynge the month with ij lampis on at the fete the tothir At the hed of graue As the vsage ys

[4.] Jtem the Suffrygan to haue the vantage of the Crossis[2]. that is to sey for euery Corse that decessith in the paryssh —— iiij.d.

[5.] All-so the Suffrygan to haue the vantage of the virgyn on Alhallon day. Where fore he muste se dayly that the westmentes of the hy Auter be foldyd when masse is do. & so y-put upp &c

[6.] Also where hit was of old vsage that the vantage of weddyngges was longgynge to the Clerke. Therefore to put A-way Al varyans in tyme to come. Hyt is ordeynyd by the Agrement of the parysshons with the will And consent of the Clerke and Suffrygan. That the Suffrygan hens-forward shuld haue the Awaylys of Weddyngges. And the Clerke to haue for A knowlegge of the same. Halfe the A-vantagge for the leyenge of Al maner Herses that shal-be leyde on the Church Except for Al such herses that ys zerely kepte of olde fundacion longyth to the Suffrygan only &c.

[1] The fees for ringing the bells, and publishing banns.

[2] That is, for carrying the cross before the funeral procession.

APPENDIX IV.

NOTES OF THE PAYMENT OF THE CLERK AND SEXTON AT ST. MARGARET LOTHBURY IN 1434 AND 1571.

[The first of these two documents is taken from Mr. James Christie's *Some Account of Parish Clerks*, privately printed in 1893. It may be found on p. 21, and it is said to be copied from a document of the Commissary Court of London. I regret that I cannot trace it further.

The second is taken from Dr. Edwin Freshfield's edition of *the Vestry Minute Book of the parish of St. Margaret Lothbury in the City of London, 1571–1677*, privately printed in 1887 by Messrs. Rixon and Arnold. The items begin on p. 1.]

[1434.]

This is the Ordenaunces and the settyng that the pryncipall Maysters and Wardeynes and aller the hole Parichouners hathe ordenyde and sette unto the Clerkes wages of Seynt Margaretes in Lothbury, to have quarterly a quarter and [1]her sensyng decesyd[1] theye to hold hem to theyre quarterage, John Cosler and William Denman then being Churchwardens.

Be hit hadden in mynde that the 7th day of Fevereller, in the yere of our Lorde, 1434, that Robert Large, Alderman of London, and Sir John Hockle, Parson, withe alle the pryncipall Maistres and Wardeynes, with alle the comontie of the Pariche of Seynte Margaretes, in Lothebury, hath ordenyde and chosyn foure honeste men of the same Pariche, to sette every house of the Pariche after his quantite that he beryth of his howse hyre:

first, a howse of 3*s.* 4*d.* be yere, one halfpenny a quarter to both Clerkes;

also a howse of 6*s.* 8*d.* be yere to both Clerkes one penny a quarter;

also a howse of 10*s.* be yere to both Clerkes one penny halfpenny a quarter;

also a howse of 13*s.* 4*d.* be yere to bothe Clerkes two pence a quarter;

also a howse of 16*s.* 8*d.* be yere to bothe Clerkes two pence halfpenny a quarter;

[1]—[1] The reading seems to be corrupt.

also a howse of 20*s.* be yere to bothe Clerkes three pence a quarter;

and also a howse of 23*s.* 4*d.* be yere to bothe Clerkes three pence halfpenny a quarter;

and so goying upwarde every nobyll one penny, the whiche was ordened and sette be thes foure men and thes been here namys: Thomas Babthorpe, Thomas Eston, Watir Adam, John Coddam, and whan these foure men had wrytyn and sette this quarterage in this maner they browte yt up to all the principalles and all the comonte of the sayd Pariche forsayd; and all they were accordyd thereto.

[1571.]

Ordinances mad by the hole consent of the parrishiners in the parrishe of Sainct Marget in Lothberie

iij° Die February anno 1571 [*in m.*]

* * * * [fo. 14

Item the clarcke shall have for his wages for the hole yeare the some of	4 13 4
Item the clarcke shall kepe the regester of cristeninge weddinge and buryinge perfectlye, and shall present the same everie sondaie to the churche wardens to be perused by them, and shall have for his paines in this behaufe yearelye	0 03 4
Item the Sexton shall have for his wages and for ringinge the bell eveninge and morninge as he is accustomed, yearlye the some of	1 00 00
more for candells to ringe with evening and morninge	00 00 08

/Item it is ordayned that whose sonne or servant shalbe [fo. 14. *b.* found to misuse Ihon a Wood sexton, in word or dede wherbye he maie not quietlye execut and accomplishe soche servis, as the parish hathe appointed him to doe, the parentes or masters of soche sonnes or servant shall paie the churche warden for the time beinge xijd. a yeare to the use of the powre for everie soche default. And if anye soche do denie, to paie the same xijd. beinge of them reasonablely requiered, and complaint mad therof to the Masters of the parishe at a vestrie, he or theie shalbe dismissed, from his or theire pewe or pewes in the churche. And if yet he or they shall continewe obstinat, and not paie the same some of xijd. as is aforesaid, then further complaint, shalbe mad therof, to the busshop, or his ordinarye.

Theise men whose names are heare under written are appointed side men for this yeare this 3 daye of Februarie 1571.

Mr Carpenter
Mr Langwithe
Abraham Smithe
Edward Fawkener

Item it is graunted, by the consent of the vestrie holden this present .3. daie of Februarie 1571. uppon good consideration ther uppon had, that the churche warden shal be allowed, the some of eyght shillinges, for a recreation or dinner, for the churche wardens and the side men, at the daie of the Archdeacons Visitacion yearelye to be donne.

Mr. George Smithe is appointed by the consent of the vestrie, to accompanie and assist Ihon Pelsant now churche warden, in the collection and gatheringe upp, of the clarkes wages for the yeare past, whiche the said George Smith left uncollected in his time the yeare past.

* * * * *

/An order or rate to be paied by the parrishioners in this [fo. 15. *b.* parrishe for weddinges cristeings churchinges and berrialls.

The profit of the great bell and the chardgis is for the parishe.

Item for ringinge one howers knell wythe the great bell to the parrishe	xijd.
Item for ringinge the great bell a fore nowne or after nounes knell to the parrishe	iijs. iiijd.
Item the clarcke shall have of the church warden for ringinge the great bell for one howers knell	ijd.
Item the clarcke shall have for ringinge a fore nownes knell or after nownes knell of the warden	viijd.
Item the parishe shall have for breakinge the grownd for a pyt, in the side chanselles	xs.
Item the parrishe shall have for breakinge the grownd for a pit in the churche	vjs. viijd.
Item the clarcke shall have for takinge upp the stones and savinge them hoale and makinge the pyt in the churche or chansell	ijs.
Item the clarcke shall have for a fore nowne or after nownes knell as heare after followeth	
For the fore bell	xijd.
For the second bell	xvjd.
For the third bell	xxd.
Item the clarck shall have for the pit at soch a buriall being in the churche yard one the north side of the churche	viijd.
And being one the south side for the pit and makinge of the pavement againe	xxd.
Item the clarcke shall have for one howers knill and for the pit of a childe, or person not passing the age of xiiij yeares	xd.
/Item the clarcke shall have for the like pit and [fo. 16 knell for one above xiiij yeares of age	xvjd.
Item the clarcke shall have, for cristeninge and churchinge for them bothe	iiijd.
Item the parson and the clarcke shall have at every weddinge, in the daie	xvjd.
Item the clarcke shall have for tolinge the passinge bell everie time	iiijd.
Item the clarcke shall have for pit and knell, and for a poore bodie not able to paie more	xd.

Item the clarcke shall find rope and bawdrickes and bear all chardges of the iij lesser belles and shall ringe a peale at the passinge bye of the queines majestie, by water or land

[1]Excepted the breking of the belles, wheles or frames or clapers wich the parrishe shall ber the charges of.

Iteme the clark shall have for Ringenge of Every peale att a Buryall yf they will have it thatt pay the funeralles the some of viijd.[1]

[1]—[1] added by another hand.

APPENDIX V.

THE OFFICE OF THE PARISH CLERKS AT FAVERSHAM IN 1506, 1548, AND 1593.

[By the kindness of Mr. F. F. Giraud I have been allowed to inspect the documents now under his care that belong to Faversham. Those now printed are contained in two folio volumes, 16 by 10½ inches. They have been spoken of by Mr. Riley in the *Historical Manuscripts, Sixth Report* . . . Part i. p. 500.

The rules of the time of Henry VII. and of Edward VI are in the volume labelled on the back : *A.* 1448 *to* 1606 *Wardmotes accounts,* and bound in half rough calf.

The Elizabethan rule is in the other volume, labelled on the side *Feversham † Wardmote Book begining † in the 1st of Queen Elizabeth and ending in Ye 9th year of K. Charles Ye 1st.*

The use of capitals by the scribe is capricious and I do not feel at all sure that I have rightly interpreted his letters. My aim has been to reproduce the text exactly, but I have only seen the manuscripts once.

Mr. Giraud has edited these in *Archaeologia Cantiana* 1893, vol. xx. p. 203 for the first time with any exactness and completeness. Edward Jacob (*History of the town and port of Faversham,* London, 1774, p. 166.) printed the two duties of 1506 but somewhat inexactly, and with no attempt at representing the old spelling.]

[The Parish Clerk's duties in 1506.]

/✠ [fo. 6

The[1] Articles of the Office of the Parish Clarks of the Parish Churche of Fauersham by them to be fulfilled and executed by them as hereafter folowoth whych Articles ware made and enacted at a comon Wardmote holden at Fauersham forsaid the Sonday next after the fest of All Seynts the xxijth yere of the reigne of Kyng Henry the vii byfore me Robert Wythiott Mayor of the same towne togeder with the Iurattes and Comons of the same.

[1.] In primis[2] the said Clarkis or one of theym dilygently shall intende vpon the Vicar or his depute in mynystracion of the Sacrements and Sacrementallis at all tymes both be daie and nyghte as

[1] Orders for the Clarkes of the church 1506 ; *written in margin in later hand.*
[2] j. cla : *in margin.*

oft as nede shall requyre and to be delygent and obedient to the Vicar or his depute in all suche lefull thynggs and comaundements as shall belong to their office to be don.

[2.] Item[1] The said clerkis or one of theym shall daily intende in his Rogett[2] at morowe masse and at high masse. apparell the auters and to Revest the prests syngyng the said masses and see that lighte or fire be contynually in the chaunsell or chirche before none euery day while their is any masse to be songe as of olde tyme hath be acustomed.

[3.] Item.[3] the said clerkys or one of theym daily shall apparell the auters wher any prests is to syng masse after the morowe Masse and bere and bryng to the auters the chalice masse boke and cruetts with wine and water. and bere a gayne to the vestry the same masse boke chalice and other ornaments whoche shalbe occupied at the said masses as of olde tyme hath be acustomed.

[4.] Item[4] the said clerkys at euery masse be note shall syng the grayle at the vpper dexte in the body of the quyer and the pistell. and to be dylygent to syng all the office of the masses be note. and to be dilygent to syng and doo ther dute at all seruyces to be songe be note. and to bryng forth suche bookis in to the quyer as shalbe necessarye as well for masses to be songe in the said chirche as any other seruice ther to be song be note. and to bryng forth in to the quyer att euery principall feste surplyces. rochetts. coopis and other ornaments as shall proue for the conuenyent seruyce accordyng to the solempnyte of the /fest and to ley the same books half on the oon side of the [fo. 6 b. quyer. and the other halff of theym on the other side. and at euery pryncipale feste the said clarkis and euery of theym shall dilygently come to the wardeyns [5]of the wardeyns[5] of the said churche for the tyme beyng and shewe theym what ornaments shalbe necessary to be occupied for the pryncipall fest. and theruppon to helpp theym to fett the same ornaments out of the tresour house in to the vestrye and ther dilygently to gyde theym and order theym as of olde tyme hath be accustomed. and after the pryncipall fest is past to folde vp the coopis and other ornaments manerly and bryng theym agayne dilygently in to the said tresour house.

[5.] Item[6] the said clarkis or one of theym at all tymes whanne ony seruyce shalbe don by note shall sett the quyer not after his owne brest but as euery man beying a synger may synge conuenyently his part. and wher playn songe fayleth one of theym shall leve faburdon and kepe the playne songe vnto the tyme the quyer be sett agayne

[6.] Item[7] the said clarkis or one of theym dayly shall fett and putt in to the cruetts freshe water for the prestis to synge with and see the said cruettis to be made clene within.

[7.] Item[8] the said clarkis or one of theym euery weke shall make clene the quyer the trynite chapell[9] and specially ouer the auters and

[1] ij. cla: *in margin.*
[2] Rochet.
[3] iij. cla: *in margin.*
[4] iiij. cla: *in margin.*
[5]—[5] *Thus, repeated.*
[6] v. cla: *in m.*
[7] vj. cla: *in m.*
[8] vij. cla: *in m.*
[9] *several words erased, the first of which is* and; *the last* chapell.

about theym and brusshe away the cobwebbis as well as ouer the auters in the quyer and chappellis as ouer the wallis and wyndowes of the same and shall apparrell all the said auters ayenst euery pryncipall fest with suche apparrell as belongith to theym.

[8.] Item[1] the said clarkis or one of theym or a sufficient man for theym shall lye nyghtly in the churche stepill. and from all hallowtide vnto the fest of the annunciation of our lady they or one of theym or ther sufficient depute shalbe in the churche euery nyght by .vii. at clok. and from the fest of the annunciacion of our lady vn to the fest all hallow the same clarks or one of theym or their sufficient depute shall nyghtly be in the said churche by .viii. at clok at the forthest.

[9.] /Item[2] the said clarkis and either of theym shall be [fo. 7 obedyent to the Mayor Juratts and Comons of the said towne and not to haue no sklaunderous words ne make none occasion of debate in words nor in dede bitwene the curatt and parisshyns ne betwene parisshen and parisshen.

[10.] Item[3] the said clarkis or one of theym asmoche as in theym is shall endeuour theymself to teche children to rede and synge in the quyer and to do seruice in the churche as of olde tyme hath be accustomed thei takyng for their techyng as belongith therto.

[11.] Item[4] the said clarkis and either of theym at all tymes whan the sextayne of the said church shall lak helpp to ryng to Evynsong mateyns or masse thei and either of theym for lak of suche help shall helpp the said sextayne as moche as in theym is to ring for the spedynes of the seruice ther to be don.

[12.] Item[5] the said clarkys and either of theym or their sufficient depute euery sonday in the yere shall beer haly water to euery mannes house as of olde tyme hath be accustomed. and if the same clarkis or any of theym make defaute in bering of holy water in the said forme. thanne he or thei so makyng defaute shall forfaite for euery suche defaute viiid. and this mony to be levied by the churche wardeyns for the tyme beyng to thuse of the said churche. Prouided alway if the said clarks or any of theym be occupied with any besynes for the parisshe or if ther fell any pryncipall fest on the sonday. then the said clarks and either of theym shalbe excused in beryng of holy water the same pryncipall fest and discharged of their penalte for euery suche pryncipall fest.

[13.] Item the said clarkis and euery of them shalbe alway delygent to the church wardeyns of the same churche for the tyme beyng and obedient to theym and dilygently do and execute all such lefull commaundements as to theym or to any of theym shalbe commaunded by the said wardeyns or any of theym for any thyng concernying the well of the said parishe and as shalbelong to their office.

[14.] /Item the said clarkis and euery of theym shall skoure [fo. 7b.

[1] viij. cla : *in m.*
[2] ix. cla : *in m.*
[3] x. cla : *in m.*
[4] xj. cla : *in m.*
[5] xij. cla : *in m.*

and kepe clene the holy water stoppis of laton and the basyn and ewer whoche be ordeigned for christenyng of childern and theym so kepe and skoure and make clene as often as nede shall requyre in that behalue.

[15.] Item from hensforth euery clark when he is admytted to th- office of the clerkshipp in the said chirche shall swer vpon a booke that he on his behalf shall endevor hym self as moche as in hym is truly to fulfill and execute all the said articles and eueryche of theym.

[The Sexton's duties]

/✠ [fo. 8

The articles of the office of the Sextayne of the parishe of Fauersham be hym to be fulfillid and executed as hereafter folowyth which articles war made and enacted at a comon wardmote holden at Fauersham forsaid the Sonday next after the fest of the Epiphany of our Lorde the xxii yere of the raigne of Kyng Henry the viith by fore me Robert Wythiott then being Mayor of the said towne togeder with the Iuratts and comons of the same towne.[1]

[16.] In primis[2] the said sextayn or his sufficient depute euery nyght shall lye in the said churche stepill.

[17.] Item[3] the said sextayn or his sufficient depute euery nyght from all halowtide vn to the fest of the annunciation of our lady nyghtly shalbe in the said churche or stepill by .vii. at clok in the euyn and ther shall contynue abyde and lye from that howre vnto .vii. at clok on the next morowe. and from the annunciacion of our lady vnto all halowtide the same sextayn or his sufficient depute nyghtly shalbe in the church' or stepill by .viii. at clok in the euyn and ther shall contynue and ly from that howre vnto .v. at clok in next mornyng. and euery nyght the same sextayn or his sufficient depute at .viii. at clok shall ryng couurefewe by the space of oon quarter of an hour with such a bell as of olde tyme hath be accustomed.

[18.] Item[4] the said sextayne or his depute euery day in the mornyng in somer shall open the churche doores at .v. at clok and in wynter at .vi. at clok.

[19.] Item[5] the said sextayn or his depute euery saterdaie seynts Euyns and pryncipall fests shall ryng noone with as many bells as shalbe conuenient for the Saterdayes seynts Evyns and pryncipall fests and as shalbe longe accordyng to the tyme. and at afternoone at eueryche of the said daies ryng to evynsong with as many bellys as belong to the tyme at a conuenyent hour as of olde tyme hath be accustomed. and on the morowe of eueryche of the said daies to ryng to matyns and masse and evynsong accordyng as belongith at conuenyent hours and as many

[1] Orders for the sexton to observe 1506 *added in hand of eighteenth century.*
[2] ja cla : *in m.*
[3] ij. cla : *in m.*
[4] iij. cla : *in m.*
[5] iiij. cla : *in m.*

peelys/ as of olde tyme hath be accustomed. and on the werk [fo. 8b. daies to ryng euery daie to masse at a conuenyent hour as shalbe requyred by the vicar or his depute as of olde tyme hath be accustomed.

[20.] Item[1] the said sextayn or his depute whan he shall rynge noone or to the first Evynsong matyns masse and last Evynsong or to any other seruice he and such persons as shall ryng with him shall rynge in dewe ordor and in as good tyme as they may or can. and not to rynge to long tyme our to short tyme but as it is conuenyent.

[21.] Item[2] the said sextayn or his depute euery werke day shall toll three tymes to the morowe masse with the iiijth bell at .v. of the clok in somer and at .vi. at clok in wynter. and at the first tollyng he shall strike xxx strokis with the claper of the same bell. at secund tollyng within a quarter of an hour after xv. strokes. and at the third tollyng vi. strokis and after as sone as the parish clark hath ronge all in to the morowe masse with the litell bell the same sextayn or his depute shall toll yn iii. strokis with the said fourth bell. and besides this the same sextayn or his depute euery werkeday shall tolle to the sakeryng of the high masse with the first bell the ij^{de} bell and the iii^{de} bell as hath be of olde tyme.

[22.] Item[3] the same Sextayn or his depute euery daie shall make provision for the lightyng of the lampe in the quyer bifore any prest goo to masse and so to se it contynue as long as ony masse is to be songe ther. and besides this the same sextayn or his depute daily and nyghtly shall kepe the lamp in the quyer to brenne if he have oile therfore. and if he lak oile thanne he or his depute diligently to complayne to the churchwardeyns for the tyme beyng or to som of theym for the spedy reformacion therof.

[23.] Item[4] the said sextayn or his depute euery holy evyn at the first evynsong mattyns. masse and last euynsong shall light the tapers and bemys accordyng to the solempnyte of the fest and custome of the said churche he takyng for his labour for lightyng of euery of the said bemys as of olde tyme hath be accustomed and vsed.

[24.] /Item[5] the said sextayn or his depute euery saterday at [fo. 9 none shall fell the holy water stoppis in the body of the churche with fresshe water and as often in the weke as nede shall requyre and euery day in the mornyng to see the churche made clene for skomeryng[6] of doggs.

[25.] Item[7] the said sextayn or his depute euery weke shall make cleen the body of the churche and the crosse Ilis[8] from dust or other filthes and also on the evyn of euery pryncipall fest and brusshe away all the cobwebbis and make cleen ouer and about all the auters wallis and wyndowes in the body of the said churche as often tymes as nede shall requyre.

[26.] Item[9] If their com any bestis in to the churcheyerd by

[1] v. cla : *in m.*
[2] vj. cla : *in m.*
[3] vij. cla : *in m.*
[4] viij. cla : *in m.*
[5] jx. cla : *in m.*
[6] evacuation.
[7] x. cla : *in m.*
[8] aisles.
[9] xi. cla : *in m.*

escape or non closure of the churche wallis thann the same sextayn or his depute shall dryve theym out in as hasty tyme as he can and if any person or persones of his or their wilfull mynde putt any best in to the said churche yerd ther to pastur then the same sextayn or his depute in the namys of the churche wardeyns for the tyme beyng curtesly shall goo to the owner or owners of the said bestes and requyre theym to fett them away and if the same owner or owners vppon suche request refuse to do then the same seytayn or his depute immediately after suche refusell made shall dryve the said bestis to the lordıs pounde and ther to remaigne vn to the tyme the owner or owners of them haue agreed with the Vicar or his depute for that offence the same sextayn takyng for his labor for euery best so offendyng and dryuen to the pound ıd.

[27.] Item[1] the said sextayn and his depute shalbe diligent to the Vicar and his depute and diligently shall doo and obserue all leful commaundements concernyng his office whoche to hym or his depute shall be commaunded by the said Vicar or his depute.

[1548.]

/Statut for makyng of Lawes within the Towne of Fauersham. [fo. 48

*   *   *   *   *

Anno 1548 E vj ij tempore Thome Ardern Maioris [*in m.*]

*   *   *   *   *

And whereas there hath bene, tyme wherof no mannys mynde hath bene to the contrarye Twoo Clercks,.whiche haue hadd at the equall charges of the Towne iiij^{li} euery of theym of whiche viij^{li} hath bene recowped and taken toward the fynding of one sexten xxvi^{s} viii^{d} for as moche as thise payments hath growen in consideracon of suche great travayll as the clerks haue heretofore susteyned in thexecucion of their office which travaills, for asmoche as they be decreased[2] and dymynisshed so the Inhabitants of the said towne having respect thereunto haue thought it mete to abate not onely the clerks wages but the number of the clerks, and yet not mynding to haue the same somes so abated to be extincted and discharged, but to remayne to good vses as the same did before conclude establisshe and agree that it shalbe ordeyned and decreed in manner and forme folowyng That is to saye

[1.] that there shalbe no moo clercks then one within the said parisshe churche and that the same clerk shall haue for his wages yerely liij^{s} iiij^{d}

[2.] and that also there shalbe a sexten within the said parisshe, which said sexten shall yerely haue for his wages xxvj^{s} viij^{d}

[3.] and the other iiij^{li} sterling shall yerly for euer be paid to and for the wages of the Comon caryer[3] before rehersed

[1] xij. cla: *in m.* [2] godes honor mynisshed: *interlined in later hand.*
[3] The common caryer was the scavenger.

[4.] and euery parisshoner. to paye and make contribucion for the payment of the said viij^{li} so appoynted, to and for the payment of the parisshe Clerk Sexten and Carter in /lyke forme and after [fo. 48b. suche seuerall porcions as here tofore they or any of theym haue paid and bene assessed or taxed when they hadd ij Clerkes and that it shalbe lawfull for the mayor for the tyme beyng, to commytt to warde euery such person refusing to paye to the same as they haue done before there to remayne, till they haue paid ytt.

[1593.]

/An act touchinge the Sexten of the Church *in m.* [fo. 36

[1.] Yt ys agreayd bye the foreseide Maior Iuratts and Comynaltye here assemblyd and gatheryd together that the Saxten from henceforthe shall giue attendance at the Churche and rynge to Seruyce as heretofore of late tyeme hathe byn vsyd within the same towne

[2.] and that the same sexten shall yerelye for hys wages haue payed hym bye the Churchewardens of the same Towne for the tyeme beinge xl^{s} of lawfull monye of Inglande quarterlye at the fower vsuall feaste dayes of the yere viz. at the Feaste daye of the Natyvytie of our lorde God, The Annuncyacion of our ladye St Marye the Vyrgyn the natyvytye of St John the Baptyste and St Mychaell the archangell bye euyn porcions, and also that the same saxten shall lykewysse yerelye haue payed hym bye the Chamberleyns of the same towne for the yere beinge xl^{s} of lawfull monye of Inglande at the foreseide feaste dayes bye the lyke porcions for ringynge to sermons

[3.] and further that the same Sexten shall haue hys accustomed fees for towlynge of the passinge bell ringinge of knelles ryngynge to buryalls makynge of graues as well in the Churche as in the Churchyard as ys allreadye sett downe in a Table now hangynge in the churche for that purpose, and moreouer for the rynginge of the greate bell to euerye funerall sermon/ the some of vi^{s} viii^{d} [fo. 36b.

[4.] In consyderacion of which hys foreseide wages and fees to be payed as aforeseide the seide Sexten shall dayelye througheout the whole yere rynge Curfewe with the fowreth Bell at eyghte of the Clocke in the Euenynge bye the space and tyme of one quarter of an hower

[5.] And also that the same Saxten shall daylye thorowhe the whole yere rynge the fowerthe Bell for a daye Bell at fower of the Clocke in the mornynge bye the lyke space and tyme.

APPENDIX VI.

RULES FOR THE PRIESTS AND CLERKS AT ST. MICHAEL'S CORNHILL BEFORE 1538, WITH AN ORDER MADE IN 1587.

[These are taken from a book edited by Messrs. A. J. Waterlow and W. H. Overall, privately printed about 1871. The title is: *The accounts of the churchwardens of the Parish of St. Michael, Cornhill, in the City of London.* The transcript is taken from a copy of the work now in the Library of the Society of Antiquaries.]

/Rules of the Church [p. 206

Hereafter Followe the Rewles whiche must be obserued and kept of all the pristes and Clarkes belonging to the same Churche of Saint Michell.

[1.] /You muste pray For the Beneffactors of this Churche of [p. 207 Saynt Michaell and specially for the sowle of Richard Atfeld some tyme Parson of this Churche, the which forsayde Richard with the consent and agrement of the Bysshop of London and other worshipfull men of the same parishe hath ordened and establysshed matens, hie Masse and evynsong to be celebrated and song daily in the foresaide churche to the honor of God and of saincte Michaell begynnyng in the yere of oure Lord 1375 Anno E: 3: 48

Item tempus a quo regule fuerunt composite erat 163 . Ante annum christi 1538.

[2.] Furst he hathe ordened due howres of ringing to seruice That is to say to ring in to matens at seuen a clock, To hie Masse at nyne a clock, to Evynsong on workdayes at ij a clock and on holy dayes according to the lawdable custome of the Citie.

For the Clarkes.

[3.] Also he hathe ordened that the Clerkes shall kepe the dew howres of ringing according as they have used in old tyme, and that the saide Clarkes shall not goe owt of the quyre into the bodie of the Churche nor into the Churche yard to walk at the tyme of devyne seruyce Where as they should be than present without a reasonable cause of payne to forfett ijd.

[4.] Also they shall provyde For Fyre at all such Feastes as incense is accustomed to be offered vnto Allmightie God with other thinges necessary to the office according to the solempnyte of the Feaste.

[5.] Also they shalbe redye at all visitacions accustomed and used to dooe theire diligence and servyce in payne of Forfeating ijd.

For the prystes and clarkes

[6.] Also that aswell Pristes as Clerkes by and by after the thryd peall shalbe present in the quyre in theire shurples singing theire from the beginnyng of Mattens, Masse and Evynsong unto the end of them all, without a reasonable excuse in payne of Forfeating as oft as they shall so doo ijd.

[7.] Also hathe decreede that one discrete preste shalbe/ [p. 208 chosen by the Parson or in his absens by his deputye to be a *Ruler* or *Deane* of the quyre in executing and seying the dyvyne seryce executed according to the lymytacion or assignement of the ordinall.

[8.] Also he hathe ordened that there shalbe two Rectors every highe or solempne Feast as the Deane shall appoynte them.

[9.] Also he hathe ordened that there shalbe every dowble feast at the hye Awlter and Masse a Deacon and a Subdeacon standing at the hie Altare with the Prist according to thassignement of the Deane. And at all other holydays a Deacon onely to be with the Prist.

[10.] Also that every Pryst disposed to celebrate shall say Masse before the hie Masse except there be a bodie present to be buryed or els some other reasonable cause doo lett it.

[11.] Also that as well Prystes as other Ministres shall not *jangle* nor talke one with an other in the tyme of devyne servyce nor doo any thing els but his dutye and that no Minister of this Churche shall sytt in the quere without his shurples in the tyme of dyvyne servyce.

[12.] Also that the Pristes shall not absent themselues from Matens, Hie Masse nor Evynsong whan as they ought to be there for any trentall or other derege except he have lycence of the Deane. And as oft as anny be from Mattens Masse or Evynsong for eche of them to Forfett ijd.

[13.] Also that the Pristes according to theire cowrse shall have two and two of them every weke one day of recreacion and that on the worke day from the hiest to the lowest of bothe sydes by the lycence of the Deane.

[14.] That yf ony of them that belongeth to the quyre taking wages, be absent from Matens, Masse or Evynsong shall Forfett as oft for eche of them ijd.

* * * * *

/1587. [p. 245

1st November [*in m.*]

Hit is orderyd that the clarke and Sexton duringe the hole tyme of sarvyse and sarmons shall not departe out of the churche upon the payne of iijs. iiijd for every default and that yf the Churchwardens do not see this order executyd then the Churchwardens to paye iijs iiijd to the use of the poore.

* * * * *

/It is agred that the youngest Churchewarden shall have the [p. 246 kepynge off the belles and the Clarke shall have the lowance set downe by the tabell For the belles as he hath had beffore, and he to beare the chargis off all the ropes and bawdryckes For the belles so often as nede shale requyre at the appoyntemente off the Churchewardene.

APPENDIX VII.

THE DISPUTE ABOUT THE CLERK AT MOREBATH IN 1531 AND 1536.

[This was partly edited in the *Western Antiquary*, Plymouth, 1893, vol. xi. p. 186, and an account of the dispute appears in the churchwardens' accounts printed by the Somerset Record Society in 1890, p. 222. It has been more completely edited by the Rev. J. Erskine Binney in *Devon Notes and Queries*, 1903, April and July. This transcript has been compared with the original manuscript but the proof not. The manuscript when examined was in the custody of Mr. Binney at Exeter, but it is still the property of the parish of Morebath.

It is a very curious account of a prolonged quarrel as to the dues to be paid to the clerk, caused apparently by a mere handful of parishioners.]

/Not the clerkescheppe of Morebath. [p. 356

Memorandum that anno domini 1531 at mychelmas: Sir christofer trychay that tyme beyng Vicar here and this parrysse they cowde not a gre for a clerke: by cause the clerke cudde not haue hys duty: there fore the Vicar at that tyme wolde fynde them no clerke no longer: where a pon the Vicar and this parrysse dyd so a gre that the order of this clerke scheppe: was putte vn to the Vicar . and to .v. men chosyn by the parrysse: and as this v men and the vicar cudde a gre a pon the clerkescheppe: so the parrysse wolde be contendyd to performe the same: so a pon this: at laste the vicar and thes v men were this agreyd that fro thens forth . for the loue of god . and to incresse the more loue yn hys parryssyn: the vicar was contendyd to fynde them a clerke as he hadde don be fore: and the clerke schulde be chardyd with no thyng: but to keppe on challis and the key of the churche dore . as he wyll keppe hys one: thys were we a greyd.

[1.] Item more ouer a gayn: thes v men dyd this a gre: that fro thens forth when seruys ys don: with yn halfe a nowr after . the clerke or on for him schall knoke the churche dore: and yff there be any perssons with yn the churche when he dothe knoke: and yff they wyll not cum forthe then by and by: but they wyll tary styll with yn the churche: where a pon at laste preuenture[1] when they cum forth . they lett stonde oppe the churche dore all the nyzth after: and yff any

[1] *sic.* (p').

suche fortune there be. Where by the churche doo take any hurte . . the payne and the iupardy schall reste to them . and not to the clerke: that doo remayne yn the churche . after warde the clerke hath knokkyd the church dore.

[2.] More ouer a gayn: we were this agreyd: that fro thens forthe the clerke schall have .j.*d.* a quarter of euery howsse holder.

[3.] Item a gayn we were this a greyd: that the clerke here after this schall haue hys hyre mette at ester of euery howse holder when he dothe in quyre for hyt.

[4.] Item a gayne we be this a greyd . that fro thens forth . the clerke schall haue a steche of clene corne to euery howsseholde: and for lacke of clene corne to pay on steche of suche as he hathe [1]and yff he have no corne: then schall he pay ij*d.*[2] erely for hys steche and a coter ij*d.* and no mor.[1]

[5.] /More over a gayn . by cause besenys hath byn oftyn [p. 357 tymys yn payment of this steche yn tymys paste, ther fore now we be this agreyd: that fro thens forthe: when the clerke dothe sende for hys steche: he schall have hem and yff he be cutte: and yff the clerke be not servyd when he dothe cum for hys steche: the owner of that corne schall keppe the clerk ys steche saffe . tyll the clerke doo sende for hem a gayn: and yff hyt be hurtyd when the clerke dothe cum for hyt a gayn: then hyt schall be to the clerke hys plesure where he wyll take the steche that ys sett owt for hem: or ells to leve the steche . and the owner of the corne schall pay hem iiij*d.* yff rye be a bow viij*d.* a bossyll: and yff yt be under viij*d.* a bossyll he schall pay the clerke iij*d.* for hurtyng of hys steche:

[6.] Soo now a pon all thes powyntis: ys the vicar and ys v men full a greyd: and ys v men have promyssed vn to the vicar substanssially . that they wyll se the clerke truly payd of all suche dutis as ys expressyd be fore with out any trobyll or vexacion anno et die predict.

Thys byth the v men namys William tymwell at Wode Richard Raw Iohn norman at corte richard hucly and Thomas norman.

* * * * * * * *

/Nota: that here follyzth a fresse warde madyn[3] a pon [p. 92 the clerkescheppe of morebath madyn by m. John sydam and by 3 men of the parysse: (chosen for the same causse: and[4] by the consent of the hole parysse:) that was William tymwell at Wode and John norman at corte and Ric hucly.

[7.] Memorandum that anno domini 1536 . at mychelmas tyme . William leddon wolde not pay hys steche of corne un to the clerke . a cordyng to the warde that was made by v men of the parysse anno domini 1531 at mychelmas tyme: (as hyt apperyth a pon the boke of a cowntis the same ere:) vt supra . and also William sceley and brochole

[1]—[1] *added in different ink.*
[2] ii. *added before the* ij.
[3] *struck through.*
[4] *different hand.*

[1]when they hadde no corne: they[1] wolde not pay the ij*d.*[2] for a steche . a cordyng to the warde: Nother the ij cottis at exbryge dyde not pay there quarter lage truly [1]vn to the clerke[1]: but they ij [1]howssholdis at exbryge[1] payd ij*d.* for there steche truly y now [1]ons a ere[1]: both John Don and John nicoll also: a cordyng to the warde of the v men: and also a cordyng to the warde of Sir William trystram sum tyme Vicar of bawnton: and by John norman at Wode:) where a pon now[3] for lacke of tru payment: the vicar that fownde the parysse a suffycyent clerke be fore that tyme: wolde not[3] mell no more with the clerkscheppe: by cawsse he cowd not have hys duty truly payd with out dysplesir takyn of hys parryssen: Wherefore to a voyd ther dysplesure . the vicar warnyd out the clerk at crystesmas follyng after the date of this present wrytyng: desyryng the parrysshe hole to be contendyd to provyde hem a new clerk agayn our lady at lent than follyng: for he wolde melle no more with hyt: so a pon thys our lady day . then beyng a pon pall[4] sonday: was cum: and clerke the parrysse hadd prouydyd none: where a pon for lacke of a clerke a gayn the besy tyme of ester: the parrysse vniuersall desyryd the vicar that he wolde fynde them a clerke tyll lytell ester day then follyng a pon a better prouision: and so dyde he at there desyre: and when that day was cum: communicacion was hadd and they coude not a gre a bowte a clerk: where a pon hyt was put forth at Visitacion the thursday follyng thoo at Vplumman[5] (where as our auctorite was grawntyd out at that tyme: that iiij honyst men chosyn by the hole parrysse . schald rule and gouerne the parrysse yn all causis concernyng the welthe of the churche: as hyt apperyth a pon the cownte bok anno predicto . Vnder the offycyall ys sele) A pon the wyche complaynte: they ware commaundyd that came at that visitacion[6] (that was the vicar Sir christofer trychay: and john Norman at cowrte: and harry hurly wardyn: and thomas Rumbelow . that spelyd John swyzth at that tyme:) to goo home and take /[7]and [p. 93 desyre[7] Mr. john sydam[8] vn to them: and all suche order as mr. john sydam . and iiij men of the parrysse: by the hole parrysse electyd . doo make a pon the clerke scheppe: the vicar and the parrysse schalbe contentyd with all: A pon this ther was a fresse day sett of communicacion to be hadd: that was in vigilia sancti georgij . beyng a pon a sonday: and so at that day: came thether mr. john sydam[8] and mathew the sumner: and askyd of euery man of the parrysse by name: Whether they wolde be contendyd to chewse iiij men of the parysse: and all suche ordor as mr. sydam and this iiij men doo make a pon the clerkescheppe . the reste to be contendyd with all: (now how say ye to this the parrissyn [9]they said[9]) a pon this they sayd they were contendyd: where a pon the iiij men ware chosyn by the hole parrysse that schulde se a ordor takyn[10] with mr. Sydam a pon the clerkescheppe: (the wyche iiij men:

1—1 *interlined.*
2 *altered to* iiij.*d.*
3 *interlined.*
4 palm.
5 Uploman.
6 Borrage Webber Emyn (?) Drue (?) was put yn at this visitacion.
7—7 *added in m.*
8 *The word which I read* sydam *stands in the manuscript thus*: sydm *with* a *over the* m.
9—9 *interlined.*
10 *interlined.*

ware the same selfe perssons: that ware chosyn a fore: and admyttyd by the ordinary to rule and gouerne the churche gooddis as ys expressyd a pon the boke of a countes and[1] under the ordinaris auctorite) and when thes men ware all chosyn then was the parryssyn hole axsemynyd[2] a gayn: to kno there mynddis whether they wold be contendyd to byde all suche ordor as mr. Sydam and thes iiij men doo make . or noo: and there ware xxvj yn on parte that was contendyd that mr. Sydam and thes forsayd iiij men[1] schuld se a nordor takyn a pon the clerkscheppe: and there was v men of the other part that wolde not be orderyd by no man: [3]quod essent Thomas norman Ric Webber william norman and John at borston[3]: where fore at this tyme they cowde not a gre a bowt a clerk; yn so moche that we hadd no clerk tho at eu[en]song follyng: nother the morow: that was sent iorge ys day: for lacke where of the church was holy sirvyd that day: yn so moche that the morow a pon sent iorge ys day: when the vicar schulde say mas for markis chylde at exbryge: tho mark was glade to goo to iohn at cowrtis to fett the churche dore key and the challys: and also he fette the wolde john watervs to helppe the vicar to mas: be fore he coud haue ony mas sayd for hys chylde: and all was for lacke of a clerke: And when[4] mas was don: we went to William at tymwellis to the be trothyn of margyd tymwell and william tayler: and there all that day we resonyd schamfully a bout our clerkscheppe: yn so moche that mark and william leddon ware a most by the eris for the same cawsse: by cawsse that william leddon hadd not brosth homme hys corne be fore mychellmas: as well as he dyd the tuysday a fore the visitacion (the wyche was halfe a bossyl of rye and the laste pec by hyppe [)] / so yn conclusion the [p. 94 parrysse hole concludyd there and sayd lett vs haue a fresse day of communicacion and we wolle be orderyd every on of vs: where a pon they desyryd the vicar to finde them a clerke a gayn. tyll a fresse day of communicacion and at the parryssyns desyr so dyde he tyll the sonday a fore rogacion wyke: and yn the mayne space mr hu powlytt kept cowrte at morebath: and he exortyd thes for sayd v perssons and so dyde mr hu stycly also: that they schulde be contendyd to be orderyd as the moste parte of the parrysse ware: and yff they wolde not: he wolde ordor them he sayd: so a pon this there was a fresse day sett[5] of communicacion to be hadd: a gayn the wyche day there was sett owt a cytacion to a cyte all such perssons as wold not be orderyd by mr Sydam and by the iiij men: so yn conclussion when the day was cum that this mater schulde by resonyd a gayn: the wyche was the Sonday a fore rogacion wyk. as ys expressyd be fore: there was the parrysse syngulerly demawndyd a gayn by name to kno whether they wolde be contendyd that mr Sydam and iij of thes men electyd by the parrysse: schuld se a nordor takyn yn this clerkscheppe or no: (for the iiijthe man was syke that tyme: that was Robert at hayne) and they sayd ye: all that ware yn the churche that tyme: (and there lackyd no moo that

[1] *interlined.*
[2] examined.
[3]—[3] *interlined.*
[4] *interlined.*
[5] *interlined.*

day but william at tymwell and william leddon and william scely: and by cawsse that euery man was contendyd to byde the ordor of mr iohn Sydam and of this iij men: the cytacion that was fett[1] was voyde: so a pon this: mr sydam and thes iij men at the parryssyn ys ynstans: toke the mater yn hande: and so with mr sydams advysse this was the ordor that they dydde make: and so concludyd and sayd: that fro thens forth this schalbe the clerkes duty by owr a ward to have (what so euer he hath hadde a fore this) to this entent: to haue the more vnite and pece a mongg vs: and to haue the churche the better seruyd) this hyt ys:

[8.] primo he schall have a steche of clene corne of heuery howsse: where as there ys corne a pon the bargan: (as brochole and wother moo) and he that hath noo clene corne schall pay a steche of wotis: and that hath no corne schall pay the clerke iij*d.*[2] for hys steche: [3]and ij*d.* a coter[3] as hyt hath byn yn tymis past. And vnder this maner the clerke schall demande hys steche: and he schall cum for hem and yff he be a redy: and yff not: he schall cum a gayn: and then yff the steche be not sufficyent: he schall leue hem: tyll that sum of /the parssons that made the warde doo se the steche: and then [p. 95 yff the steche be sufficient after there iustment: then the clerke schall fett hem: and yff he be not sufficient: then the clerke with owt any besenys schall fette a steche with Richarde hucly (and yf hyt be yn the weste parte of the parrysse) and yff hyt be yn the yeste parte of the parrysse: he must fett hys steche with John norman at cowrte: for this ij men be surty to the clerk: to se all hys dutis payd truly vn to hem that this men have orderyd: with owt any trobyll or vexacion: and the hole parryssyn hath made there ansswer vn to this for sayd ij men: that they wyll were them harmlis: and yf any frowarde felow wolle not pay hys duty to the clerke acordyng to this a warde. And also and yff the clerke be warnyd to fett hys steche and preuenture he can not cum fore him by and by: then the ouner of the grownde schall keppe him tyll he cum:

[9.] Also he schall haue j*d.* a quarter of every howssholder:

[10.] And the clerke schall haue at every weddyng ij*d.*:

[11.] Also at euery corsse present and at every monyzth ys end that ys song by note the clerke schall haue ij*d.*:

[12.] Also the clerke schalbe chargyd with no thyng sauing ondly with on challis and with the churche dore key: this for to keppe and hyde as he wyll doo hys one:

[13.] Also he schall goo a bowt the parrysse with hys holy water ons a ere when men have schorne there scheppe to gether sum wolle to make him cotte to goo yn the parryssyn ys lyuery and here fore the clerke schall helppe the wardyn to make up the vestmentis and to dresse the auters &c.

[14.] Also this ere ondly for losyn of hys duty yn tymys paste: the parryssyn shall helppe to drenke him a cost of ale the sonday a pon

[1] *sic.* [2] *altered to* iiij.
[3]—[3] *interlined* Coter is a quarter.

trinite sonday (et sic factum esset et ibi essent omnes. duntaxat: Borston et scely: Webber et William Norman)

also at euery ester [1]her after[1] the clerke schall gether hys hyre mett: and then the parrysse schall helpe to drenke him a coste of ale [1]yn the churche howsse.[1]

[15.] and this ys all the warde that mr iohn Sydam and William tymwell at wode and Iohn norman at cowrte and Richard hucly dyde make a pon the clerke scheppe anno et die predicto: before the parryssyn and iohn dysse: then beyng bayly there under mr hu powlytt and Mathew the sumner: &c.

In wyttnyssyng where off: this notte was made here a pon this cownte boke to testyfy truly the clerke ys duty and owr award to a voyd all other vnconueniens.

[1]—[1] *interlinea.*

APPENDIX VIII.

THE DUTIES OF THE PARISH CLERKS AND SEXTON AT ST STEPHEN'S COLEMAN STREET IN 1542.

[This account of the duties of the parish clerks has already been printed by Dr. Edwin Freshfield in *Archaeologia*, 1887. vol. l. p. 49. with a number of other documents illustrating the history of this church. Dr. Freshfield has given me every help in collating the manuscript with the proof and I am much indebted to him for his courtesy.]

/The Inuentory. . . . To thentent the tow parish Clarkes [p. 15 of the same churche shall haue charge and kepinge of them att all tymes hereafter shall be redye and deliuer agayne or to be delyuerd. To the saide vicar and Churche wardens. Or to their successours all the same goodes Iuels and ornamentes when they or aiether of them shall be therto required.

* * *

The Sexton's Devtie/ [p. 148

[1.] Also the sexton shall swepe the Churche and the yelle therof euery weke ons at the least and cast water on the grounde for Rasynge of dust.

[2.] Also he shall light the candulls euery sounday and holyday yn the yere and doo them owt ayene as tyme requiereth.

[3.] Also he shall Rynge curfie whan it ys rounge with one bell and call for help whan it ys rounge with moo.

[4.] Also he shall blow the Organs euery. sounday and holyday in the yere.

[5.] Also he shall bere the crosse on procession. and carie holywater euery sounday and fete[1] fyre in tyme of nede.

[6.] Also he shall make the pittes for dead bodies depe I nough for corrupte heyers.[2] that is to say for men and women .iiij. fote depe and for children iij fote deep.

[7.] Also he shall swepe the churche roffe .liij. tymes yn the yere the churche fyndyng bromes and polles therfor

[8.] Also whan any procession is about[3] . . . . .

[1] fetch.
[2] against corrupt airs, to prevent escape of foul gas.
[3] *A cross in the left margin; the sentence breaks off here at the bottom of the page.*

/The Devtie of the tow Clarkes [p. 149

[9.] Also they shall clenesse the founte and feille it agayne with clene water twysse yn the yere at paschall and att witsountyd and after yf nede requier

[10.] Also they shall euery weeke Certifye to the Curat and the churche wardens all the names and sir names of them that be wedded Christened and burried in the same parish that weeke sub pena of a j^{d} to [be] paid to the churche

[11.] Also the goodes of the churche that belongeth to ther kepyng they shall treat and kepe it in the most best maner and savynge it from harme or perisshinge to the vttermost of ther powers.

[12.] Also that the saide clarkes to be at noo tyme owt of the way but one to be alwayes redy to mynester Sacramentes and sacramentalles what soo euer shall nede. to wayet vpon the Curat and to geve hym warnyng.

[13.] Also that none of the saide Clarkes shall goo or ryde owt of the towne with owt speciall lycence hadde of the vicar and churche wardens.

[14.] Also vpon euery sounday and other holydayes to helpe the sexton to Rynge the secounde pele to matens in deve tyme and to masse Evensonge and yn the lent tyme to complene. and also in the absence of the sexton to rynge curfie.

[15.] Also they shall dayly bringe forthe the Bookes that be longe to the quier and Receyve them agayne to ther savegarde as they will answer for them on principall dayes and other festiall dayes they shall bringe forth the Coppes vestementes and apperellis for the aulters in the Churche with the Ivelles[1] to be set on the saide aulters and they to dysaray them agayne as the tyme requireth. and bringe the sayd Ivelles and Ornamentes into ther owne kepynge for the discharge of them selffes.

[16.] Also they shall serve the Curat and preest with the coppes and see fier fet[2] and redy in the sensours afore it nede and to set children to do service in the saide quier.

[17.] To light the tapers to the sensours and to see them borne or revesterid and the quier to be senced and many moo small thinges as syngyng and Redyng and preparing the bookes and Turnyng[3] theroff to the dyvine service afore it begyne as of a laudable and an Auncient custome hath ben vsed in tymes past.

[18.] Also they shall bere holywater euery sounday in the yere.[4]

[19.] Also the clarkes shall fette and bringe in all such casuelltes[5] as be longeth to the Churche wardens [and] to the churche be hoveffe[6] and iff any casuelltes fall yn any churche wardens absence as beynge owt of towne they shall apply them selffes to bring them yn to the said churche wardens for the tyme being.[7]

[1] Jewels.
[2] fire fetched.
[3] *The* [2] *interlined.*
[4] *An asterisk follows this word.*
[5] fees.
[6] behoveth.
[7] End of p. 149. All this written in bookhand.

/Statutum[1] De officio Clericorum et quomodo se [p. 154
habebunt erga Curatum presbiteros et parochianos omnes.

[20.] In primis Clerkys in ther office shal fynde sufficient Surete to the Curatt and Chirche wardens to kepe alle Bokys all vestmentes all Ivellys and se to alle the avter clothes and wasschynge of hem. and to the amendynge of hem at alle tymes as thei wer thayre owne.

[21.] Item they schal be obedient to the Curate and to alle the prestys in the Chirche. doynge to hem reverence. and be redy Day and Nyght and at alle tymes to goo with the Curate or his Debite[2] to visitte the seeke. and to help to mynystrynge of the Sacramentes gladly.

[22.] Item they shal be diligent and redy dayly both holiday and warkeday to alle Diuine seruice that is don in the Chirche of seynt Stephan and not rangelyng nor tale tellynge in tyme of diuine service bot exemplar of Deuocion.

[23.] Item thei shal be redy to mynyster Bokys. vestmentes. Chalyces and all other thynges necessary to the Curate. to the morning masse preste and to all other prestes of the sayd Chirche, that is to say[3] to rynge .iij. pelys with the lest Bells to the morowe masse and be for the last pele warne the morow masse preste and aske hym if he shal rynge alle in. And so to do to the Curate or his Debite[2] on sondays and holidays after the gode custom of london.

[24.] Item they shall opon the Chirche dores in somer att .vj. of the belle and orden fressch water wyne and bredde. And ryng to morning masse in somer at .v. of the belle. in wynter at halfe owre be fore .vj. so that the masse may be sayd be .vij.

[25.] Item thei shal help the morning masse preste to say masse in a surpelis, and at hyz masse dayly. And no nodur preste [4]in the chyrch bin at his ovyn wyll[4] except the Curatt say masse at a side awter on of the parissch Clerkes shal help hym to say masse or se that he haue on.

[26.] Item thei shal be redy to ryng to all maner of diuine seruice at dewe owre assyngned of the Curate or his debite affter the vse and the custom of london the Cite of. and not to ryng the laste pele vnto the Curate or his debite be present.

[27.] Item thei shal swepe all the ymagys and glasse wyndowys of the Chirche .ij. tymes of the yere atte Pasch and at the Translacion of sent Stephann. and pare the alyes[5] of the chirche yerde. and suffer no[6] grave nor pitte to be made in the procession way in payne of .xij. d without gret nede.

[28.] Item they shal be redy euery sonnon day affter matens be sayd to orden water and salte/ and[7] to cutte the holi loffe .s. [p. 155

[1] *This is in a different hand courthand, and in the left margin an asterisk precedes the first line.* [2] Deputy.

[3] *Here are some marks to fill up the space.*

[4]–[4] *These words are written over an erasure and I cannot be certain what they are. I give Dr. Freshfield's reading.* [5] prepare the alleys.

[6] *A letter erased here.* [7] *The page is headed* The devtie of the clarke.

ij d ob, and a ob loffe for the Cantelle subpena of a j^{d} to the Chirch to be payd.

[29.] Item thei shal see the profett of the Curate in offeringys in wax. in wyne. in brede. In purificacions and in alle other Rightes and Dewtys that longe to the avter of god in Incresynge multiplyinge at ther power.

[30.] Item thei shal make no contencion nor baate nor hevenesse betwene the Curate and the Parisschons nor of no other Preste. And if thei here any Confeterice or Imagynacion or Sklawndyr of malice a gaynce the Curate or of any other preste that longes to the said Chirch in all haste thei shal in confession telle hit to the Curate. and the namys of the personys that so ymagynn.

[31.] Item thei[1] be obedient in all lefull thynges to alle the Parisschons and curtes in beryng in behauyng hem selfe. In answer to higth and to lowe as seruauntes and membris of the Chirche of Godde askynge theyre quartage. their Casuallys.[2] and other thynges that long to hem be right. ameabully. and if any man or woman contraye and will not pay ther dewty to informe the Curate and the Chirch wardens and they shal sette remedy with grace of God.

And yf ony persone be breker of this good and goodly ordinaunce. The Indyngnacion of Almyghty God falle he Inne. Amen/

Dat' etc.

[1] *A mark of omission, and* shal *is written in the margin.*

[2] The fees. *See above, p.* 69, *last line but one: and p.* 91, *line* 5 *from bottom.*

APPENDIX IX.

[Taken from Number 21 of a *Collection of Records . . . referred to in the Second Part of the History of the Reformation of the Church of England*, by Gilbert Burnet, London, 1680, p. 126. The manuscript from whence these injunctions are taken is said to belong to Dr. Johnson. They are reprinted from Burnet by Wilkins (*Concilia*, iv. 29), by whom they are assigned to the second year of King Edward VI. But I feel some hesitation in accepting this date.]

Injunctions given by the King's Majesty's Visitors, to all and every the Clergie and Laity, now resident within the Deanry of *Duncastre.*

* * * * *

Item. You shall every *Sunday*, at the time of your going about the Church with Holy Water, into three or four places, where most audience and assembly of People is, for the declaration of the Ceremonies, say, distinctly and plainly, that your Parishioners may well hear and perceive the same, these words,

Remember Christ's Blood-shedding,
by the which most holy sprinkling,
of all your Sins you have free pardon.

And in like manner, before the dealing of the Holy Bread, these words,

Of Christs Body this is a Token ;
which on the Cross for our Sins was broken ;
wherefore of his Death if you will be partakers,
of Vice and Sin you must be forsakers.

And the Clarke in the like manner shall bring down the *Paxe*, and standing without the Church Door,[1] shall say loudly to the People these words ;

This is a Token of joyful Peace, which is betwixt God and Mens Conscience : Christ alone is the Peace-maker, which straitly commands Peace between Brother and Brother.

And so long as ye use these Ceremonies, so long shall ye use these Significations.

[1] Is this a misreading for *choir door*?

Item. The Church-Wardens of every Parish-Church shall, some one *Sunday*, or other Festival day, every Month, go about the Church, and make request to every of the Parish for their charitable Contribution to the Poor; and the sum so collected, shall be put in the Chest of Alms for that purpose provided. And for as much as the Parish-Clark shall not hereafter go about the Parish with his Holy Water as hath been accustomed, he shall, instead of that labour, accompany the said Church-Wardens, and in a Book Register the Name and Sum of every Man that giveth any thing to the Poor, and the same shall intable; and against the next day of Collection, shall hang up some-where in the Church in open place, to the intent the Poor having knowledg thereby, by whose Charity and Alms they be relieved, may pray for the increase and prosperity of the same.

APPENDIX X.

The Holy Loaf at Stanford in the Vale, Berkshire, in the Reign of Queen Mary Tudor.

[This document has been already edited from the registers of the parish by Mr. Walter Haines and printed in the *Antiquary*, 1888. vol. xvii. p. 70. By permission of the Rev. H. Aldrich Cotton I have collated this edition with the registers at Stanford in the Vale.]

/The Fyfte parte of this boke. [fo. x.

Here Followyng ys the ordre of the geueyng of the looffes to make holy bred with videlicet of where hyt begynith and endythe what the hooll valure ys in what porsyons hit ys deuyded and to whome the porsions be dew and thowgh hit be written in the fyuet parte of the dyvision of the boke before in the begynning with thes worddes (how monay shall be payed towardes the charges of the Communion) [1]ye shall vnderstande that in the tyme of Scysme when this Realme was deuyded from the Catholyc Churche the wiche was in the yer of owr lord god 1547 in the second yer of Kyng Edward the syxt all godly ceremonyes and good vsys were taken owt of the Churche with in this Realme and then the monay that was bestoyd one the holy bredde was Turned to the vse of fyndyng brayd and wyne for the Communyon and then the olde order beying browght[2] vnto his prystyne state before this boke was wrytten cawsyd me to wryte with thys terme.

(The ordre of the geuying of The loofes to make holy bredde of.)[1]

Inprimis the geuing of the holy lofe takyth his begynnyng at a pece of Grownde caulyd Ganders at the wrytting here of in the Tenure of Thomas collens. The whiche pece of ground cavled ganders ys a cottage and when that grownde caulyd ganders doth begyn then doo all the cottages in the Towne geue in ordre with the other grounddes and howsses Rownde abowte vntyll that come to[2] the sayd ground caulid ganders agayne and theyre leuyth.

And at the seconde goyng abowte the Towne yt begynnethe at Rychard Snodnams howse the yonger wyche howse ys next to the vicarage one the northe syde and then dothe all yardlandes halffe yardlandes cotsettulls[3]

[1]–[1] The passage is crossed out in the original by a later hand. The word "Scysme" is almost obliterated.

[2] *interlined.*

[3] Cotsettulls = Cotsethlands. Under this see Murray's *New English Dictionary*. Also Cottager's lands, Cotlands.

and meeses geue vntyll hit hathe gone Rownde a gayne and be comm to ganders. and theyre and then begyneth the Thyrde tyme and so Rownde a bowte the Towne a gayne. So that cotages geue but at euery seconde tyme goynge abowte. There be sum howsses in the parishe that hathe notte geuen the holy looffe at eny tyme that euer eny of the parishe at this wrytting [1]knew of[1] and they be theys The parsonage. The vicarage. The ferme cavled the manor howse a cottage belonging to the vicarage. a smythes forge one the Greene and the churche howse cauled the Gylde hawll.

Here after followyth the ordre of geuyng of the wholl Townesheepe as well cottages as others with the names of Them that helde suche growndes and howssis at the wryttinge here of with an addyson one theyr heddes who hathe a cottage to avoyde varyans when theyr Tyme to geue for the holy Loofe shall come.

[Here follow the names of one hundred parishioners, which are now omitted.]

Thus endyth geuyng of the breade to make holy bredde off Throwgh the whole Towne bothe wher yt begynneth and endyth.

The wholl valure of The carges[2] cumyth to ij*d*. ob and yt ys Thus devided.

The offer to the curates hand Too peny worth of bread with a halfepeny candull or a halfepeny for the candull putte in to a Taper and browght vppe to the preste at the hyghe altar. of the Too penyworthe of bredde they Resyue a halfepeny lofe wholl for to be delyuered to The next that shall geue the holy loofe for a knowledge to prepare agaynst the soomeday folloyng. And thus I make an ende of this matter.

[1]—[1] *interlined.* [2] charges.

APPENDIX XI.

Extracts from Visitation Articles, Injunctions, and like Documents.

Iniunctions exhibited by Iohn [Parkhurst] *by gods sufferance Bishop of Norwich,* London, John Day [1561.]

¶ *For Clarkes and theyr dutie.* [B. iii

WHether that the songe in the Churche be modest and distincte so deuised and vsed that the ditte may plainly be vnderstand.

2. Whether they vse to sing any nomber of psalmes, dirige lyke, at the buryall of the deade or do any other thing otherwise then it is appointed by the comon order of the seruice boke.

3. Whether they vse to ring oft or longe peales at the buryall of the dead or vse muche iangling in festiuall daies in ringing none or curphew.

Articles . . . in the Metropoliticall Visitation of . . . Edmonde [Grindal] *Archbishop of Yorke,* London, William Seres, 1571.

39. Whether anye Parishe Clarke be appoynted agaynst the good will, or without the consent of the person, vicar, or curate, whether he be not obedient to the person, vicar, or curate, especially in the time of celebration of diuine seruice, or of the Sacraments, or in any preparation therevnto. And whether he be able, and readie to read the first Lesson, the Epistle, and the Psalmes, with aunswere to the suffrages as is vsed, and whether he keepe not the bookes, and ornaments of the Church, fayre and cleane, and cause the Church and Queere, the Communion Table, the Pulpet, and the Font to be made decent and cleane, agaynst seruice time, the communion, sermon, and baptisme?

Constitutions and Canons Ecclesiasticall . . . Imprinted at London by Robert Barker, Anno 1604.

¶ Parish Clearks

xci.

Parish Clearks to be chosen by the Minister.

NO Parish Clearke vpon any vacation shal be chosen within the Citie of London, or elsewhere within the Prouince of Canterbury, but by the Parson or Vicar: or where there is no Parson or Vicar, by the Minister of that place for the time being: Which choyce shall be signified by the saide Minister, Vicar, or Parson, to the Parishioners the next Sunday following in the time of Diuine Seruice. And the said Clearke shallbe of twenty yeeres of age at the least, and knowen to the sayde Parson, Vicar or Minister to be of honest conuersation, and sufficient for his Reading, Writing, and also for his competent skill in singing (if it may be.) And the saide Clearks so chosen, shall haue and receiue their ancient Wages, without fraude or diminution, either at the handes of the Church-wardens at such times as hath been accustomed, or by their owne collection according to the most ancient custome of euery Parish.

Articles .. Diocesse of Exeter . . . Joseph [Hall] *Lord Bishop of Exeter*, London, Thomas Harper, 1638.

[Parish Clarke *in m.*]

61 *Item*, Whether in the absence of your Minister, or at any other time, hath your Parish Clark, or any other Lay person, said Common Prayer openly in the Church, or any part of the Divine Service, which is proper to the Priest?

62 *Item*, Whether your Parish Clark or Sexton hath had due regard to the Ornaments of your Church, and to the clean keeping of your Church, and the Seats and Pews therof from dust or anything which might be noysome?

63 *Item*, Is your Parish Clark of the age of twenty yéere at the least, and of honest conversation, and sufficient for his reading, writing and competent skill in singing, and doth hee usually weare his Surplesse or Rochet in the time of Divine Service, and whether hath any detained his accustomed wages at the accustomed time of payment? And is the said Clark approved by your Ordinary, and sworn to obserue and execute his said office accordingly?

64 *Item*, What wages or what quarterly or yéerly payment in mony, or what other benefit is your Parish Clark to have, according to the ancient custome of your Parish? Declare and specifie the same in your presentment.

Articles to be enquired of in the Ordinary Visitation of the Right Worshipful Iames Marsh, D.D. Archdeacon of Chichester. Holden Anno Dom. 1640. London, B.A. for Richard Meighen, 1640.

Of Parish Clarkes and Sextons. [B. 2. *v.*

HAue you a fit Parish Clarke aged twenty yeares at least, of honest conversation, able to read and write, diligent in his office, seruiceable to his Minister: is he approued by the Ordinary: hath he taken his Oath as is required?

2 What wages hath your Clarke and Sexton according to the ancient Custome of the Parish: are the wages duly payed, or by whom kept backe?

3 Doth your Clarke and Sexton doe their duty in keeping the Church cleane, the doores locked, or is anything lost or spoil'd in his Church through his default: doth he suffer any vnreasonable ringing, or any prophane exercise in your Church?

4 Hath your Parish Clarke or Sexton taken vpon him to meddle with any thing aboue his office, as Churching of women, burying of the dead, or such like?

Articles to be enquired of within the Diocese of London . . . William [Juxon] *Lord Bishop of London*, London, Richard Badger, 1640, Sign. 4. *b*.

Whether do you the Churchwardens of every Parish within the Citie and Suburbs of London (according to the Kings Majesties Letters Patents, under the great Seal of England in that behalf granted) suffer your Parish Clerk to gather his wages himself, in as full and ample manner as the same hath formerly beene gathered, in or by colour of his name, without diminution, upon pretence of pewage, or the like, and without any manner of disturbance or interruption or forbidding anyone so to pay the same unto him, and whether do you assist your Clark in collecting his wages (if need be) according to his Majesties said Letters Patent: and whether doe you duely present all such persons of your Parish as refuse to pay the said Clarkes accustomed wages, as by his Majesties said grant, you are required and commanded?

Articles . . . in the first Episcopal Visitation of . . . John [Cosin] *by Divine providence Lord Bishop of Durham*, London, T. Garthwait, 1662, p. 10. Titul. v. *Concerning Parish Clerks and Sextons*.

1. HAVE you belonging to your Church or Chappelry a Parish Clerk aged 21 years at the least? Is he of honest life and Conversation? and sufficient or able to perform his duty in reading, writing and singing? Is he chosen by your Minister, and doth he duly attend him in all divine Services at the Church? Doth he wear a Gown when he so attendeth and a Surplice over it, if heretofore the Custome hath been such among you? Are his wages duly paid unto him? or who with-holdeth the same from him?

2 DOTH he or your Sexton (if there be any such appointed in your Parish) diligently look to the doors of your Church, that they be locked and opened at due time? And doth he keep your Church or Chappel clean from noysome dust, cobwebs, litter, straw, or any other annoyance? Doth he toll or ring the Bells at the due accustomed hours before the beginning of divine Service Morning and evening, that the people may be warned to come unto the Church? And when any person is passing out of this life, doth he upon notice given him thereof, go and toll a Bell, as hath been accustomed, that the neighbours may thereby be warned to recommend the dying person to the grace and favour of God?

Articles of Visitation and Enquiry within the diocess of Ely, in Second Episcopal Visitation of . . . Peter [Gunning] *by Divine Permission Lord Bishop of Ely in the fifth year of his Translation,* London, S. Roycroft, 1679.

[Can. 91. *in m.*] [p. 16

VIII. Have you a Parish-Clerk aged 20 years at the least, chosen by your Minister, of honest life and conversation, and sufficiently able to perform his duty in reading, writing and singing? and doth he duly attend the Minister in all Divine offices at the Church? doth he keep clean the Church, and carefully look to it, and to the Books? and is he payed the ancient and usual wages as hath been accustomed?

[Can. 92. *in m.*]

IX. Doth your Clerk, or your Sexton (if there be any such in your Parish) diligently look to the doors of the Church, that they be locked and opened at due times, and that the Bells be toll'd and rung at the due and accustomed hours before the beginning of Morning and Evening Service, that the people may be warned and invited to come to the Church? and when any person is passing out of this life, doth he upon notice given thereof toll a Bell as hath been accustomed, that devout and charitable persons may thereby be warned to recommend the Soul of the dying person to the grace, mercy, and peace of God Almighty?

[Can. 67. *in m.*]

X. Do they at the instance of any, make any grave in any part of the Church (except in such Isles where some person hath propriety) without the express consent of your Minister?

Anno Regni Jacobi II. Regis . . . Primo.

An Act for Erecting a new Parish to be called the Parish of St. *James* within the Liberty of *Westminster.*

* * * * * * * [p. 16

likewise to nominate a fit Person in like Orders [Priests] to be Clerk of the said Parish and Parish Church, and one or more Sexton or Sextons, to which Clerk and Sextons respectively there shall be such and the like Dues, Fées, Perquisites and Profits paid and allowed as are or have at any time been paid or payable or belonging to the Clerk and Sextons of the said Parish Church of St. *Martin* respectively; which said Preacher, assistant, Clerk and Sexton or Sextons and every of them shall con-/tinue in his said place during his or their Natural Lives, if they [p. 17 shall so long inhabit there, except for some Offence or Misgovernment by them or any of them committed, (and unless for Cause reasonable proved) they shall be displaced by the said Rector for the time being by and with the Consent of the said Vestrymen or any six or more of them.

And be it Enacted That the Churchwardens of the said Parish of St. *James* for the time being, shall and are hereby Required from time to time to pay the yearly sum of Thirty pounds to the Clerk to be appointed as aforesaid out of the Profits of the Pews in the said Church. . . .

Articles of Enquiry . . . William [Fleetwood] *by Divine Permission Lord Bishop of St. Asaph*, 1710.

p. 56. 4. Have you a Parish-Clerk of the age of 21 years of Sober Life, and well Qualified for his Office?

5. Is he Paid his accustomed Salary, Dues, and Perquisites, belonging to his Place?

6. Doth he keep the Church clean, and carefully look to the Books, and all Things committed to his Charge?

7. Doth he Open and Shut the Church Doors at due Times, and Toll the Bell, or Bells, at the usual Hours before Prayers, that People may have sufficient warning to come to Church?

4, 5, 6, 7. 'Tis very fit that all who any ways relate to the Church, be of sober Life, and rightly qualified for their Office. The *Parish-Clerks* were heretofore in some low sort of *Orders*, and had their part in *assisting* at the Divine Service, and they still keep the name of *Clerici*, and ought to be of exemplary and good Behaviour. And if they discharge their Office well, especially that part of it of *keeping the Church clean*, they will deserve, and ought to have their Salary duly paid, and none of their accustomed Perquisites withheld. But if they are negligent, or slovenly in their Churches, or live not soberly, they are to be *presented*, and, if they are found incorrigible, they are to be *removed* from their Places, to make room for those who will live, and do their Business better.

7 and 8 Victoria, Cap. 59. An Act for better regulating the offices of Lecturers and Parish Clerks, [29th July, 1844.]

11. And be it enacted, That when and so often after the passing of this Act as any Vacancy shall occur in the office of Church Clerk, Chapel Clerk, or Parish Clerk, in any District, Parish, or Place, it shall be lawful for the Rector or other Incumbent or other the Person or Persons entitled for the Time being to appoint or elect such Church Clerk, Chapel Clerk, or Parish Clerk as aforesaid, if he shall think fit, to appoint or elect a Person in the Holy Orders of Deacon or Priest of the United Church of *England* and *Ireland* to fill the said office of Church Clerk, Chapel Clerk, or Parish Clerk; and such Person so appointed or elected as aforesaid shall, when duly licensed as herein-after provided, be entitled to have and receive all the Profits and Emoluments of and belonging to the said Office, and shall also be liable in respect thereof, so long as he shall hold the same, to perform all such spiritual and ecclesiastical Duties within such District, Parish, or Place as the said Rector or other Incumbent, with the Sanction of the Bishop of the Diocese, may from Time to Time require; but such Person in Holy

Orders so appointed or elected as aforesaid shall not by reason of such Appointment or Election have or acquire any freehold or absolute Right to or Interest in the said Office of Church Clerk, Chapel Clerk, or Parish Clerk, or to or in any of the Profits or Emoluments thereof, but every such Person in Holy Orders as appointed or elected as aforesaid shall at all Times be liable to be suspended or removed from the said Office, in the same Manner and by the same Authority, and for such or the like Causes, as those whereby any stipendiary Curate may be lawfully suspended or removed ; such Suspension or Removal nevertheless being subject to the same Power of Appeal to the Archbishop of the Province to which any stipendiary Curate is or may be entitled.

* * * * *

V. And be it enacted, That if at any Time it shall appear, upon complaint or otherwise, to any Archdeacon or other Ordinary that any Person not in Holy Orders, holding or exercising the Office of Church Clerk, Chapel Clerk, or Parish Clerk in any District, Parish, or Place within and subject to his Jurisdiction, has been guilty of any wilful Neglect of or Misbehaviour in his said Office, or that by reason of any Misconduct he is an unfit and improper Person to hold or exercise the same, it shall be lawful for such Archdeacon or other Ordinary forthwith to summon such Church Clerk, Chapel Clerk, or Parish Clerk to appear before him, and also by Writing under his Hand, or by such Process as is commonly used in any of the Courts Ecclesiastical for procuring the Attendance of Witnesses, to call before him all such Persons as may be competent to give Evidence or Information respecting any of the Matters imputed to or charged against such Church Clerk, Chapel Clerk, or Parish Clerk as aforesaid ; and such Archdeacon or other Ordinary shall and may, if he see fit, examine upon Oath, to be by him administered in that Behalf, any of the Persons so appearing or attending before him respecting any of the Matters aforesaid, and shall and may thereupon summarily hear and determine the Truth of the Matters so imputed to or charged against such Church Clerk, Chapel Clerk, or Parish Clerk as aforesaid ; and if upon such Investigation it shall appear to the Satisfaction of such Archdeacon or other Ordinary that the Matters so imputed to or charged against such Church Clerk, Chapel Clerk, or Parish Clerk are true, it shall be lawful for the said Archdeacon or other Ordinary forthwith to suspend or remove such Church Clerk, Chapel Clerk, or Parish Clerk from his said Office, and by Certificate under his Hand and Seal directed to the Rector or other officiating Minister of the Parish, District, or Place wherein such Church Clerk, Chapel Clerk, or Parish Clerk held or exercised his Said Office, to declare the said Office Vacant, and a Copy of such Certificate shall thereupon, by such Rector or other officiating Minister, be affixed to the principal door of the Church or Chapel in which the said Church Clerk, Chapel Clerk, or Parish Clerk usually exercised his said office ; and the Person or Persons who upon the Vacancy of such Office are entitled to elect or appoint a Person to fill the same, shall and may forthwith proceed to elect or appoint some other Person to fill the same in the Place of the said Church Clerk, Chapel Clerk, or Parish Clerk so removed as aforesaid: Provided always, that the exercise of such Office by a sufficient Deputy who shall duly and faithfully perform the Duties thereof, and in all respects well and properly demean himself, shall not be deemed a wilful Neglect of his Office on the part of such Church Clerk, Chapel Clerk, or Parish Clerk, so as to render him liable, for such Cause alone, to be suspended or removed Therefrom.

APPENDIX XII.

Draft of a licence to a parish clerk to read prayers, church, and bury.

[This document has been copied from MS. Rawlinson D. 818 in the Bodleian Library. It is the draft of a licence to Thomas Dickenson, parish clerk of Waltham Holy Cross, given by Dr. John Mountain, Bishop of London, sometimes to read prayers, church women, and bury the dead.

I owe my knowledge of the document to the Rev. W. D. Macray, Litt.D.]

John by the providence of God Bishop of London To all[1] [f. 174. our welbeloved in Christ, Thomas Dickenson parishe Clerke of the Churche and parishe of Waltham holy crosse in the Countie of Essex and of our Dioces and iurisdiccion of London sendeth greting in the Lorde

Whereas we have receyved certificate from the right worshipfull Master Joseph Hall Doctor of Divinitie Deane of the Cathedrall Churche of Worcester and preacher at Waltham holy crosse aforesayd that the parishe of Waltham aforesayd is very spacious and large many of the howses in the same parishe being far of from the Churche by reason whereof the Curate [2]of the same Churate[2] of the same Churche cannot at all tymes be had to performe the[3] duetye[2]s etcetera of his office and calling[2] in visiting the sicke buriall of the dead churching of women and other busines belonging to his office and calling without further helpe he being called vppon to performe seuerall services at one and the same tyme

and therevppon petition hath byn made to vs and our say[1] Chauncellor [4]in regard of the multitude of Churche busines there[4] to graunt our[1] licence and aucthoritie to you the sayd Thomas Dickenson [4]sometimes in absence of[4] [2]to assist[2] the Curate there [2]in burying [f. 174b of the[2] [4]to reade praiers churche and bury[4] dead corpses in that parishe [2]in the absence of the Curate there, or when he cannot conveniently in his owne person performe the same,[2] and our sayd Chancellor hath decreed[5] the same to be graunted

[1] *struck through.* [2]—[2] *struck through.*
[3] The *struck through and* his *written in margin.*
[4]—[4] *interlined.*
[5] *a* w *beginning the line has been written before* creed *and then struck out.*

We therefore the Bishop aforesayd in regard of the necessitie of this service to be performed and to thintent that the Curate there may have more libertie and the better oportunitie to visit the sicke and performe the other dueties of his calling have and doe for the reasons before expressed licence and aucthorize you the sayd Thomas Dickenson now parishe Clerke of that Churche and parishe from tyme to tyme hereafter [1]in the absence of the Curate there or when the Curate cannot conveniently performe his duetie in his owne person [2]sometimes to reade prayers[2] to bury such[1] [3]sometimes to reade praiers in the Churche of Waltham holy crosse aforesayd and to church women and to bury suche[3] dead Corpses as hereafter shalbe to be buryed in your parishe Churche or Church yard in the absence of the Curate there or when the Curate cannot conveniently performe the same duetie[4] in his owne person, so as in the same premisses[5] you observe and kepe the wordes and order prescribed in the booke of common prayer now by lawe established and not otherwise.

In witnes whereof we have caused the seale of our Chancellor [3]which we vse in this behaulfe[3] to be set to these presentes.

Dated at London this 12 of January according etcetera. 1621.

[1]—[1] *struck through.* [2]—[2] *interlined and struck through.*
[3]—[3] *interlined.* [4] *interlined.*
[5] burialls *struck through and* premisses *interlined.*

APPENDIX XIII.

JOHN GODOLPHIN ON THE RIGHT TO ELECT THE PARISH CLERK.

Of Parsons and Parsonages.

* * * * *

CHAPTER XVII.

* * * * *

Whether the Parson may appoint the Parish Clerk?

(15.) At a Synod in 44. *Ed.* 3. a Canon was made, That the Parson of every Church of *England* shall appoint the Parish-Clerk. And at another Synod held in *An.* 1603. a Canon was made to the same effect; and yet it doth not take away the Custom where the Parishioners or Church-wardens have used to appoint the Clerk because that is Temporal, which cannot be altered by a Canon.[1] If the Clerk of a Parish in *London* hath used time out of mind to be chosen by the *Vestry*, and afterwards Admitted and Sworn before the Archdeacon, and he refuse to Swear such Clerk so Elect, but Admits another chosen by the Parson: In this Case a Writ may be awarded, commanding him to Swear the Clerk chosen by the *Vestry*. 22 *Jac. Walpool's* Case. The like Writ was granted for the Clerk of the Parish of St. *Fosters*, *London*. Mich. 16. *Car B. R.* between *Orme* and *Pemberton*.[2] The Parishioners of the Parish of *Alphage* in *Canterbury* prescribed to have the Nomination and Election of their Parish Clerk, and the Parson of a Parish by force of a Canon, upon voidance of the place of the Parish-Clerk, elected one to the Office: The Parishioners by force of their Custom elected *C.* the Parson, supposing this Election to be Irregular, for that it was against the Canon sued *C.* before Dr. *Ne*[w]*man* Chancellor of *Canterbury*, and the said *C.* was by Sentence deprived of the Clerkship of the Parish, and another Clerk of the Parish Admitted. *C.* moved for a Prohibition, and had it granted by all the Court; for it was held, That a Parish-Clerk is a meer Lay-man, and ought to be deprived by them that put him in, and no others; and the Canon which willeth that the Parson shall have Election of the Parish-Clerk, is meerly void to take away the Custom, that any person had to Elect him. *Vid. Stat.* 25 *H.* 8. That a Canon against Common Law, confounding the Royal Prerogative of the King, or Law of God, is void; and Custome of the Realm cannot

[1] M. 24 Jac. B. R. Walpole & Gale, *per cur.* & Roll. Abri. ver. Prerogative, lit Y.
[2] Roll ib. lit L.

be taken away but by Act of Parliament. *Vid.* 21 *Ed.* 4. 44. And it was Resolved, That if the Parish-Clerk misdemean himself in his Office, or in the Church; he may be Sentenced for that in the Ecclesiastical Court to Excommunication, but not to Deprivation: And afterwards a Prohibition was granted by all the Court; and held also, That a Prohibition lieth as well after Sentence in this Case as before.[1] And in *Germin's* Case, Whereas the Church-wardens and Parishioners of *K.* surmized they had a Custom to place a Clerk there by the election of the *Vestry*: the Parson sued them in the Ecclesiastical Court, to have his Clerk placed there, according to a late Canon made: It was the Opinion of the Court, that it was a good Custom, and that the Canon could not take it away; wherefore a Prohibition was granted.[2]

(John Godolphin, *Repertorium Canonicum*, Chap. xvii. § 15, London, Atkins for Chr. Wilkinson. Third ed. 1687. p. 192.)

[1] Pasch, 8 Jac. C. B. *Gaudy* vers. Dr. *Newman*. Brownl. Rep. par. 2. [This is almost word for word as in Richard Brownlow's *Reports* (*a second Part*) London, 1652. p. 38.]

[2] Trin. 21 Jac. B. R. *Jermin's* Case Cro. par. 2.

APPENDIX XIV.

The Office of the Parish Clerk of Barrow on Humber about 1713.

[The following transcript was made by Mr. Robert Brown, Junior, F.S.A. from the Town's Book of Barrow on Humber; and it has been very kindly placed at my disposal for the purposes of this work. The book from which the extract is taken is a manuscript of forty-eight pages and is in the old vellum binding; it appears to contain a complete list of the parishioners and landowners in A.D. 1709. On p. 1 is "the Towns Book of Barrow containing the Dues and customs belonging to the said Town One Thousand seven Hundred and nine" also "the ministers Tiths and Dues 1713."

On p. 4 begins "the office and Duty of the parish Clerk."

On the last page of the book the sections which relate to the clerk's wages are repeated.

The book, says Mr. Brown, who has added several notes, is a compilation of different dates. One page is headed "the Townes paines maid and Agreed by the Iury in Barrow Court Anno Dom. 1553," and the entry may be of that date.

The document has been printed by Mr. Christopher Wordsworth in the *Lincoln Diocesan Magazine* for May and June, 1901, from a transcript found by accident and apparently made many years ago; which, however, does not accord in all particulars with the text as now edited. The same may be said of that printed by the late Mr. Thomas North, F.S.A. in the *Antiquary*, 1880, vol. ii. p. 95.]

/The office and Duty of the parish Clark. [p. 4

[1.] Item.—He is to atend the Church or within the parish when he is officiated in his function: he ought carefully to lay up the Comunion Cloth Carpet and Surp[lice] Cloath Cushun Books and other things Appertaining to the Church.

[2.] Item.—He is to see that the Church Chan[c]ell and seats be swept and keep hansome and Deasent; he ought to attend the Church at such times as there is any manner of Churching or buriall and to tole a bell and Ring a lettle According to the accustome manner; he must be carfull that no boys or Idle persons Janle the bells or abuse the Church or windows; he shall or is to pike grease or oyle and keep the Bells in good order; and if they be defected in any thing he is to aquant the churchwardens that they be mended in convenient time.

[3.] Item.—He is to Ring a Bell att nine a Clock in the morning and at 4 at afternoon every working day from munday in the first whole week of Lent untill Easter. E.x.[cep]t such days as there are praye[r]s in the Church.

[4.] Item.—He is to Ring a bell every working day in the mo[rn]in break of the day and continue the Ringing thereof untill allst[1] day and also to Ring a Bell every eve about sunseting till Harvest be fully ended; which bells are to begin to [ring] from the first begin[ning]. of Harvest.

[5.] Item.—He is to provide and pay a workman for mowing [p. 6. and stowing upon the 14 acre dale belonging to the westcote and to see the ordering and bringing to the Church before midsumer day and to pay the waineman for Loading there of every Load four pence; he is to give notice to the owner or farmer occupior of Wistcote (*sic*).

[6.] Item.—About a week before Christmas and Easter that hee before other of those feasts send one Load of strow to the Church stiell where the Clark shall receive It and take care to Lay it in ye seats and in[2] and in[2] Like maner pay the wainman for every Load 4*d.* which strewing of strow shall at Last belong to the Clark.

[7.] Item.—He is to ring a bell for the ringing of the Corphew begining at St. Andrews eve and ending at Candlemas eve and provide Candles for the Ringers and continue in the bell House all the time of ringing and be carefull that nothing their Suffer abuse or Damage.

/The Clark's Wages 1715 May 12th. [p. 7

[8.] Item.—Hee is to Receive at Easter for every plough Land eight pence; and after that rate for every greater or Lescer quantity: Likewise of every Cottager 3*d.* except such as do recive Colliction.

[9.] Item.—for every plough Land he is to have for ringing 9 a Clok Bell 4 of the Clok Bell and night bell and Day Bell 2 pecks of wheat and rye or masheldine[3] and after the rate for a greater or Lesser quantity of Land.

[10.] Item.—He is to have at every wedding or marrige in the parish 6*d.* for every passing bell 4*d.* for every soull knell 4*d.*: If the friends of any deceased person desire to have the great bell Rung a little before the Corps be brought to the Church the Clark for Ringing the bell shall have one shilling; If any person shall willingly or carefully over turn Λ [a] bell the Clark may demand of him one shilling for that offence which if he denys to pay the Clark may sue for it in the Cort and be Jnsested by the parishoners therin 1715.

[1] All Saints? [2]—[2] and in: *repeated.* [3] *Cf.* mashlum, mixed grain.

NOTES.

P. 1. Over the top of the title page is written : hic [*two words illegible*] liber Feb. 25, 1602. Rector de Gawsworth.

Dr. Scott thinks that the two words which cannot now be read, even after the application of ammonium sulphide, may be *William Brownall*, who according to George Ormerod was Rector of Gawsworth in 1597. (*History of . . . Chester*, London, 1819, vol. iii. p. 294.) The latter word certainly appears to end in *ell*.

On the right hand edge is written vertically : William Moreton.

P. 2. No. VI. of the table of contents gives no mention of confirmation, which occurs immediately after the communion on p. 34, below. As a matter of fact no order for confirmation appears in this book, though in the order for confirmation of Edward VI.'s first book there are versicles and responds in which it might be supposed that the clerk took a part. The word confirmation probably slipped into p. 34, by carelessness.

The Prayer Books that appeared before the publication of this book had no psalter attached to them. The last paragraph *Here is to be noted*, therefore, is needed to explain the way to find the psalms of the day.

P. 3. *The ordre how the Psalter, &c.* appears in full in Edward VI.'s first book : the last paragraph *This is also to be noted* is taken from *the Ordre howe the rest of holy Scripture, &c.* a leaf beyond.

P. 4. This is also identical with the table in Edward VI.'s first book.

PP. 5-16. *The Kalendar.* I do not detect any important difference between the Kalendars of the two books.

P. 17. In the margin a seventeenth century hand has written the references to the psalms from which *O Lord open thou my lips* and *O God make good speed to save me* are taken. Similar references are scattered in the margin, together with tryings of the pen, of which no notice will be hereafter taken in these notes.

The ordre for Mattyns is that in Edward VI.'s first book.

P. 24. *Ordre for Euensong* is that of Edward VI.'s first book.

P. 26. This headline *Evensong* over *Quicunque vult* is to be found in the first book of Edward VI.'s, and in the Durham book (see above, p. xiv.) and in the Elizabethan edition of 1559, the headline is *Euening prayer*. But in editions of 1596 and 1615, it has become *Quicunque vult*. This was again altered in 1661, and became *At Morning prayer*.

The version of *Quicunque vult* is that of Edward VI.'s first book, not of the psalter of 1548.

Grafton's edition of Edward VI.'s first book, Mense Martii, has instead of *Christian veritie* the words *Christian unitie*. (B.M. C. 25 m. 14.)

P. 28. The text of the Litany is that of Edward VI.'s first book, not of the psalter of 1548, which retains the invocation of the mother of God, the angels, and saints generally. But its place is not the same. In Edward VI.'s first book it comes after the order for the Communion. Here it comes immediately before.

P. 34. *All that appertein*, &c. has *Confirmacion* immediately after *Communion*, but the book does not contain the order for Confirmation, and the table of contents (p. 2.) also omits the word in the list.

After this place Edward VI.'s first book is no longer followed verbally. Those parts which are read or sung by the clerk become prominent, while the priest's part is often omitted. The variation shows itself early; for the Introit is marked as coming first of all and nothing is said of the Lord's prayer, which the priest repeats at the opening of the Order in Edward VI.'s first book, though the cue of the collect follows after the introit.

P. 35. Here, after *Let us praie*, there is again a somewhat unintelligent following of Edward VI.'s first book, as the collect of the day which came before the collect for the King is wholly omitted, and only the collect for the King has its cue.

The epistle, it should be noted, may be read by the priest or clerk.

The creed is left imperfect.

P. 36. *The Offertorie.* The offertory sentences are from Edward VI.'s first book.

When I was young it sometimes happened that the clergyman who read the epistle read the offertory sentences, but this custom now seems entirely to have died out.

The two exhortations before them in Edward VI.'s first book are omitted here.

P. 38. The Preface being the priest's part is left out, and only *Sanctus* given in full in which the clerk joins. The whole of the canon (as it is called) is omitted, together with the confession: the latter omission is remarkable, as the confession might, under the rubric of Edward VI.'s first book, very reasonably be recited by the clerk. It runs thus: *Then shall this generall confession be made, in the name of all those that are mynded to receaue the holy Communion, either by one of theim, or els by one of the Ministers, or by the Priest him selfe.* The absolution, comfortable words and prayer of humble access, as might be expected, are not given. John Merbecke's *Booke of Common praier noted* (Grafton, 1550) does not contain the confession, but the canon is given at length.

P. 39. *Agnus Dei* and the anthems at the Communion are as in Edward VI.'s first book.

P. 41. Here again only the cue for the thanksgiving after Communion appears; and none of the *Collects to be said after the Offertory, when there is no Communion* is printed. These, however, appear in the Durham book. (See above, p. xiv.)

The cue is *Almighty and euerliuyng*, while in one of Edward VI.'s first books it is *Almighty and everlasting*. (B.M. C. 25, m. 14.)

P. 42. Of the Form for Matrimony, nothing is printed until the psalm, when the clerk joins in its recitation; the *Kyrie*, Lord's prayer, and versicles are printed, as the clerk joins in these.

The psalms are not given in full as in Edward VI.'s first book, for the clerk would have them at hand in the psalter at the end of the book.

P. 43. Only the cue of the first of the final prayers appears. There is nothing of the final exhortation.

P. 44. *Peace be within this house* is somewhat different from the early books of Edward VI. which have *Peace be in this house.*

The versicles and responses appear, but only the cues of the priest's parts are given.

P. 46. In this Communion of the sick is shown very markedly the desire to omit whatever is not said by the clerk. The epistle is given at length, being read by the clerk ; but the collect and gospel and canon have nothing but the cues.

The *Kyrie*, to which in Edward VI.'s first book is added the note, *without any more repetition*, is wholly omitted ; though it might be expected that the clerk would have taken his part in answering once *Christ have mercy upon us.*

P. 48. In Merbecke's *Booke of Common praier noted* (Grafton 1550, sign. Q. ii.) these three opening verses are treated as response with a versicle. So also is *Man that is borne* with *In the middest.*

I commende is struck out and in the margin is written *For as much* ; *almightie* is also struck out and after is written : *For as much as it hath pleased Alm. god to tak vnto himselfe the soule of this our brother.* These are attempts in the seventeenth century, perhaps early, to accommodate the book to the Elizabethan prayer book.

P. 49. In margin opposite *Let us praie* is [*O*]*mit al that foloweth.* This is again a signal to the user of the book in the seventeenth century.

In the lower margin under ps. C. xlvi. is written *Huc* [usque].

These notes appear to be in the same hand as the writing of the top of the title page.

The lesson is given at length for the benefit of the clerk.

P. 50. In lower margin of sign. d. iv. *b.* is written in a hand like that on sign. d. ii. *b.*

Alm. god with whom do live the sp. of the depart. hence in the lo : and in wh. the soule of thos that be elect.

Alm. god who art the resurrection and life in whomsoever bel. sh. liue.

P. 51. Parallel with the head line is also written : *omit alle the end.*

P. 52. The epistle is given at length for the benefit of the clerk.

P. 53. Under *Purificacion of women* is written in same hand as before : *For as much as it hath pleased god to give you safe deliverance and hath.*

After *O almightie God etc.* is written : *which hast safly deliver.*

P. 54. Nothing is given of the homily or of the "Curses," to which the answer of *Amen* might have been led by the clerk.

Notes to Appendix I.

P. 57. It will be seen from the items of this Appendix that the "deacons" at Coventry performed duties very similar to those of the parish clerk. At Ludlow, also, from 1541 to 1564 there were "deacons" who rang the bells, read the first chapter, wore surplices, and had a "deacons chamber." Thomas Higges, being deacon, was paid £5. 6. 8 for a whole year's wages.

(*Churchwardens' accounts of the Town of Ludlow*, ed. Thos. Wright, Camden Society, 1869, pp. 8, 35, 47, 119, 134, 139, and elsewhere.) All that we know of them points to the Ludlow "deacons" being parish clerks, as those at Coventry were. It seems to be much the same at St. Nicholas Bristol where bequests to "the deacon and suffragan" and "the clerk and suffragan" occur in wills, apparently meaning the same officers. (T. P. Wadley, *Notes or Abstracts of the Wills . . . at Bristol*, Bristol and Gloucestershire Society, 1886, p. 11.)

The deacon and suffragan are also spoken of in 1401, at St. Mary Redcliffe. (p. 61.)

§ 1. Vestment here includes all the mass vestments, and is not limited to the chasuble.

P. 58. § 7. Compare the order at St. Michael's Cornhill in 1596: "It is ordred that the Saxton shall after service don presently carry in the Bible and service books to the vestry to be locked for the better saffetie of them and that the Church dore shalbe kept shut in the week daies after service times whereby boys and others maie be kept forth frome doeing damage." (Waterlow and Overall, *Accounts . . . St. Michael Cornhill*, 1872, p. 253.)

§ 9. See below Appendix III. § 13, Appendix VI. § 3.

§ 10. This section seems to suggest that in the beginning the "deacon" was a man in deacon's orders, and thus able to read the gospel himself: that he ceased to be in holy orders and became a mere clerk, when he had to find a real deacon to perform this part of his duties. See also below, § 34. The practice of setting men in minor orders, or no orders at all, to do the office of sub-deacon or deacon seems very widely spread. The singing men at Worcester and Winchester in the seventeenth century read the epistle and gospel. (See Introduction, p. xxiii.)

Or the opposite may be suggested. In St. Cyprian's days the reader read the gospel. (*Epistolae*, xxx. and xxxiv. ed. Migne.) Is it that when first instituted the clerk read the gospel as his fellow read the epistle, but that an increasing desire to limit the service of the altar to men in holy orders was the cause of the clerk being made to find a deacon to sing the gospel?

§ 12. At St. Ewen's Bristol, in 1457–8 they paid ij*d.* "for the clansyng of the gutters of the churche whan the grete snow was" (*Transactions of the Bristol and Gloucestershire Archæological Society*, 1890–91, vol. xv. p. 168.) Similar items may be met with elsewhere. But at Coventry the clerks had to do this work. See § 53. Also at Bledlow in 1782.

§ 13. The priory door at Coventry may be the same as the priory gate of which Thomas Pennant speaks: "Pass by *Cookstreet Gate*, on the outside of the city, and a little further, by the *Three Virgins*, or *Priory Gate*, between which there is a complete part of the wall." (*Journey from Chester to London*, London, 1782, p. 150.) In Hamper's copy of Dugdale's *Antiquities of Warwickshire*, preserved in the British Museum [C. 45. k. 2.] there is a plan in the first volume with *priory gate* marked to the north of Holy Trinity Church.

The form was very likely a thing at which the priest could kneel, what we now call a litany desk. It was easily moveable, for it was to be brought away from the priory door to the body of the church before the rood. The Rev. Dr. Fowler has pointed out "a forme to serve in procession tyme" at Cheswardine, Salop, in the time of Queen Mary Tudor.

(*The Ornaments of the Rubric*, Alcuin Club Tracts, 1897, p. 48, by J. T. Micklethwaite, quoting from the Rev. Dr. J. T. Fowler, *Church Times*, December 7th, 1883, p. 901. col. ii.)

And at Syon they had on Ash Wednesday for the seven penitential psalms "a lytel forme" for the priest and his ministers, taken away when the seven psalms were ended. (G. J. Aungier, *History and Antiquities of Syon Monastery*, Westminster, 1840, p. 343.) Also, after compline, before taking holy water, there was a "forme or deske" that "the president only may lene to" and kneel. (*ibid.* p. 334.)

If they followed at Coventry the Sarum processional, the priory door might well be the place of the first station, during which the *executor officii* had to kneel, and thus might be glad of the support of a "form." In like manner, the priest had to kneel at *Ave rex noster* sung before the rood. (*Missale ad usum . . . Sarum*, Burntisland, 1861-1883, col. 262.)

Ave rex noster is an anthem found in many parts of western christendom; in Spain, Germany, and France, as part of the procession on Palm Sunday.

At Bristol they made in 1572, a charge of two pence for "4 legs and 4 ballusters to the forme to kneele at procession tyme." (J. F. Nichols and John Taylor, *Bristol past and present*, Bristol, 1881, vol. ii. p. 37.) The litany in Elizabeth's time was thus still called procession, and Robert Burton later on uses the same word: "We may doe well therefore, to put this in our precession† amongst the rest: *from all blindnesse of heart, from pride, vaine-glory*" etc. (*The Anatomy of Melancholy*, Part i. Sect. 2, Memb. 3, Sub-section 10, at end. Oxford, 1621, p. 143.)

§ 14. The holy water stock would seem to be moveable; what is now called the holy water bucket.

§ 15. At Easter and Whitsuntide the font was hallowed, and fresh water brought. See below § 20.

This towel is spoken of in the Sarum manual. "Verumtamen in sabbato sancto pasche et in vigilia penthecostes peracta consecratione fontium non infundetur oleum neque crisma: nec ulterius in officio baptismi procedatur nisi forte aliquis assit baptizandus: sed lintheamine mundo cooperiantur: et usque ad completorium pasche et penthecostes reseruentur. ut si forte his diebus aliquis baptizandus aduenerit: fecundatis et sanctificatis fontibus olei et crismatis infusione baptizetur." (*Manuale ad usum insignis ecclesie Sarum*, Rothomagi, Ioan. Richardus, 1501, fo. xliii. *b.*) About 1850 the custom still prevailed at West Luccombe in Somerset of covering the font with a linen cover after the water was poured in for baptism. (*Hierurgia Anglicana*, ed. Vernon Staley, London, 1902, vol. i. p. 10.) At Milan a sort of linen canopy is hung over the font continuously.

§ 16. *Rex sanctorum angelorum* is a metrical hymn, called a litany in the Sarum books, sung returning from the blessing of the font at Easter and Whitsuntide. The Sarum rubric directs that it shall be sung by three clerks of the upper grade in silk copes, two of which are to be red, the third white. (*Processionale ad usum . . . Sarum*, ed. Henderson, Leeds, 1882, p. 90.) This also favours the idea that at Coventry the Sarum Missal was in use, as the other printed missals do not have *Rex sanctorum angelorum.*

§ 17. This carrying of holy water gave his name to the clerk, *aquaebaiulus;* and was a source of profit to him. See Introduction above, p. li. and Lyndwood, *Provinciale*, Lib. iii. tit. *De concessione praebendae*, cap. *a nostris*, Oxon. 1679, p. 142.

§ 18. On Sundays the holy cake was blessed after the blessing of the holy water, and then distributed, (*Missale . . . Sarum*, ed. F. H. Dickinson, Burntisland, 1861-1883, col. 33** and 36**) "cut according for every man's degree."

The xii. day is the twelfth day after Christmas, the Epiphany. See § 59, below. The mending of the surplice doubtless became a mere excuse for demanding a Christmas box.

§ 20. This takes one back to a time not so very long ago when there was no system of waterworks, and water laid on in every building. There used to be in English villages a man who came with a horse and butt, the bitter, who brought potable water to peoples' houses.

The water on Easter even and Whitsun Eve was for the new water that was to be blessed in the font. That on Shere Thursday (Maundy Thursday) was for the washing of the altars. A birche besom for this (§ 26) was to be provided by the first deacon, and wine and a holy water bucket were to be had ready by the second (§ 69.)

"1509. For water for the funt on Wytson-yevyn. . . .

"1520. For water to be halowed on Maundy Thursday for the alters and Estureven for the fountain." (? Font: St. Mary Hill, 1520, in Nichols, *Illustrations*, London, 1797, pp. 105 and 108.

"1549–50. Paid for water for the Founte for one yere Sm' vj*d.*

"1550–51. P'd to the water bearer for water viij*d.*

"1556–57. Payd For wattar For the Fontt at Whyt sonteye i*d.*"

(Churchwardens' accounts for St. Matthew, Friday Street, edited by W. Sparrow Simpson, *Journal of the British Archæological Association*, 1869, vol. xxv. p. 361.)

P. 59. § 23. This is further evidence that the palms and branches hallowed and distributed on Palm Sunday furnished the ashes for the following Ash Wednesday. It was so at Syon. (G. J. Aungier, *History and Antiquities of Syon Monastery*, Westminster, 1840. p. 343.)

§ 24. The palm on Palm Sunday seems more often to have been found by the churchwardens. The charge, including cake and bread, appears in the churchwardens' accounts.

"Flowrs obleyes, and for box and palme ayenst Palme sondaye o. o. 6."

"For palme flowrys and cake on Palme Sonday o. o. 10."

(St. Mary Hill, in Nichols, *Illustrations*, London, 1797, pp. 111 and 105, 1486 and 1510.)

"Paide for palme, boxe, yewe, flowers, and cakes for Palme Sondaie viijd. ob."

(Waterlow and Overall, *Accounts . . . St. Michael Cornhill*, London, about 1872, p. 128.)

"Paid for Syngyng brede on Palm Sonday ij."

(Charles Kerry, *A history . . . St. Lawrence Reading*, Reading, 1883. p. 49, year 37–38 of Henry VIII.)

"1521. Item spent uppon palme sonday for caks, flowers, box and palm, vijd."

"1556. Item for palme flowers and cakes for palme Sondaye xijd."

(St. Peter cheap, *Journal of the British Archaeological Association*, 1868, vol. xxiv. p. 261 and 263.)

There is a description of the Palm Sunday procession contained in a dialogue given below. Though the conversation is somewhat onesided, yet by leaving out the interpretation of the ceremonies and questions upon them, a tolerably consecutive account of the procession can be supplied. It is written from a standpoint not scoffing at, nor yet wholly approving of, the old ceremonies, and it appears amongst the collected *Workes* of one Thomas Becon printed in 1563. If it be Becon's, it may be evidence of the grave deterioration of character that took place in ten years when he wrote *The Displaying of the Popish Mass*.

"In the begynnynge of the Procession the people goethe oute hauynge euery one a Palme in theyr hand followynge the Crosse which is couered with a clothe . . . that whiche they beare in dede in theyre handes, is not properlye called a Palme, for they are the bowes of a Salow tree, but bycause we haue no Palmes growinge in this londe, therfore do we beare them in stede of Palmes . . . Than go they forthe withe the Crosse, vntyll they come vnto a certayne stedde of the Chyrche yearde, where they stonde styll, and in the meane season, the preste rede the gospell . . . The Gospell beynge once done, than goth the people forthe withe the crosse that is couered, and euen streyghtwayes not farre from them come other people and the preste wyth the Sacrament, whyche haue wyth them a crosse bare and vncouered, prycyked ful of grene Oliues and Palmes . . . ye shall note, that there come forthe certayne chyldren before the naked Crosse, syngynge a certayne songe, whiche begynnethe, *En Rex uenit.* Beholde the Kynge commeth . . . After the songe of the chyldren, the Preste goeth forthe with the Sacrament and certayne people also wythe the naked Crosse, vntyll hey mete wythe that Crosse, that is obuelated and couered. They are not so soone met, but the bumbled Crosse vanyshe awaye, and is conueyed from the company streyghtwayes. Than all the whole people enclose togyther wyth great ioy, syngyng and makyng melody triumphantly followynge the naked crosse, bearynge in theyr handes euery one a Palme, in some places also they beare grene herbes in the stede of Oliues . . . These thynges once done, than the people gothe somewhat further vnto the chyrche dorewarde, and there stondeth styll . . . Immediatly after certayne chyldrenne stondyng vpon an hygh place right agaynste the people, synge wythe a lowde voyce a certayne Hympne, in the prayse of oure Sauioure Iesus Christ, whych begynnethe, *Gloria laus* . . . At the end of euery verse, the chyldren caste downe certayne cakes or breades wythe floures . . . These thynges once done than gothe the procession forth vntyll they come to the chyrche dore whyche, whan they come vnto it, is sparred, and certayne chyldren in the chyrche syngyng. The songe beyng once done, the Preste taketh the crosse in his hand, and putteth the dore from hym with it, and so openeth it, and entreth in with all the other people after him . . . Whan they are once entred into the chyrche, whereby heauen is signifyed, than dothe all the people knele downe, and the prest pluckyng vp the clothe, wher with the crucifyxe was couered, and makyng it open to all that are there presente, syngethe a certayne songe, the people in the meane season prayeng and gyuynge thanckes vnto God. And so endeth the Procession."

(*A Potacion or drinkynge for this holy tyme of Lent* . . . by Theodore Basille, London, John Mayler for John Gough, 1543. Brit. Mus. C. 21. a. 7. This is printed among Thomas Becon's *Workes* in the edition of 1563.)

The "bumbled Crosse" would seem to be the cross that is covered. Bumbles are a bandage or blindfolding, for blinkers for horses. See Dr. Murray's *New English Dictionary*, s.v.

There is an allusion to the meeting of the two crosses, and the casting of cakes in another work written in the form of a dialogue, but altogether on the protestant side.

"They haue their laudable dumme ceremonies with lenten crosse, and vptide crosse, and these two must iustle, til Lent breake his uecket. Then cakes must be cast out of the steple, that al the boys in the parish must lie scambling together by the eares. tyl all the parish falleth a laughing, . . . But Lord what Apes play made thei of it in great Cathederal churches, and Abbaies?

"*Nich.* What did they there?

"*Oliu.* One comes forth in his albe, and his long stole (for so they call their girdet that they put aboute theyr neckes) thys must be leashe wise, as hunters weares their hornes. This solempne syre, played Christes part, a gods name. Then another companye of singers, chyldren and al, song in priksong, the Iewes part. And the deuil (the deacon I should haue said) read the middel text.

"*Nicho.* What dyd the prest at the alter al this while?

"*Oliu.* He stood mum, and played Iudas, that betrayed his Mayster.

And in the meanetime, because it was teadiouse to be vnoccupyed, such playne soules as thou art, made crosses of palme, to set vpon your dorss, and to beare in your purses."

(*A Dialogue or familiar talke between two neighbours*, Roane, Michael Wodde, 1554. sig. D. iii. Brit. Mus. C. 25. c. 26.)

§ 25. The sepulchre, wherein after Evensong on Good Friday were deposited the Eucharist and the cross (*Processionale Sarum*, ed. Henderson, Leeds, 1882, p. 72.) was watched by the second deacon on Good Friday night (§ 65.) and by the first deacon on Easter Even, until the procession which preceded the Mattins of Easter Day. (*Breviarium . . . Sarum*, ed. Procter and Wordsworth, Cambridge, 1882. fasc. i. col. dcccvii.)

The Lenten cloths that covered the images and the crosses during Lent were taken down after this procession, and before Mattins. (*ibid.* col. dcccix.)

At St. Helen's Abingdon in 1555 they paid the sexton eightpence "for watching the sepulter two nyghtes" (Nichols, *Illustrations*, p. 141.) So at St. Michael's Worcester, he had in 1543 twopence beyond his wages. (John Amphlett, *Churchwardens' Accounts of St. Michael's in Bedwardine, Worcester*, Oxford, 1896, p. 12.) If the clerk were paid more as a rule for this watching of the sepulchre, we see why it is expressly said at Coventry that the watching is to be part of his duties, so that he could not claim an extra fee.

§ 26. The rites at the washing of the altars on Maundy Thursday will be found in the Sarum Processional, ed. Henderson, 1882, p. 59.

"Aftyr hygh masse, or els aftyr mete, al the autyrs schal be made bare, and the mynyster of the sextry schal ordeyn for two bysoms made of boxe and ewe that was halowyd on palme sonday for waschyng of the autyrs, and he, or els the mynyster of high masse, schal helpe the sextayn to halowe the holy watyr, and ordeyn for cruettys of wyne and cuppys for to powre watyr up on the autyr." (G. J. Aungier, *op. cit.* p. 348.)

§ 27. The discipline rods were for use on Good Friday. Sir Thomas More speaks of the lady who wept when she remembered "that the priest had on good friday with the dyspelying roade beaten her hard vppon her lylye white hands." (Quoted by D. Rock, *Church of our Fathers*, London, 1853. vol. iii. part ii. p. 241. as in controversy with Tindal. I have been unable to find the quotation.)

In 1510 at St. Mary at Hill together with the "watur of Mawndy Thursday and Estur ewe" they bought "disseplynyng roddis, and nayles, for the sepulchre." (Nichols, *Illustrations*, p. 105.)

"Palme stickes, Iudas bels with candels blowen out at the ende of euery Psalme and lesson, crepinge to the crosse with egges and apples, dispelinge with a white rodde, wasshinge of aultares."

([Io. Olde.] *A short description of Antichrist*, fol. 8. British Museum G. 11, 694.)

The mention of the discipline rods is with other things connected with passion tide: palm, tenebrae candles, creeping to the cross, and washing of altars. William Lambarde likewise speaks of them with other Lenten ceremonies: "their takinge of Ashes, coveringe of Images, strewinge of Flowers, bearinge of Palmes, soundinge of Clappers, beatinge on Bookes, disciplinge on the Heades and Handes, ceasinge of Belles at one Tyme, and soundinge with Belles, Voyce, and Organs, like a black Sanctus at an other Tyme." (*Dictionarium Angliae Topographicum*, London, 1730. p. 459, *sub voce* Wytney.)

"For disciplining rods and trash for the sepulchre, 1*s.* 1*d.* For keeping clean the Pardon Churchyard, 16*d.* For Easter Even a quarter of coals for the holy fire, 5*d.*" (T. B. Murray, *Chronicles of a City Church . . . St. Dunstan in the East*, London, 1859. p. 13. accounts for 1494.)

Discipline rods were used also at other times, as we may see at Rome at the present day.

"This yeare, the Sondaie after All-hallowe daie, did certene prestes ther penaunce at Poules, and went before the procession, ech of them in a whit shirt, with a tapere in one hand, and a whit rode in the other. In the procession, the busshopp came and displed them, and then kyssed them. Then they stode before the preacher at Poules Crosse till the praiers were made; then did the preacher disple them, and so they put of ther whit vesture, and stode all the reast of the sermond in ther clothes." (J. G. Nichols, *Narratives of the . . . Reformation*, Camden Society, 1859. p. 289. in 1555, perhaps 1554.)

§ 28. John Meneley was appointed Vicar of Holy Trinity in 1443: he was also a canon of Lichfield. Robert Melborn had an anniversary by an indenture dated in 1440. (Thomas Sharp, *Illustrations of the History . . . Holy Trinity Church Coventry*, Coventry, 1818, pp. 5 and 18.)

See also note to § 81.

§ 29. At St. Michael's Bath, it was the churchwardens who found the grease for the bells: in 1460, "in campanis unguendis per an. iij*d*." and in 1474 "pro unguento empto pro campanis per an. ij*d*." (C. B. Pearson, *Church wardens Accounts . . . of St. Michael without the North Gate, Bath*, Somersetshire Archaeological and Natural History Society's Proceedings, vol. xxiii. Taunton, 1878, pp. 54 and 70.)

§ 32. There does not seem to have been more than one lamp in the church. Rushes were much used in the middle ages to put on the floor whether in churches or dwelling houses. See App. XIV. p. 110, for a continuance of the custom into the eighteenth century. Mr. Cuthbert Atchley informs me that it is continued at St. Mary Redcliffe to this day, but only at Whitsuntide.

§ 33. The sermon by a doctor was marked in other ways than by the mere covering of the pulpit with a cloth. There is a scurrilous tract on the mass printed at Strassburg in 1554, which contains these lines:

But looke ye call your selfs master doctor
And Graduate of the vniuersite,
Preache in your hoode, and set forthe your honor
And so declare what learned men ye be.

(Hugh Hilarie, *The resurreccion of the masse*, Strasburgh, 1554, sig. C. iii.)

The precedence of a doctor of divinity is marked at the trial of Ridley and Latimer. Latimer was thought not to have taken this degree. When Ridley was examined, a cloth was laid on the table before him; it was removed when Latimer took his place. (J. Fox, *Actes* &c. 1555. October, ed. 1563, p. 1372. The pulpits in the frontispiece have cloths hanging over them.)

§ 34. After evensong in the Easter week there was a procession to the font, two deacons at Salisbury bearing the *oleum catechumenorum* and the *chrisma*. (*Processionale . . . Sarum*, ed. Henderson, Leeds, 1882, p. 94.) In a parish church it seems likely that both these oils were kept together in one chrismatory, so that one deacon sufficed.

§ 35. The church holy day is doubtless the feast of dedication which lasted a week. Whether the banner were hung from the steeple and whether on the banner were blazoned the vicar's arms cannot be told from this description.

At St. Margaret Pattens about 1506 they bought "a lynen with a Redde crosse to hynge up on the dedycacon day." (W. H. St. John Hope, *Archaeological Journal*, 1885, vol. xlii. p. 320.)

§ 36. See below § 61. It would seem to have been the usual practice for the clerk to accompany the parish priest visiting the sick. See above Introduction, p. xxvi.

§ 38. The pictures and images in the church as well as the altar and rood were covered with white linen veils from the first Sunday in Lent to Easter. Abundant evidence of this use of white cloths in Lent has been brought by Mr. W. H. St. John Hope. (*Transactions of the Saint Paul's Ecclesiological Society*, 1886–90, vol. ii. p. 237.) The vail in the quire was hung between the presbytery and the quire.

"This tyme of Lent, whiche is a tyme of mournyng, all thynges that make to the adournement of the chyrche wherof the Images are parte, are either layde asyde or els couered, to put vs in remembraunce that we ought nowe to lamente and mourne for oure soules dead in sinne, and continuallye to watche, praye, faste, giue almes, and do such other workes of Penaunce." (Theodor Basille, *A Potacion or drinkinge for this holy tyme of Lent*, London, 1543, fo. lix.)

P. 60. § 39. As early as the time of Ælfric's Canons, food was not taken in Lent till after evensong; (B. Thorpe, *Ancient Laws . . . England*, 1840. p. 487, Canon xl.) and accordingly in laxer times evensong in Lent was sung early, so that men might go to dinner much at their usual time.

Thus Sir Thomas More tells us that evensong in Lent was sung before noon (*The apology*, Ch. xxxi. in *Workes*, London, 1557, p. 895.) as it still is abroad. But compline remained at the same hour as usual, so that the bell on Saturday had still to be rung.

§ 41. "But that men vse in saturdaies and vigilies to ryng holy at midday compellith nat men anon to halowe, but warnythe them of the haliday followynge." (*Dives and Pauper*, the thridde precept, xiv. chap. London, Pynson, 1493, sign. l. i. *b*.)

In 1540 at Fairstead the churchwardens were to "ryng to even-songe on Saterdaiis and other festivall evens." (W. H. Hale, *Series of Precedents . . . extracted from Act-Books of Ecclesiastical Courts in the Diocese of London*, London, 1847. p. 114.)

In 1541 at Tey parva they complain of the parson that "he saith non evyn-songe upon the Saterdaie at any time in the yere." (*ib.* p. 123.)

§ 45. Twopence seems a large sum for the hire of the surplice; but if we believe Chaucer it can hardly have been a venial sin to relieve so bad a man of some of his ill gotten gains.

> "*Radix omnium malorum est cupiditas.*
> Thus can I preche agayn the same vice.
> Which that I use, and that is avarice."

(*Prologue of the Pardoner*, 140–143, ed. Richard Morris, iii. 89.)

In 1519, Lestrange of Hunstanton gave the pardoner threepence the first Sunday in Lent, and a penny on the third Sunday. (*Archaeologia*, 1834. vol. xxv. p. 420.) Yet at Christmas only fourpence was offered. (p. 449.) Payment by the parishioners at the same rate must have greatly enriched the pardoner.

§ 46. At Ashburton in Devonshire, they collected in 1498–9 the sum of xixd. for the bells on the eve of All Souls. (J. H. Butcher, *Parish of Ashburton in the 15th and 16th centuries*, London, 1870 p. 11.)

This ringing of bells on All Hallows' day at even continued late into the sixteenth century. John Hooper tried to stop it at Gloucester in 1551. (*Injunctions*, § xxxv. in *Later Writings*, Parker Society, 1852, p. 147.) But it continued in some places until 1569, for it is forbidden in that year by John Parkhurst, Bishop of Norwich. "3. Item, that vppon all sainctes daye and other like times, ther be no ringing of belles after Euening prayer, or any other superstitious ceremony vsed, to the maintenaunce of poperie, or praying for the dead, and that if any such shal be hence forth vsed, the same with the names of suche as shall offende therein, to bee presented to the Ordinary." (*Second Report of the Commissioners . . . Rubrics, Orders, Directions*, 1868. Appendix E. p. 404. See also Aylmer, Bishop of London, in 1577. p. 419. Article 8, and many others to the same effect.)

P. 61. § 49. The ordinal usually means the Pie, the *Directorium Sacerdotum*, which Mr. Christopher Wordsworth edited for this Society in 1901 and 1902. But in the Sarum pie the directions for bellringing are not prominent, if they exist at all. In this case, the word ordinal probably refers to some local custom that was written down, and thus could be said to specify.

§ 53. Compare §§ 11 and 12 above.

§ 54. This second clerk had to be sub-deacon himself and read the epistle while the gospel was only to be read by a deacon whom the head clerk had to find. (See above, § 10.)

P. 62. §§ 56–68. Compare corresponding sections in the head clerk's duties.

§ 63. The new fire had to be blessed on this day at the beginning of the ceremonies of Easter. A charge for coals at Easter is very common. As example of such there is :

" For two quarters of colis for the fire to be hallowed o. o. 11."

(St. Mary Hill in 1517. Nichols, *Illustrations*, London, 1797, p. 107.)

" Item for colis to be hallowed on Easter yeve 1d."

(W. L. Nash, *Churchwardens' account book for the parish of St. Giles Reading*, Reading, 1881. p. 13. anno 1520.)

Other entries make it possible that some of the coals were used for keeping the watcher of the sepulcre a little warm. Thus at Ludlow in 1540 they paid fourpence "for colis agaynst Chrystmas, Ester, Whitsontyd and Alhalontyd to sense with and to weeche the sepulcre."

(*Churchwardens' Account for the town of Ludlow*, Camden Society, 1869, p. 5.)

P. 63. § 69. See above, notes to § 26.

§ 70. See above, notes to § 46.

§ 71. There is a noteworthy coincidence with this at Reading. At St. Lawrence, in 1506, they paid " for sysis to the holy bush at Christmas, ix *d*." (C. Kerry, *History of St. Lawrence, Reading*, Reading, 1883, p. 52). Sysis are small wax tapers. Here the churchwardens seem to have paid for these decorations ; at Coventry, the Vicar. At St. Ewen's Bristol, in 1456–57, the churchwardens paid "for condels and bowes a geyne Cristesmas." (Sir John Maclean, *Transactions of the Bristol and Gloucestershire Archaeological Society*, 1890–91, vol. xv. p. 168.) Till the middle of the nineteenth century it was the custom for the clerk or sexton to deck the church with holly at Christmas. We may remember the rebuke, recorded in Washington Irving's *Sketch Book*, that was given by the parson to the sexton for setting mistletoe among the greens with which he had decorated the church, and the clerk's musical duties which Master Simon, the cousin of the squire, so well discharged.

§ 73. By the Roman *Rituale* of Paul V. the woman, as she kneels to be churched, holds a lighted candle in her hand ; but I do not find any direction for this in any of the English manuals that I have looked at ; nor could Mr. Cuthbert Atchley in his careful Essay on the Ceremonial use of lights (*Some Principles and Services of the Prayer Book historically considered*, Rivingtons, 1899, p. 26, note 2), find any but incidental notices.

The York Manual (*Manuale . . . Ebor.* Surtees Society, 1875, p. 22 see also p. 214*), however, speaks of the holy bread to be blessed and given to the woman, in accordance with the following canon :

Item, quando mulieres post puerperium venerint ad purificationem, sacerdotes tantummodo dent eis panem benedictum, et corpus Domini nullo modo eis proponatur, nisi expresse petant, et prius confessae fuerint. (Council held at Durham 1220, D. Wilkins, *Concilia*, London, 1737, t. i. p. 579.)

§ 79. See above, notes to § 39.

§ 81. Apparently the eating and drinking at these dirges took place in the church.

In 1506 at St. Mary at Hill they paid a penny " For hyryng three gallon pots to bere drinke about the chirche for the pepyl of the parish [which is the deceaseds wyll ; and he that spendyth more to pay it out of his own purse without any allowance.] " (Nichols, *Illustrations*, p. 104.)

See above, § 28.

Some of the details of this kind of drinking at dirges are shown in the following extract from Strype's edition of Stow :

" *Margaret Atkinson*, Widow, by her Will, *October* 18. 1544, orders, That the next *Sunday* after her Burial, there be provided two Dozen of Bread, a Kilderkin of Ale, two Gammons of Bacon, three Shoulders of Mutton, and two Couple of Rabbits. Desiring all the Parish, as well Rich as Poor, to take their Part thereof: And a Table to be set in the Midst of the Church, with every Thing necessary thereto."

(John Stow, *A Survey of the Cities of London and Westminster*, edited by John Strype, London, 1720, vol. i. p. 259. In margin : *Regist. Lond.*)

Notes to Appendix II.

P. 64. *Memorandum*, etc. Compare the first paragraph of Appendix IV. p. 71, and the dispute at Morebath in Appendix VII. p. 84. There is in both these a committee of the parishioners who are chosen to look after the affairs of the church.

§ 1. The care of the vestments, books, and jewels, the opening and shutting of the church doors are the duty of the clerk in many other places. It was the Sexton's at St. Michael's Cornhill, in 1596. (See note to Appendix I. p. 58, § 7.)

The church was to be searched also at St. Nicholas, Bristol (Appendix III. p. 66, § 1.) and at Morebath. (Appendix VII. p. 84, § 1.)

P. 65. § 2. This care for lost goods is not to be found in any of the other rules.

Notes to Appendix III.

The notes to which the initials C. A. in square brackets are attached are by Mr. Cuthbert Atchley.

This set of rules is remarkable for the fines set out for any neglect of duty.

P. 66. § 3. The two lamps would be the lamp before the rood, mentioned in the accounts for 1521–22, 1534, and 1539–40 ; in 1547–48 it is " the lampe that dyd brene befor the Rodlofft " : and that " within the ynterclows " (1523) *i.e.* in the quire before the high altar. The lamp before the Lady-altar was bought in 1532. [C. A.]

P. 67. § 10. The dressing of the altars meant putting on the front and over front, and the ridells, and displaying the "Jewels" on the reredos. "Jewels" included all such things as images, caskets, monstrances, etc. The practice is still retained in royal chapels. Besides the high altar the accounts mention our Lady altar and St. John's altar. In 1556, the accounts mention the "four altars": and there were four in 1432. (*Vestry-book*, fol. 12). [C. A.]

In later times the clerks were paid for brushing the cobwebs and dust from the altars and imagery: 1527, for Brusshyng of the highe aulter and the Rode loffte, xxd. There was begun in 1468, a notable new work over the high altar in the quire, called a "Reredors." It contained an image of St. Nicholas on the north side of the altar, one of St. Blaise on the south, and in the middle an image of the Trinity above and of our Lady below; all gilt. (*Vellum-leaved Vestry-book*, fol. 24.) In 1542 43 are payments for makyng and gilding the images of Adam and Eve and the Angel, and a mitre for an image of St. Clement. [C. A.]

§ 13. To the amount of a full half of quarter of an hour. Curfew seems to have been rung at St. Nicholas for the whole town. [C. A.]

§ 14. For the boy bishop. The Mayor and Corporation attended both evensongs and mass of St. Nicholas, 6. December, listened to the boy-bishop's sermon and received his blessing. After dinner they waited his coming at the Gildhall, playing dice the while; and when he arrived, his chapel (*i.e.* choir) sang, and he and they were served with bread and wine. (*The maire of Bristow is Kalendar by Robert Ricart*, Camden Society, 1872. p. 80.) In 1528. Pd. to the clarke for dressyng vp the byshopes stale, viij*d*. [C. A.]

§ 15. The Host and a Crucifix were buried in the Sepulchre from Good Friday till Easter morning. 1530: Pd. to the Clerkes to sett vppe the sepulcur, x*d*. Similarly in 1520. [C. A.]

P. 68. § 30. The under suffragan, at this date called Lymner, appears to be a different person from the suffragan; probably a third clerk. [C. A.]

§ 35. It would seem that only one torch was to be ready for each mass. During the middle ages it was very common to have one light only at the altar during the celebration of the Eucharist. There is abundant testimony for this from the canon law, liturgical writings, and pictures.

P. 70. § 2. *Sospitati dedit aegros olei perfusio. Nicholaus naufragantum affuit praesidio* is the beginning of the prose that used to be sung in the Sarum use after the ninth respond at mattins on the feast of St. Nicholas, 6. December. Evidently the clerks went round the parish singing this hymn after the fashion of the Waits and Carol-singers of later days, and the "avails" or "tips" obtained on this occasion went to the parish-clerk. [C. A.]

For the text of *Sospitati* see Procter and Wordsworth, *Breviarium . . . Sarum*, Cambridge, 1886. fasc. iii. col. 36. For numerous other references see U. Chevalier, *Repertorium Hymnologicum*, Louvain, 1889–97, sub voce *Sospitati dedit*.

It may be remembered that parish clerks are under the patronage of St. Nicholas. The London Company was the Fraternity of St. Nicholas.

§ 3. The following was the distribution of the "blacks" at Christchurch Canterbury in 1614, November 25th.

"It is agreed that the Blacks of funeralls shalbe disposed as followeth vizt.

"That the herse cloth which compasseth the rales of the solemne herse where soever in the church shalbe for the sacrist

"The Stoole cloathes shalbe to the vestiars

"And the Bere cloath which lyeth ouer the graue shalbe to the Bell ringers." (*Acta Capitula*, 1608–28. p. 131, in the Treasury at Canterbury.)

See also above, Introduction, p. lvii.

§ 5. What is the vantage of virgin on All Hallows' day? The fee would seem to have been of some amount; for in return the suffragan was to perform a daily service.

Notes to Appendix IV.

P. 71. The expression *quarterage*, which holds so large a place in the payment of the clerk, here makes its appearance in 1434. This document shows a very interesting process going on of rating houses according to their value for the benefit of the clerks.

The Elizabethan table of wages may be compared with that given in the Introduction, p. lvii.

Notes to Appendix V.

P. 76. § 2. In 1506 it was not so easy to obtain light or fire as now, when lucifer matches are everywhere at hand. At St. Mary Ottery, for example, they kept a light continually burning in the church, not only for reverence of the body of Christ, but also for those who might want fire. (G. Oliver, *Monasticon Diocesis Exoniensis*, Exeter 1846, p. 273, § 2.)

It has been said that a light was necessary for the due celebration of mass: at least one candle had to be burning, usually on or near the altar. It is just possible that the light or fire which was to be continually in the chancel before noon every day was to serve for all the masses said in the church.

See below, note to § 22, on p. 79, where the sexton has to keep the lamp in the quire burning day and night.

The clerk is to wear a rochet as in so many other cases. (See above, Introduction, p. xxxix.)

§ 3. There does not appear to be any ceremony indicated here, such as was practised at Sarum at high mass after the introit, when bread, wine, and water were brought to the altar. (*Missale . . Sarum*, Burntisland, 1861–1883, ed. F. H. Dickinson, col. 589.) We are dealing here with the ceremonies of low mass, and it will be noticed that the clerks brought in the chalice and took it out again into the vestry; nowadays the priest carries it himself. As at Faversham so did the suffragan at St. Nicholas Bristol, (see above, p. 67, § 17) but at high mass. In Mr. Percy Dearmer's *Dat Boexken vander Missen* (Alcuin Club, 1903, p. 8), there is a Flemish woodcut showing the subdeacon bringing in the cruets, and the deacon the chalice, to the altar.

§ 4. Mr. Giraud has pointed out to me the place at the west end of the parish church, which is called the treasury. Above it is the room in which the sexton is said to have slept. See note to § 8.

§ 5. *Breast* here is the voice; see Shakspere, *Twelfth Night*, II. iii. 18. "The fool has an excellent breast . . . so sweet a breath to sing, as the fool has." Also line 54. Cf. Dr. Murray, *New English Dictionary*, sub voce.

Faburdon is faux-bourdon, "a simple kind of Counter point to the Church Plain Song." (Geo. Grove, *Dictionary of Music*, 1880, Macmillans.) The same authority tells us that it was much in use in England in the fifteenth century.

§ 6. *To synge with* is *to sing mass with*, that is, the fresh water was to be used for the mixing of the chalice, and for rinsing it out after the communion of the priest.

Probably the cruets were of metal, not, as in our more economical days, of glass, and therefore there would be the greater need of careful cleansing of the inside.

P. 77. § 8. It was not unusual for a man to sleep in some part of the church to guard against thieves. At Ludlow they had a deacon's chamber in Elizabethan times. (*Churchwardens' Accounts . . . of Ludlow*, Camden Society, 1869, p. 139.)

§ 10. To teach children to read implied in 1506, instruction in the rudiments of Latin, especially if they were also to help in the quire and service in the church.

P. 78. § 14. *The bason and ewer which be ordained for the christening of children* may be found elsewhere. In 1522, Agas Herte of Bury bequeathed "to the chyrche of Seynt Jamys a basen and a ewer of pewter hamerd, to be vsyd at crystnyng of chyldern in the seyd chyrch as long as it will indure." (*Wills . . . of Bury*. ed. by Samuel Tymms, Camden Soc. 1850, p. 116.) Also William Holme, Vicar of Mathesay, left in 1466, "j. pelvim cum lavacro; et volo quod huiusmodi pelvis et lavacrum deserviant temporibus baptizationis infancium." (*Testamenta Eboracensia*, Part ii. Surtees Soc. 1855, p. 279.)

§ 15. This oath is apparently different from that to be taken at admission to the office by the archdeacon; it is a separate promise to observe the local order.

§ 16. See above, notes to § 4.

§ 19. See above, notes to § 41, of Appendix I.

P. 79. § 22. See above, note to § 2 on p. 76.

§ 24. *skomeryng of doggs*. The expression is found in Elizabethan writers. The following quotation shows the word used much in the same sense as in the text:

> a brace of grey hounds,
> When they are led out of their kennels to scumber.
>
> Massinger, *The Picture*, V. i. 61.

Notes to Appendix VI.

The fines for neglect of duty appear again in this set of rules, but not so uniformly as at Bristol. (Appendix III.)

P. 82. § 2. Whatever may have been the practice in cathedral churches and monasteries, this is evidence again that mattins were not sung at midnight in parish churches, but much later in the day. Here at St. Michael's it is seven in the morning. This may also have been the hour at Coventry; certainly not before half past six, for this was the time at which the second clerk had to ring for mattins. (See above, p. 61. § 48.) Nine o'clock is the usual hour for high mass, but evensong was often sung at three, not at two o'clock. It was at three at Coventry. (§ 5. of Appendix I.)

P. 83. § 7. The ordinal in this case is most likely the Sarum Pie, or *Directorium Sacerdotum*. It has been lately edited for this Society by Mr. Christopher Wordsworth.

§ 9. High mass on holidays not doubles was served only by a deacon. It seems likely that one of the clerks took upon him the office of subdeacon, and read the epistle.

Notes to Appendix VII.

P. 84. This is a very interesting and unusual document. Morebath, a small parish on the borders of Devonshire and Somerset, under 3,500 acres in extent, "in the hundred of Bampton, and in the deanery of Tiverton, lies about two miles from Bampton, and nine from Tiverton. The small village of Exebridge is partly in this parish, and partly in that of Brushfield, in Somersetshire." (Lysons, *Magna Britannia*, vol. vi. Devonshire, London, 1822. p. 355.)

P. 85. § 4. *A steche of clene corne.* See F. H. Stratmann, *Middle English Dictionary*, by Henry Bradley, Oxford, 1901. *Sub voce* Stücche, a piece, fragment, *frustum.* But in this document it would seem to have a more definite meaning.

line 12 from bottom.

Timewell, East and West, are shown close to Morebath on the 25-inch Ordnance map.

P. 86.

line 6. *Sir William Trystram* Vicar of Bawnton *i.e.* Bampton which is near to Morebath.

line 12. The vicar seems here to have discharged the clerk on his own authority.

line 14. *Our Lady at Lent* is the annunciation, March 25, which fell this year on Palm Sunday. Here we pass into 1537: Easter day being on April 1.

line 19. *Lytell ester day* seems to have been Low Sunday.

line 9 from bottom. *Vigilia Sancti Georgii*, April 22. St. George is the patron saint of Morebath.

P. 87.

line 20. We see how needful a clerk was for the celebration of mass.

line 15 from bottom. In 1532 Sir Hugh Paulet was in the commission of the peace for Somerset. (*Cal. State Papers*, Henry VIII. vol. v. No. 1694. Entry ii.) He was the eldest son of Sir Amias Paulet. (*Dict. Nat. Biography.*)

line 13 from bottom. *Mr. Hu Stycly* may be Hugh Stukeley, one of the family of Stukely of Affeton. A Sir Hugh Stucley died in 1560. (*Dict. Nat. Biography.*) He seems to have been a man of some local importance, as he is joined with Hugh Paulet in trying to quell the disturbance. A Hugh Stucle came into Affeton in the fifteenth century by marrying the heiress. (Thomas Westcote, *View of Devonshire*, Exeter, 1845, p. 470. note.)

Notes to Appendix VIII.

P. 91. § 9. The clean water is for the blessing of the font at Easter and Pentecost. They bought water at Coventry for the font at these seasons. See above Appendix I. p. 58. § 20.

§ 10. This is in obedience to the injunctions of Thomas Cromwell. (See Introduction p. xxxv.)

§ 14. *In Lent time to compline.* Evensong was said in Lent before dinner. See the notes to § 39 of Appendix I.

§ 15. The jewels which adorned the altars were any kind of plate, gold or silver. The high altar of Westminster Abbey was adorned in this way for the coronation of King Edward VII. and the effect is said to have been magnificent. (See *Guardian*, 1902. August 13. p. 1149. col. iii.)

P. 92. § 27. It may be supposed that by the translation of St. Stephen is meant his invention, celebrated on the 3rd of August.

P. 93. § 30. *Shall in confession tell it to the Curate and the names of the persons &c.* Does this mean sacramental confession?

Notes to Appendix IX.

P. 94. In a blank column of a Sarum Breviary written in the fifteenth century, there has been added by a later hand the following verses, as an anthem to a part of *Miserere* in the vernacular. The manuscript is now in the British Museum. (Add. MS. 32,427. fo. 141.)

Remember your promys made yn baptym
And crystys mercyffull bloud shedyng
By the wyche most holy sprynklyng
Off all your syns youe haue fre pardun.

Attention was called to these verses in 1879 by the Rev. H. T. Kingdon, who has since become bishop of Fredericton. A facsimile of the anthem with the musical notes is also given. (*Wiltshire Archæological and Natural History Magazine*, Devizes, 1879, vol. xviii. p. 62.)

The verses were also known to Latimer:

What maister Latimer being bishoppe of Worcester taught al them of his dioces to say, in geuing of holy water.

¶ Remember your promise in baptime,
Christ his mercy and bloudshedding,
By whose most holy sprinkeling
Of al your sinnes you haue free pardoning.

What to saye in geuing of holy bread.

¶ This is a token of ioyfull peace
Betwene God and mans conscience.

(John Fox, *Actes and Monuments*, London, 1563. p. 1348.)

Notes to Appendix X.

P. 96. Strictly speaking January 28th, 1548, to January 28th, 1549, is the second year of Edward VI. but this note, almost contemporary, strengthens the suspicion that the ceremony of the holy loaf had been put down before the issue of Edward's first book.

line 8 from bottom. In Queen Mary's reign, J. Whayre and T. Colens were churchwardens. (Lewin G. Maine, *A Berkshire village*, Oxford, 1866, p. 102.)

last line. *Yardlands.* Yardland "is a quantity of land, different according to the place or country; as at Wimbleton in Surrey, it is but fifteen acres, in other counties it is twenty, in some twenty-four, and in others thirty, and forty acres." (Giles Jacob, *New Law Dictionary*, London, 1772.)

Cotsettulls. "The piece of arable land (of about 5 acres) held along with his cot by the Old English cotset or cottar." (Murray's *New English Dictionary*, sub voce *Cotland.*)

P. 97.

line 1. *meeses*, messuage, dwelling house with garden.

line 4. Some of the houses that have not given the holy loaf can still be traced. The parsonage to the north of the church had at the time of my visit only just passed out of the hands of the Ecclesiastical Commissioners into private hands. It was called the rectory. The vicarage, close to the rectory, is inhabited by the Vicar. The farm called the manor house is to the south of the church, and was once the property of the family of Knollys and still shows traces of its former estate: and there is yet a smith's forge on the green. But I could not identify the church house, or Ganders.

Of the Church house Aubrey says: "In every Parish is, or was, a church howse, to which belonged spitts, crocks, etc., utensils for dressing provision. Here the Howsekeepers met, and were merry and gave their Charitie: the young people came there too, and had dancing, bowling, shooting at buttes, etc., the ancients sitting gravely by, looking on. All things were civill and without scandall." (John Aubrey, *Topographical Collections*, ed. by J. E. Jackson, Wiltshire Archæological and Natural History Society, Devizes, 1862. p. 10.) Mr. Jackson remarks in a note that "in many parishes in Wiltshire there is still to be met with some old house called 'The Church House' where this took place." At Stanford in the Vale there is still a feast kept by the people on the day of St. Denys, in whose honour the church is dedicated.

NOTES TO APPENDIX XIV.

P. 109. Barrow-on-Humber is in Lincolnshire, opposite to Hull, and close upon 6,000 acres in extent.

§ 1. I think this means that the clerk is to attend the parson at the church or anywhere within the parish when the clerk is officiating in his function, as helping in visiting the sick, baptising infants in peril of death, or any other duty away from the church.

P. 110. § 4. We may compare the following extract from a newspaper. "The parish clerk of Driffield attained his eightieth birthday last week; and on Saturday he completed his fifty-fifth year of ringing the harvest bell at five o'clock every morning for 28 days during harvest." (*Standard*, September 22nd, 1903, p. 8, col. 4.)

§ 5. Mr. Christopher Wordsworth suggests very reasonably that it would be better to leave out the *item* before § 6 and to make a fresh paragraph or item at "he is to give notice": so that the item would run thus:

§ 6. He is to give notice to the owner or farmer occupier of Westcote about a week before Christmas and Easter, etc.

In the text I have preserved the arrangement of the manuscript.

§ 6. "The Rushbearing. . . . This ceremony consists of carrying to church the rushes intended to be strewed on the clay floor under the benches, which are piled neatly up in a cart, and a person constantly attends to pare the edges with a hay knife, if disordered in progress." (G. Ormerod, *History of . . . Chester*, London, 1819, vol. i. p. liv.)

§ 8. "Plowland . . . in respect of repairing the highway is settled at £50 a year." (Giles Jacob, *New Law Dictionary*, London, 1772.) But see the third Essay in F. W. Maitland, *Domesday Book and beyond*, Cambridge, 1897.

INDEX.

List of Works already issued.

1891.* I. MISSALE AD USUM ECCLESIÆ WESTMONASTERIENSIS. fasc. i. Edited by Dr. J. WICKHAM LEGG, F.S.A. 8vo. [Dec. 1891.]

III. THE MARTILOGE, 1526. Edited by the Rev. F. PROCTER, M.A., and the Rev. E. S. DEWICK, M.A., F.S.A. 8vo. [May, 1893.]

1892.* II. THE MANNER OF THE CORONATION OF KING CHARLES THE FIRST, 1626. Edited by the Rev. CHR. WORDSWORTH, M.A. 8vo. [Dec. 1892.]

IV. THE BANGOR ANTIPHONARIUM. Edited by the Rev. F. E. WARREN, B.D., F.S.A. Part I. containing complete facsimile in collotype, with historical and palæographical introduction. 4to. [Aug. 1893.]

1893. V. MISSALE AD USUM ECCLESIÆ WESTMONASTERIENSIS, fasc. ii. Edited by Dr. J. WICKHAM LEGG, F.S.A. 8vo. [Aug. 1893.]

VI. OFFICIUM ECCLESIASTICUM ABBATUM SECUNDUM USUM EVESHAMENSIS MONASTERII. Edited by the Rev. H. A. WILSON, M.A. 8vo. [Aug. 1893.]

1894. VII. TRACTS OF CLEMENT MAYDESTONE, viz. DEFENSORIUM DIRECTORII and CREDE MICHI. Edited by the Rev. CHR. WORDSWORTH, M.A. 8vo. [Oct. 1894.]

VIII. THE WINCHESTER TROPER. Edited by the Rev. W. HOWARD FRERE, M.A. 8vo. [Nov. 1894.]

1895. IX. THE MARTYROLOGY OF GORMAN. Edited by WHITLEY STOKES, D.C.L., Foreign Associate of the Institute of France. 8vo. [July, 1895.]

X. THE BANGOR ANTIPHONARIUM, Part II. containing an amended text with liturgical introduction, and an appendix containing an edition of Harleian MS. 7653. Edited by the Rev. F. E. WARREN, B.D., F.S.A. 4to. [Nov. 1895.]

* The books issued for 1891 and 1892 are out of print.

1896. XI. THE MISSAL OF ROBERT OF JUMIÈGES, BISHOP OF LONDON, A.D. 1044–1051, AND ARCHBISHOP OF CANTERBURY IN A.D. 1051. Edited from a MS. in the Public Library at Rouen, by the Rev. H. A. WILSON, M.A. 8vo. [July, 1896.]

XII. MISSALE AD USUM ECCLESIÆ WESTMONASTERIENSIS, fasc. iii. Containing an appendix giving certain Offices from Westminster MSS. in the Bodleian Library and the British Museum, together with full indices, notes, and a liturgical introduction. Edited by Dr. J. WICKHAM LEGG, F.S.A. 8vo. [Nov. 1897.]

1897. XIII. THE IRISH LIBER HYMNORUM. Edited from MSS. in the Libraries of Trinity College, and the Franciscan Convent at Dublin by the Rev. JOHN H. BERNARD, D.D., and ROBERT ATKINSON, LL.D. Vol. I., Text and Glossary.

XIV. Vol. II., Notes and Translations of the Irish Prefaces and Hymns. 8vo. [July, 1898.

1898. XV. THE ROSSLYN MISSAL. An Irish manuscript in the Advocates' Library, Edinburgh. Edited by the Rev. H. J. LAWLOR, D.D. 8vo. [April, 1899.]

XVI. THE CORONATION BOOK OF CHARLES V. OF FRANCE. With reproductions in collotype of the 38 miniatures which illustrate the ceremonies, and facsimiles of seven of them in gold and colours. Edited by the Rev. E. S. DEWICK, M.A., F.S.A. 4to. [Dec. 1899.]

1899. XVII. MISSALE ROMANUM, Milan, 1474. (The first printed edition of the Roman Missal.) Edited by the Rev. ROBERT LIPPE, LL.D. Vol. I. Text. 8vo. [Oct. 1899.]

XVIII. THE PROCESSIONAL OF THE NUNS OF ST. MARY AT CHESTER. With English rubrics. Edited by Dr. J. WICKHAM LEGG, F.S.A. 8vo. [Oct. 1899.]

1900. XIX. THREE CORONATION ORDERS: (1.) The Coronation Order of William III. and Mary II. (2.) An Anglo-French version of the English Coronation Order. (3.) Consecration of the Anglo-Saxon King. Edited by Dr. J. WICKHAM LEGG, F.S.A. 8vo. [Feb. 1901.]

XX. CLEMENT MAYDESTONE'S DIRECTORIUM SACERDOTUM. Edited by (the late) Rev. Canon COOKE, M.A., and the Rev. CHRISTOPHER WORDSWORTH, M.A. Vol. I. 8vo. [Feb. 1901.]

1901. XXI. FACSIMILES OF HORÆ B.M.V., reproduced in collotype from English MSS. of the 11th Century. Edited by the Rev. E. S. DEWICK, M.A., F.S.A. **4to.** [Jan. 1902.]

XXII. CLEMENT MAYDESTONE'S DIRECTORIUM SACERDOTUM. Edited by (the late) Rev. Canon COOKE, M.A., and the Rev. CHRISTOPHER WORDSWORTH, M.A. Vol. II. 8vo. [March, 1902.]

1902. XXIII. CUSTOMARY OF THE BENEDICTINE MONASTERIES OF ST. AUGUSTINE, CANTERBURY, AND ST. PETER, WESTMINSTER. Edited by Sir EDWARD MAUNDE THOMPSON, K.C.B., LL.D., D.C.L., V.P.S.A. Vol. I. Containing text of Cottonian MS. Faustina C. xii. 8vo. [October, 1902.]

XXIV. THE BENEDICTIONAL OF ARCHBISHOP ROBERT. Edited by the Rev. H. A. WILSON, M.A. 8vo. [Jan. 1903.]

1903. XXV. THE CLERK'S BOOK OF 1549. From the unique copy in the British Museum. (C. 36. d. 1.) Edited by Dr. J. WICKHAM LEGG, F.S.A. 8vo. [Feb. 1904.]

XXVI. THE HEREFORD BREVIARY. Edited by the Rev. W. HOWARD FRERE, M.A., and LANGTON E. G. BROWN, sub-Librarian of the Hereford Chapter Library. Vol. I. Psalterium, Commune Sanctorum, Temporale. 8vo. [Feb. 1904.]

The following Works are in preparation:

CUSTOMARY OF THE BENEDICTINE MONASTERIES OF ST. AUGUSTINE, CANTERBURY, AND ST. PETER, WESTMINSTER. Edited by Sir EDWARD MAUNDE THOMPSON, K.C.B., LL.D., D.C.L., V.P.S.A. Vol. II. Containing text of Cottonian MS. Otho C. xi. and of part of Gonville and Caius College MS. 211. 8vo. [In the Press.]

A MISCELLANEOUS VOLUME OF TRACTS ON THE MASS. Edited by Dr. J. WICKHAM LEGG, F.S.A. Containing:—

Ordinarium Missæ Sarum. From an early 14th Century Missal formerly in the possession of the late Mr. WILLIAM MORRIS, F.S.A.

Langforde's *Meditatyons for Goostly Exercyse in the tyme of the Masse.* (Bodleian MS., Wood 17.)

Alphabetum seu Instructio Sacerdotum. (Bodleian, Douce 14.) Collated with four other editions.

Dominican Directions for High Mass. From a 13th Century MS. (Brit. Mus. Add. 23,935.) With an Appendix on Low Mass from a Dominican Missal printed at Lubeck in 1502.

Ordo Missæ of John Burchard, Rome 1502, collated with a shorter recension from a Roman Missal of 1501.

And other pieces. 8vo. [In the Press.]

FACSIMILES OF EARLY MSS. OF THE CREEDS, including an early copy of *Quicunque vult*, from an Irish MS. in the Ambrosian Library at Milan (O. 212, sup.). Edited by the Rev. A. E. BURN, M.A. 4to.

THE LITURGY OF ST. JAMES. Edited by the Rev. F. E. BRIGHTMAN, M.A.

MISSALE ROMANUM, Milan, 1474. Edited by the Rev. ROBERT LIPPE, LL.D. Vol. II. Supplement and Indices.

THE HEREFORD BREVIARY. Edited by the Rev. W. HOWARD FRERE, M.A., and LANGTON E. G. BROWN, sub-Librarian of the Hereford Chapter Library. Vol. II. Sanctorale. 8vo.

THE PONTIFICAL IN THE LIBRARY OF MAGDALEN COLLEGE, OXFORD (MS. 226), an English manuscript of the twelfth century. Edited by the Rev. H. A. WILSON, M.A.

THE SECOND RECENSION OF QUIGNON'S BREVIARY. Edited by Dr. J. WICKHAM LEGG, F.S.A.

CRANMER'S EARLY PROJECTS FOR REFORM OF THE DIVINE SERVICE. A complete Edition of British Museum MS. Royal 7 B. iv. Edited by Dr. J. WICKHAM LEGG, F.S.A.

THE MARTYROLOGY OF OENGUS THE CULDEE. Edited with a collation of the MSS., by WHITLEY STOKES, D.C.L., Foreign Associate of the Institute of France.

THE LEOFRIC COLLECTAR, an English manuscript of the eleventh century (Harl. MS. 2961). Edited by the Rev. E. S. DEWICK, M.A., F.S.A.

PONTIFICALE LANALETENSE. An English MS. of the 11th Century, now in the Public Library at Rouen. Edited by LEOPOLD G. WICKHAM LEGG, M.A.

THE COLBERTINE BREVIARY. Edited by F. C. EELES.

THE ORDINALE OF EXETER. Edited by the Rev. J. N. DALTON, M.A., F.S.A., Canon of Windsor.

THE MOZARABIC PSALTER. (Brit. Mus. Add. 30,851.)

MISSALE GOTHICUM. (Vatican MS. Reginae 317.)

MISSALE FRANCORUM, and other fragments of Gallican Liturgies.

FACSIMILE EDITION OF THE STOWE MISSAL, a manuscript belonging to the Royal Irish Academy.

THE BRIGITTINE BREVIARY OF THE NUNS OF SION, with English rubrics. From a MS. at Magdalene College, Cambridge.

THE MONASTIC BREVIARY OF THE CHURCH OF DURHAM. (Harl. MS. 4664.)

February, 1904.

Printed in the United States
210750BV00001B/13/P